CHRISTIAN SCRIPTURE

CHRISTIAN SCRIPTURE

An Evangelical Perspective on
Inspiration, Authority and Interpretation

DAVID S. DOCKERY

BROADMAN
& HOLMAN
PUBLISHERS

Nashville, Tennessee

4210–40
0–8054–1040–6

Dewey Decimal Classification: 230
Subject Heading: Doctrinal Theology \ Bible—Inspiration \ Bible—History
Library of Congress Card Catalog Number:94–36520

All Scripture unless otherwise noted is from the Holy Bible, New International Version, copyright © 1973, 1978, 1984 by International Bible Society.

Portions of this book appeared previously in different forms and are used with permission. From *Biblical Interpretation Then and Now: Contemporary Hermeneutics in the Light of the Early Church*, by David S. Dockery © 1992 Baker Book House; *The Doctrine of the Bible*, by David S. Dockery © 1991 Convention Press; and *Authority and Interpretation: A Baptist Perspective*, Duane A. Garrett and Richard R. Melick, Jr., eds. © 1987 Baker Book House.

Interior design Leslie Joslin
Cover design by Steve Diggs & Friends

Library of Congress Cataloging-in-Publication Data
Dockery, David S.
    Christian scripture: an evangelical perspective on inspiration, authority, and interpretation / David Dockery
        p.   cm.
        ISBN 0–8054–1040–6
        1.Bible—Inspiration.   2. Bible—Evidences, authority, etc.   3. Bible—Criticism, interpretation, etc. —History   4. Baptists—Doctrines.
I. Title.
    BS480.D56   1995
    220.6—dc–20   94–36520
                                                                         CIP

2 3 4 5 6 00 99 98

CONTENTS

PREFACE

This book represents fifteen years of personal reflection on the nature and authority of Holy Scripture. During that time my understanding of revelation, inspiration, and the truthfulness of Scripture has deepened. I have wrestled with issues of hermeneutics, canonicity, and authority as these affect the task of teaching the Scriptures in our contemporary context. I have struggled during this time with what it means to be Evangelical and Baptist—the tradition from which I write, both out of heritage and conviction. Much of this book has been published in earlier piecemeal forms in a variety of journals and books. I am deeply appreciative to Broadman and Holman Publishers for their encouragement and for bringing the fruit of my research and reflection into this form.

I write as one deeply appreciative of those who have gone before me throughout the history of the church. Most significantly I have been influenced by key figures in the patristic era, by the Reformers, and by many in the Evangelical, Pietistic, and Baptist traditions—particularly Chrysostom, Luther, Calvin, Manly, Mullins, Strong, Carroll, and Conner. In recent years I have been particularly challenged and greatly helped by J. Leo Garrett, Jr., Millard J. Erickson, Donald G. Bloesch, Carl F. H. Henry, Clark Pinnock, D. A. Carson, and John Woodbridge. I have chosen not to interact with the Rogers/McKim thesis (1979) since that conversation has generally been brought to a conclusion with Bloesch's balanced critique in Holy Scripture (1994), building on Woodbridge's thorough analysis a decade earlier. Thus, this volume is hopefully a constructive synthesis of much prior work.

Christian Scripture is an unapologetically biblical, confessional, and evangelical treatise.[1] The Evangelical tradition is a movement that developed from the Great Awakenings in Northern Europe and North America. David Bebbington has characterized four key elements of the Evangelical tradition as conversionism, biblicism, activism, and crucicentrism. While informed and shaped by all of these elements, this volume is focused on biblicism or the meaning of biblical authority.[2]

Perhaps the most original contribution of the volume is found in the appendix. The appendix surveys the history of biblical inspiration and interpretation in the Southern Baptist Convention (SBC) (1845–1995), which seems especially significant during this sesquicentennial celebration year. Much discussion concerning the nature of biblical authority has taken place in the SBC over the past two decades. Yet, our survey indicates that these issues have been discussed with equal intensity in previous generations, particularly the final two decades of the nineteenth century.

This work would not have been possible without the helpful support of many people. John Landers, academic editor at Broadman and Holman, has offered editorial guidance along the way. The support staff at Southern Baptist Theological Seminary has been invaluable. Particularly, I want to thank Tish Gardner and her Office Services staff. Words are inadequate to express my gratitude for the labors of Cynthia Meredith, Jane Jones, and Dianne Teafatiller. Personal encouragement has come from special colleagues: Thom Rainer, Diana Garland, Dennis Williams, Lloyd Mims, Bob Johnson, and Marsha Ellis Smith—fellow members of the academic council at Southern Seminary. Timothy George, Charles Chaney, and James E. White have offered important insights and direction along the way. Each pointed me to important sources in various areas of research.

I would like to say a special word of thanks to my family (Lanese, Jon, Ben, and Tim) and my church family (the community called "Springdale"), particularly my pastor David Butler, for their love, prayers, joyful support, and spiritual strength. I offer this work with the prayer that believers might be edified and informed, and that ministers, Bible teachers, and students might be strengthened to study, proclaim, and teach the Christian Scripture with greater confidence.

Soli Deo Gloria

NOTES

1. See the initial chapter in *Southern Baptists and American Evangelicals: The Conversation Continues* (Nashville: Broadman and Holman, 1993).

2. See Mark A. Noll, *The Scandal of the Evangelical Mind* (Grand Rapids: Eerdmans, 1994); also David Bebbington, *Evangelicalism in Modern Britain: A History from the 1730's to the 1980's* (London: Unwin Hyman, 1989).

I

CRISIS OF BIBLICAL AUTHORITY

CRISIS OF BIBLICAL AUTHORITY

Strident controversies present in both church and society in many ways demonstrate the crisis of biblical authority.[1] Whether in Roman Catholicism or Protestantism, whether in the evangelical world, the Methodist church, the Presbyterian church, or in Baptist churches, there is an ongoing crisis centered around the nature, authority, and interpretation of the Bible. Questions dealing with wide-ranging issues such as abortion, homosexuality, feminist theology, and inclusive language for God, postmodern concerns or New Age ideas point to the wide-ranging gap between the message of Scripture and the controversies raging in our society. The Southern Baptist Convention, the community of believers of which I am a part, has been embroiled in a controversy over the truthfulness and authority of Holy Scripture since 1979. It is somewhat paradoxical that the people who call themselves "the people of the book," as so described in *The Baptist Hymnal* (1991), have argued, debated, and now are seemingly fragmenting over this issue.[2]

THE CONTEMPORARY CONTEXT

Today the larger church is divided between liberal experiential-ists who make human moral experience the primary basis for the church's message and theological understanding and a rigid funda-mentalism that has equated cultural norms and forms of philosoph-ical rationalism with the truth of Scripture. This volume rejects these extreme positions and seeks to offer an evangelical under-standing of the inspiration, interpretation, and authority of Scrip-ture. Such a position unapologetically affirms the complete truthfulness and absolute authority of God's Word in our world.[3] The contemporary crisis revolves around understandings of truth,[4] approaches to interpretation, and the meaning of authority. We will focus our attention on these issues later in this volume. Before deal-ing with the issues of interpretation we will attempt to set the stage for the contemporary discussion by surveying the use of the Bible in the history of the church. We will examine the present impasse and hermeneutical quagmire that currently exists and from which we will seek to articulate a healthy position in continuity with the great heritage of the Christian church.

We will seek to offer a model for understanding Scripture that equally affirms both Word and Spirit. Evangelical theology needs to recover the unity of Word and Spirit in line with the great reformed heritage in the church.[5] We will also seek to develop a model for understanding the nature of Scripture built on a Christo-logical model that affirms the divine-human authorship of Holy Scripture.[6] In doing so, we will affirm that the Bible is the Word of God written, in which we find God's Word to His people for all times.

Many men and women who believe the biblical stories as recorded, who affirm the historical foundations of Holy Scripture, and who never doubted the miraculous claims of the Bible are nev-ertheless confused by such terms as canon, infallibility, authority, revelation, and hermeneutics. We will seek to define these terms in our discussion (a glossary will also be included in the back to help us deal with these important and sensitive matters).

Every Lord's Day, Christians around the world in churches of various denominations gather to hear the Bible read and expounded. What is true in these congregations is characteristic of the experience of most Christians as well. It is common in these churches to hear the words, "Let us stand together as we read the Word of God." Such an affirmation assumes that the Bible is a divine Word. Such an affirmation has become a major problem for many contemporary men and women who struggle with what it means to say that the Bible is the written Word of God.

A large number of present-day Christians have been taught in their homes and churches to believe that the Bible is a divinely inspired book, written by godly men. They believe that the Bible is God's revelation to men and women, and since it is God's revelation, it is to be studied and obeyed. A characteristic response among these faithful believers is: "The Bible says it; I believe it; that settles it." Such people gladly accept the biblical reports that Jonah was swallowed by a fish, that God led Joshua to lead the people into the promised land, that Elijah and Elisha performed miraculous deeds, that Jesus walked on water, and that He was raised from the dead on the third day.

Conversely, others who have been influenced by trends in contemporary philosophy and theology have great difficulty accepting these biblical accounts as miraculous without reinterpreting them. Although many have difficulty believing the miraculous accounts, they nevertheless confess that the Bible is a significant and important book. For these people the Bible is essentially a human book.[7] It is important because it is a record of humanity's quest for and experience with God. Most Christians would want to confess more than this limited affirmation, maintaining that God in some way reveals Himself through the collection of human books. Even though the books may seem to some to be contradictory, the readers believe they can still hear God's truth through these writings.[8]

In addition to these positions are numerous opinions that try to explain carefully and fairly the two-sided character of the Bible as a divine-human book. These views attempt to do justice to the mystery of Scripture's divine inspiration while maintaining its human authorship.[9] One of the key issues in developing a doctrine of Scripture is the need to maintain both the divine and human aspects of the authorship of Christian Scripture. The precise relationship between divine revelation and the human writings that comprise the canonical Scripture has been at the heart of the contention both in the church and the academy for the past decades.

I will seek to articulate in this volume what is meant by an evangelical view of the Bible, affirming its complete reliability and full inspiration for Christians today. In doing so I write as both an evangelical and a Southern Baptist. While the goal of this book is not so much restricted to Baptist thinking, it will include a survey of Baptist understanding on this subject as well as evangelical conclusions on which we can build a sure foundation.

It would be naive to think that the issues that have been so hotly debated for almost two decades in the Southern Baptist Convention are only being discussed in the Southern Baptist context, as though Southern Baptist theologians, pastors, and lay people lived in a vacuum. Some aspects of the impasse can be attributed to the cultural and sociological changes taking place among people who historically have functioned regionally and rather parochially, and now are attempting to come to grips with modernity and the broader issues of our society. But this does not tell the whole story.

In many ways the struggles in the Southern Baptist Convention parallel debates taking place in the evangelical world and in Christianity at large. For example, the German scholar Wolfhart Pannenberg, commenting on "The Crisis of the Scripture Principle," notes that the development of historical research has led to disillusion of the Scripture principle and brought on a crisis in the foundations of evangelical theology that has become more and more acute.[10] Harvard theologian Gordon Kauffman observes that only in isolated places does the Bible have "anything like the existential authority and significance which it once enjoyed throughout much of Western culture and certainly among believers."[11] James Barr, almost twenty years ago, predicted that doubt about the status of the Bible may well come to be regarded as normal in the churches.[12] The developing concern over the inspiration and authority of the Bible in church and theology has greatly intensified during the past two decades.[13] Most recently, Donald Bloesch introduced his masterful work *Holy Scripture* with a description of the crisis in biblical authority.[14]

The controversy over the Bible is not unique to Southern Baptists. The intensity of the controversy among Southern Baptists, however, is unrivaled in other Christian circles, thus creating a major impasse. It is important for readers to understand that I am writing out of that context while seeking to speak to the broader evangelical world. Before moving forward with our discussion, it will be helpful and informative to see how the Bible describes itself. This description is foundational for our larger exposition.

THE BIBLE'S SELF-ATTESTATION

"The Bible says" ends all questioning except the question "what does the Bible say?" To even ask how the Bible describes itself is, according to James Barr, "an anachronistic question." Barr, with his characteristically pointed critique writes,

> According to conservative arguments . . . the Bible "claims" to be divinely inspired. All this is nonsense. There is no "the Bible" that claims to be divinely inspired, there is no "it" that has a "view of itself." There is only this or that source, like 2 Timothy or 2 Peter which makes statements about certain other writings, these rather undefined. There is no such thing as "the Bible's view of itself" from which a fully authoritative answer to these questions can be obtained.[15]

Barr's argument is extremely articulate, but not necessarily devastating. I will suggest in this volume, that it is more than a citation of 2 Timothy 3:16 that informs our understanding of the nature of Scripture. It is rather a compounding of the biblical testimony coupled with the inward work of the Holy Spirit bearing witness by and with the written Word of God in our hearts. Acknowledging these presuppositions, let us look at the various ways Scripture describes itself.

Even before the canonization of the sacred books, importance was attached to the sacred writings. Moses wrote "all the words of the LORD" in the "Book of the Covenant" (Exod. 21–23; 24:4–7, KJV). Joshua's farewell address was written "in the book of the law of God" (Josh. 24:26, KJV). Samuel spoke words about the manner of the kingdom and "wrote them down on a scroll and deposited it before the LORD" (1 Sam. 10:25). Jesus repeatedly appealed to the authoritative Scriptures (see Matt. 19:4; 22:29). Similarly, Paul and the apostles thought of the scrolls as "the very words of God" (Rom. 3:2).

The term Scripture is a rendering of the Greek word *graphe*. The plural form identifies the whole collection of sacred writings (see Matt. 21:42; 1 Cor. 15:3–4). The singular form can mean either a specific passage (see Mark 12:10) or the constituent body of writings (see Gal. 3:22). Paul characteristically used *gramma* (writing or Scripture) to refer to the Torah or the Law. In 2 Timothy 3:15 he referred to the "Holy Scriptures" (*hiera grammata*), which Timothy had known since he was a child and which were able to make him wise for salvation. The divine author of Scripture is the Holy Spirit (see Acts 28:25), who has breathed out Scripture as a function of His creative activity. This sacred Book's instruction is divine. It is divine and authoritative for salvation and for Christian living.

We commonly refer to the Christian Scripture in English as the Bible. The English word *bible* is derived from the Greek word *biblion* or *biblia*, which means scroll(s) or book(s). English-speaking Christians use three major titles to refer to this holy Book. We call it the Bible, the Scripture or Scriptures, and the Word of God. These words, as we use them today, have a far more significant connotation than the Greek word *biblion*. *Biblion* was a roll of papyrus, a reedlike plant, whose inner bark was dried and fashioned into a writing material widely used in the ancient world. *Biblion* could be used to designate books of magic (see Acts 19:19) or a bill of divorce (see Mark 10:4), as well as sacred books. To believers the word Bible refers to the Book par excellence, the recognized source of divine revelation for contemporary believers.

In Daniel 9:2 the Greek translation used *ta biblia* to refer to the prophetic writings. Paul used the word *biblia* when he wrote to Timothy and asked him to bring the books (see 2 Tim. 4:13). He was probably referring to scrolls containing the Hebrew Scriptures, which we usually call the Old Testament. This usage passed into the postapostolic church (see 2 Clement 14:2). Sometime during this period a significant change occurred in the common usage of the plural *biblia* to the singular *biblion*. This change reflected the growing conception of the Bible as one utterance of God rather than a multitude of voices speaking for him.

THE BIBLE AS WORD OF GOD

Christian theology appeals to the authority of Holy Scripture because it sees Scripture as the written Word of God. Since the time of the Reformation, Christians have not hesitated to use the term "written Word of God." Baptists have employed this term since the Second London Confession of 1677.[16] However, this identification of Scripture with the Word of God has been called into question in recent times. Some contend that the Bible merely contains the Word of God and then only insofar as it becomes the "Word of God for me" to the individual soul. To regard the Bible in its full extent as the Word of God written would be to claim that it was composed by the superintending work of the Holy Spirit. It is this action of the Spirit over the work of biblical writers that the apostles themselves claimed (see 2 Tim. 3:16; 2 Pet. 1:19–21) and that requires the characterization "Word of God" for the sacred writings.

It is very important to recognize that the designation "Word of God" or "Word of the Lord" is appropriately used in three distinct contexts. Primarily, the phrase refers to (1) Jesus Christ; (2) though it also rightly points to the divinely disclosed message through God's spokesmen and this in principle to (3) the biblical writings. The three usages are certainly related, lying within one another in concentric circles. So the phrase belongs to Christ, the ultimate Word, through the proclamation of Christ in the apostolic church, and to the truth of Christ embodied in written form in the Scriptures.

This concept of Scripture specifies the prophetic declarations from God to and through his servants (see Num. 3:16,51; Josh. 19:50; 22:9; 2 Sam. 22:31; Prov. 30:5; Isa. 5:24) and numerous occasions in the Psalms (see Ps. 119:11,105). The New Testament appears to use the terms Word of God, Word of the Lord, Word of Jesus, and Word of Christ with similar, almost synonymous and interchangeable meanings. The Word of God, which was at first orally proclaimed, was finally embodied in written form in the New Testament.

Our Lord authenticated this usage by declaring that Scripture as the Word of God cannot be broken (see John 10:35). It is "the Word of the prophets made more certain" about which the apostles wrote, because these words were spoken from God as the writers "were carried along by the Holy Spirit" (2 Pet. 1:19–21). It is biblically and theologically right to acknowledge that the prophetic-apostolic word is God's Word written. Without their writing there would be no writing, no Scriptures, and therefore no Word of God available to us. The Bible is God's Word written. The Bible itself does not indicate what title we should use. Therefore we can use the terms the Bible, the Word of God, or the Scriptures interchangeably in this volume, even though we have selected the term Christian Scripture as the title for our book.

THE BIBLE'S STRUCTURE AND MESSAGE

The Bible has two major parts that we commonly call the Old Testament and the New Testament. What the Jewish people call the Hebrew Scriptures, Christians generally refer to as the Old Testament. The origin of these terms is related to the Bible's covenant themes.

God made a covenant with Abraham (see Gen. 12:1–3) in which He promised to bless Abraham and to make Abraham a blessing. God promised the people of Israel that they should be a "kingdom of priests and a holy nation" (Exod. 19:6). Similarly, God said, "I will walk among you and be your God and you will be my people" (Lev. 26:12). The promises of Abraham were ratified with Isaac and Jacob and reaffirmed with Abraham's descendants through Moses after the Exodus. The covenant promises were expanded with David (see 2 Sam. 7).

After the division of the kingdom, following Solomon's reign, and the conquering of the Northern and the Southern Kingdoms by Assyria and Babylon, many people thought that God had forsaken His covenant people. The prophet Jeremiah, however, proclaimed that God would make a new covenant with the nation (see Jer. 31:31–34). God's dealing with people in anticipation of the coming of Christ is the major theme of the thirty-nine Old Testament books.

The term "new covenant" appears several times in the New Testament. Jesus used it when He instituted the Lord's Supper (see Luke 22:20). With this usage Jesus sought to call attention to the new basis of fellowship with God established by Jesus' death. The apostle Paul also spoke of that new covenant (see 1 Cor. 11:25; 2 Cor. 2:14–3:18), as did the author of Hebrews (see Heb. 8:7–13; 9:11–15; 10:15–18). The description of God's dealings with people on the basis of the new covenant is the major theme of the twenty-seven New Testament books.

There was no Old Testament or New Testament before the coming of Christ, only one collection of sacred writings. But after the apostles produced another body of sacred literature, the church began to distinguish between the two. The covenant identified God's unalterable promise of the spiritual blessing and guidance of His people. Among the church fathers the Latin term *testamentum* was used to translate covenant, and from there the term passed into English. So the old and new covenants became the Old and New Testaments.

The Old Testament was written in Hebrew, though a few chapters were written in a similar language, Aramaic. Customarily, the Jewish people divided the Old Testament into three sections called the Law, the Prophets, and the Writings (Luke 24:44). Sometimes only two distinctions were employed, the Law and the Prophets. Christians arranged the Old Testament into four groups: the Law, or Pentateuch (Genesis through Deuteronomy); the Historical books (Joshua through Esther); the Poetic-Wisdom books (Job through the Song of Songs); and the Prophets (Isaiah through Malachi), divided into Major and Minor Prophets (Major referring to books that are longer and Minor referring to books that are relatively short; the terms have nothing to do with major or minor importance, only length).

If one adopts the view that Moses wrote or edited the first five books of the Old Testament (the position adopted in the New Testament, including the words of Jesus), the earliest Old Testament books were probably written between 1400 and 1200 B.C. If the final writing was Malachi (ca. 400 B.C.), then the thirty-nine books were composed over a period of about a thousand years. Probably all the writers were Jews and included prophets, judges, kings, and other leaders in Israel.

The New Testament was written in Greek, though Jesus and His disciples apparently spoke Aramaic. A few Aramaic words were scattered throughout the New Testament. The twenty-seven books as we have them in our Bible follow a generally logical arrangement. They begin with the four books called Gospels (Matthew through John) that describe the birth, life, death, and resurrection of Christ. The Book of Acts begins where the four Gospels end, describing the birth of the church and the advancement of the Christian mission and introducing the apostle Paul and his church-planting efforts. Following Acts we find a group of letters. In the Western canon we find the letters of Paul, whereas in the Eastern canon we find the general letters.[17] Following the Western canon, the first group of letters (thirteen) consists of writings from Paul to churches and young ministers, arranged from the longest to the shortest. After the Pauline letters are a group of letters called the Catholic Letters or General Letters. The last book, Revelation, is a prophetic-apocalyptic work.

The New Testament was written during a fifty-year period. There is some question whether James, Galatians, or 1 Thessalonians was the first book written. It is generally agreed that Revelation was the last book written, in the waning years of the first century. All the writers were Jews with the exception of Luke, who wrote the Gospel of Luke and Acts (Though some think that Luke was also a Jew, this is doubtful). The writers represent a variety of occupations, including fishermen, doctors, tax collectors, and religious leaders.

Together, the Old and New Testaments consist of sixty-six books. Many of these writings were not originally designed as books, in the sense of being written for publication and public distribution. Several (like Philemon) were private documents and others (2 and 3 John) were too short to be called books. But all of them have been collected and now are published in one Book, the Bible, which we call the Christian Scriptures. It is appropriate, therefore, to refer to these books as the Bible.

In addition to the major sections identified above (Law, Prophets, Poetry, Gospels, and Epistles or Letters), several other types of literature in the Bible are referred to by literary genre or type. These include poems, parables, hymns, narratives, confessions or creeds, sermons, and apocalypses. In spite of the diversity of authors, languages, genres, and composition spanning almost fifteen hundred years, the Bible has a remarkable unity. The unity is the result of the one divine Author's superintending the production of many human authors to present the divine message to humankind.

The Bible presents a message about God and His purposes. It describes the creation of the universe, including the direct creation of men and women in a paradise on earth. The Bible describes the call of Abraham, the giving of the Law, the establishment of the kingdom, the division of the kingdom, and the captivity and restoration of Israel. Scripture sees humankind as fallen from a sinless condition and separated from God. The promise of a coming Messiah who will redeem men and women and reign as King appears throughout the Old Testament. The message of the Word of God proclaims that believers are restored to favor with God through the sacrifice of Christ.

It is the confession of Jesus as the Christ, the Savior of the world, that is at the heart of the evangelical faith. This message is central to the content of Holy Scriptures. Contemporary evangelicals need not only to affirm this message, but also to affirm the Bible's inspiration, truthfulness, and normative nature. In the midst of the crisis of biblical authority in which we find ourselves, we need to evidence our concern for the matters dealt with in this book by careful theological reflection, faithful proclamation, repentance, and prayer. A confession that the Bible is fully inspired and totally truthful is important because it is the foundation that establishes the complete extent of Scripture's authority.

Contemporary evangelicals must choose to articulate a view of the Bible for the contemporary community that is faithful to and in continuity with the consensus of historic positions in the church that have characteristically confessed that the Bible is the written Word of God. Building upon that foundation block, we can relate to one another in love and humility, bringing about true fellowship and community and resulting not only in orthodoxy but orthopraxy before a watching world, because not only is there a crisis of biblical authority but a crisis of biblical piety in the church as well.[18]

ENDNOTES

1. See David S. Dockery, "A People of the Book and the Crisis of Biblical Authority," *Beyond the Impasse?: Scripture, Tradition, and Interpretation in*

Baptist Life, eds. Robison B. James and David S. Dockery (Nashville: Broadman, 1992), 17–39; also Donald G. Bloesch, *Holy Scripture: Revelation, Inspiration, and Interpretation* (Downers Grove: InterVarsity, 1994), 17–29.

2. See Nancy T. Ammerman, *Baptist Battles* (New Brunswick, N.J.: Rutgers University Press, 1990); Bill J. Leonard, *God's Last and Only Hope* (Grand Rapids: Eerdmans, 1990); James and Dockery, *Beyond the Impasse?*; and David S. Dockery, "Holy Wars, Houses on Sand and Heresies: A Review of the Inerrancy Controversy in the Southern Baptist Convention," *Criswell Theological Review* 2 (1988): 391–402.

3. Much of the information in this volume has been published previously in a different form and is herein used with permission. See David S. Dockery, *The Doctrine of the Bible* (Nashville: Convention, 1991).

4. See the helpful analysis in James E. White, *What Is Truth?* (Nashville: Broadman, 1994).

5. See Bloesch, *Holy Scripture*, 25–29.

6. See David S. Dockery, "The Divine-Human Authorship of Inspired Scripture," *Authority and Interpretation*, eds. Duane A. Garrett and Richard R. Melick, Jr. (Grand Rapids: Baker, 1986), 13–43.

7. This position was widely confessed in American Baptist life early in the twentieth century. The works of Shailer Matthews are exemplary. Contemporary statements include James Barr, *The Bible in the Modern World* (London: SCM, 1973); idem., *Beyond Fundamentalism* (Philadelphia: Westminster, 1984); D. E. Nineham, *The Use and Abuse of the Bible* (London: SCM, 1976); G. M. Tucker and Douglas A. Knight, *Humanizing America's Iconic Book* (Chico, Calif.: Scholars, 1982).

8. Such is even the case with non-evangelical works such as William Countryman, *Biblical Authority or Biblical Tyranny* (Philadelphia: Fortress, 1982); and R. P. C. Hanson and A. T. Hanson, *The Bible Without Illusions* (Philadelphia: Trinity, 1989).

9. Representative works, from which there are many, include: G. C. Berkouwer, *Holy Scripture*, trans. and ed. Jack B. Rogers (Grand Rapids: Eerdmans, 1975); Carl F. H. Henry, *God, Revelation, and Authority*, 6 vols. (Waco: Word, 1976–83); Jack B. Rogers and Donald K. McKim, *The Authority and Interpretation of the Bible: An Historical Approach* (New York: Harper and Row, 1979); Roger Nicole and J. Ramsey Michaels, eds., *Inerrancy and Common Sense* (Grand Rapids: Baker, 1980); William J. Abraham, *The Divine Inspiration of Holy Scripture* (Oxford: Oxford University Press, 1981); I. Howard Marshall, *Biblical Inspiration* (Grand Rapids: Eerdmans, 1982); Clark Pinnock, *The Scripture Principle* (San Francisco: Harper and Row, 1984); D. A. Carson and John D. Woodbridge, eds., *Scripture and Truth* (Grand Rapids: Zondervan, 1984); idem., *Hermeneutics,*

Authority, and Canon (Grand Rapids: Zondervan, 1986); and important systematic theologies by Millard Erickson (1983); Bruce A. Demarest and Gordon R. Lewis (1987); James Leo Garrett, (1990); and Donald G. Bloesch (1994).

10. Wolfhart Pannenberg, *Basic Questions in Theology*, vol. 1 (Philadelphia: Westminster, 1970), 6.

11. Gordon D. Kaufman, "What Shall We Do with the Bible?" *Interpretation* 25 (1971): 96.

12. Barr, *Bible in the Modern World*, 8.

13. See Mark A. Noll, "Evangelicals and the Study of the Bible," *Evangelicalism and Modern America*, ed. George Marsden (Grand Rapids: Eerdmans, 1984), 198–99; also see D. A. Carson, "Recent Developments in the Doctrine of Scripture," *Hermeneutics, Authority and Canon*, 5–48; and John R. Muether, "Evangelicals and the Bible: A Bibliographic Postscript," *Inerrancy and Hermeneutics*, ed. Harvie M. Conn (Grand Rapids: Baker, 1988), 253–64.

14. Bloesch, *Holy Scripture*, 17–29.

15. James Barr, *Fundamentalism* (London: SCM, 1977), 78.

16. See William L. Lumpkin, *Baptist Confessions of Faith* (Valley Forge: Judson, 1959), 249.

17. See F. F. Bruce, *The Canon of Scripture* (Downers Grove: InterVarsity, 1988).

18. See Donald G. Bloesch, *The Crisis of Piety* (Grand Rapids: Eerdmans, 1976); and Stanley J. Grenz, *The Cry for the Kingdom* (Peabody, Mass.: Hendrickson, 1986).

II

REVELATION,
JESUS CHRIST, AND SCRIPTURE

In a famous essay on revelation, Archbishop William Temple exclaimed,

> The dominant problem of contemporary religious thought is the problem of revelation. Is there such a thing at all? If there is, what is its mode and form? Is it discoverable in all existing things, or only in some? If in some, then in which, and by what principle are these selected as its vehicle? Where is it found, or believed to be found, what is its authority?[1]

The answers to these questions which were posed over sixty years ago represent the myriad of voices that constitute modern theology. The radically different ways people understand revelation is confusing, if not painful. The issues raised by Archbishop Temple are still striking issues today. We cannot address each question raised by Temple in this chapter, but we can address the major issue of how God makes Himself known to His creation. In this chapter we will focus on God's self-revelation, that is His manifestation of Himself and His will. We will make a distinction between general and special revelation, while emphasizing Jesus Christ as God's final revelation. In this work on Christian Scripture we will need to examine how the Bible serves as God's revelation for today's believers.

GOD'S SELF-DISCLOSURE

All knowledge of God comes by way of revelation. The knowledge of God is revealed knowledge since it is God who gives it. He bridges the gap between Himself and His creatures and discloses Himself and His will to them. God is the source of knowledge about Himself, His ways, and His truth. By God alone can God be known. The knowledge of God is revealed by His self-disclosure.[2]

The word *revelation* means an uncovering, a removal of the veil, a disclosure of what was previously unknown. More specifically, revelation is God's manifestation of Himself to humankind in such a way that men and women can know and have fellowship with Him. An example of revelation is found in the biblical narrative in which Simon Peter declares that Jesus is the Christ, the Son of God (Matt. 16:16). Jesus responded to this declaration, "Blessed are you, Simon son of Jonah, for this was not revealed to you by man, but by my Father in heaven" (Matt. 16:17). That Jesus is the Son of God could be known only through revelation. The veil was removed; the gap in the disciples' knowledge was bridged. God, the Father, revealed Himself to the disciples, and they perceived the knowledge of Jesus, His Son. The knowledge of Jesus' Sonship was not attained by human discovery, nor could it have been; it came from God alone.

All Christians recognize that God has revealed Himself to His creatures by acting and speaking in history. Yet opinions about what constitutes revelation vary. Is there a natural or general revelation? Is special revelation rational or meaningful? Is revelation only an experience or existential encounter? Let us turn our attention to these matters.

GENERAL REVELATION

It would be a misconception to think of physical nature as a part of God in the same way that my hand is a part of me. Yet God might reveal Himself through His actions as a person often does. Let us consider how this might occur. Besides speaking or writing, persons may reveal facts about themselves in other ways, such as through physical gestures or facial expressions. Sometimes persons' actions communicate whether they are selfish or generous, clumsy or skillful. A grimace, a smile, or a frown can often be revealing. Transferring this idea to a theological context is not simple, because God is not visible. Nature is not identical with God, or even part of God. When we say that God reveals Himself through nature, we mean that through the events of the physical world God communicates to us things about Himself that we would not otherwise know.[3]

What sort of things might God tell us in this manner? In Romans 1:19 Paul wrote that "what may be known about God is plain to them, because God has made it plain to them. For since the creation of the world, God's invisible qualities—His eternal power and divine nature—have been clearly seen, being understood from what has been made, so that men are without excuse" (Rom. 1:20). This point echoes an affirmation the psalmist made centuries earlier: "The heavens declare the glory of God" (Ps. 19:1). The psalmist saw the glory of God through the spectacles of special revelation. But it is very important to note that what the psalmist saw was objectively and authentically present. In other words, all that can be known about God in a general or natural sense has been revealed in nature. Thus, we call this natural or general revelation. General revelation is universal in the sense that it is God's self-disclosure of Himself in a general way to all people at all times in all places. General revelation occurs through nature, through human experiences and conscience, and through history. We will consider each of these avenues of general revelation.[4]

Wonders of nature. God manifests Himself in the wonders of the heavens—sun, moon, stars—and in the beauty of the earth—skies and seas, mountains and forests, grass and flowers. Whether in the smallest atom or the largest galaxy, the simplest form of life or the most complex, God reveals Himself through His works. As Jesus maintained "He causes his sun to rise on the evil and the good, and sends rain on the righteous and the unrighteous" (Matt. 5:45), thus revealing His goodness to all.[5] Likewise, Luke recorded that "the living God, who made heaven and earth and sea and everything in them . . . has not left himself without testimony: He has shown kindness by giving you rain from heaven and crops in their seasons; He provides you with plenty of food and fills your hearts with joy" (Acts 14:15–17). God makes Himself known in the continuing care and provision for humankind. The universe as a whole serves the Creator's purpose as a vehicle for God's self-manifestation.[6]

Human experience. God also reveals Himself in the experiences of men and women, who are made in the image and likeness of God (see Gen. 1:26–27). Humans, as a direct creation of God, mirror and reflect God. People are God's unique workmanship. This uniqueness is evidenced by human dominion over the rest of creation; in the capacity people possess to reason, feel, and imagine; in human freedom to act and respond; and in humanity's sense of right and wrong (see Gen. 1:28; Rom. 2:14–15). Especially through this moral sense does God reveal Himself in the consciousness of men and women. The fact that religious belief and practice are universal confirms the apostles' statements in Romans 2. Yet the creatures who worship; pray; build temples, idols, and shrines; and seek God in diverse ways do not glorify God as God or give Him thanks (see Rom. 1:21–23).[7] Nevertheless, because persons have been given the capacity for receiving God's general revelation, they are responsible for the way they respond to it.

The events of history. The combined experience of humankind and the interpretation of this experience makes up what is known as history, another source of God's general revelation. While these events are only revelatory after further reflection and interpretation on the events, nevertheless we can say that God manifests Himself in the workings of history. All of history bears the imprint of God's activity and thus has a theological character. Primarily, God is revealed in history through the rise and fall of peoples and nations. The history of nations reflects some manifestation of God at work. Paul on Mars Hill asserted that God has made Himself known in history and that He is no unknown God.[8] Rather, He is the true God who commands all people everywhere to repent (see Acts 17:22–31).[9]

Adequate for salvation? It is much debated whether or not general revelation is an adequate and sufficient source to bring one into a saving relationship with Jesus Christ.[10] We can affirm that God's general revelation is plain, whether in nature, in human conscience, or in history. However, it is often misinterpreted because simple

18

and finite humans are trying to understand the work of a perfect and infinite God.

What we have seen so far is compatible with the following: (1) religious belief is a nearly universal human phenomenon; (2) such religious belief is impacted by God; (3) all people ought to acknowledge God on the basis of what they learn from the world around them; and (4) all people probably believe in the existence of God, even though some do not admit it.[11]

No one, no matter how seemingly insignificant or limited, can be excused for missing God's revelation. Enough knowledge of God is revealed in a flower to lead a child or a scientist to acknowledge God and worship Him. Sufficient evidence lies in a tree, a fingerprint, a snowflake, or a grain of sand to cause us to glorify the one true God. But people will not do this. Instead they substitute nature, parts of nature, or their own experience for God and find their hearts darkened.

The light of nature is not sufficient to impart the knowledge of God necessary for salvation.[12] The revelation of God through nature reveals His power (see Rom. 1:20), goodness (see Matt. 5:35), and righteousness (see Rom. 2:14–15); but it does not reveal His saving grace. This grace is revealed only through special revelation. The revealed will of God, His special revelation, is necessary for men and women to know how to worship Him rightly.[13] A manifestation of God is made known in His general revelation, but human sinfulness perverts or suppresses the reception of this manifestation (see Rom. 1:18–21). General revelation is plain enough to lead all people without excuse before God; nevertheless, it does not succeed in bringing people to a saving knowledge of God. It is as if a lawyer were offered the information necessary to solve a case, yet perversely chose to ignore it. Although the information by itself would not solve the case, it could provide the means necessary for the lawyer to solve it. The purpose of God's revelation is to promote the worship of Himself. The result of the suppressing nature of sin leaves men and women without excuse (see Rom. 3:20).[14]

In summary, men and women lack the willingness to come to a pure and clear knowledge of God. They have no excuse, because the fault of rejection lies within the human heart. It is impossible to pretend to be ignorant of God's revelation. Human conscience itself convicts humankind of rejection and ingratitude. Men and women push away God's truth because they do not like the truth about God. They do not like the God to whom the truth leads them; so they invent substitute gods and religions.

The universal presence of religion on earth is evidence of this substitution, and is an evidence of the general nature of God's universal revelation.[15] God has revealed Himself to all peoples at all times in all places. Thus men and women everywhere express a need for God. This expression may be found in sophisticated laws of culture, in materialism, in the gods and goddesses of world religions, or in the bestial images of paganism or the thought world of the New Age movement.[16] These expressions support the fact that humans throughout history have consistently and willfully rejected God because they choose not to respond to Him or obey Him. Therefore, they need something or someone else to take God's place (see Rom. 1:18–32).

According to Paul, our suppression of the awareness of God and His demands warps our reason and conscience.[17] Because we reject God, He righteously reveals His wrath against humankind. Although God's general revelation does not bring one into a saving relationship with God, it reveals God to His creatures; therefore they are responsible for their responses. Thus we find ourselves neither in agreement with those who think that natural or general revelation is sufficient for salvation,[18] nor with those who think that there is no revelation of God in nature.[19] We affirm the universality of natural revelation,[20] but find it to be inadequate for salvation. God's message of salvation comes to us only through what is known as special or particular revelation.[21]

SPECIAL REVELATION

We have learned that God has revealed Himself in nature, human experience, and history. But sin's entrance into the world has changed the revelation as well as the interpretation of it. What is needed to understand God's self-disclosure fully is His special revelation. Indeed, as noted in our discussion of Psalm 19, special revelation provides the viewpoint through which we can fully understand and appreciate God's revelation. Divine truth exists outside special revelation; but it is consistent with and supplemental to, not a substitute for special revelation. General revelation is consistent with special revelation yet distinct from it.[22]

Particular revelation. In contrast to God's general revelation, which is available to all people, God's special revelation is available to specific people at specific times in specific places. This revelation is available now only by consultation of sacred Scripture.[23] Special revelation is particular in its manifestation. God reveals Himself to His people. These people of God are the children of Abraham whether by natural (see Gen. 12:1–3) or spiritual descent (see Gal. 3:16–29). Does this statement mean God confines knowledge of Himself to a particular people? Not necessarily, because God's general revelation has been given to all, though perverted and rejected by the universal wickedness of humankind. He now chooses to whom and through whom He will make Himself known. As with Abraham, God said, "All peoples on earth will be blessed through you" (Gen. 12:3). This is God's purpose in manifesting Himself in a particular manner to His people; that they will be a channel of blessing to others.

Progressive revelation. Special revelation is also progressive. In the witness of biblical history is found a developing manifestation of God, His will, and His truth in the Old and New Testaments. The development is not contradictory in any fashion. It is complementary and supplementary to what has been previously revealed. We should think of the progress not from untruth to truth, but from a lesser to a fuller revelation (see Heb. 1:1–3). The revelation of the law in the Old Testament is not superseded by the gospel, but is fulfilled in it. The latter fulfills the former. Thus we can say that God's particular revelation has been unfolded to us throughout redemptive history, ultimately being consummated in the person and work of Jesus Christ (John 1:1–18).

Personal revelation. In recognition of the human predicament, God chose from the very beginning to disclose Himself in a direct way. God has entered this world throughout the course of history. He has made Himself known to us within time and space. God has acted and spoken to redeem the human race from its own self-imposed evil. Through miracles, the Exodus, and ultimately Jesus Christ, God has revealed Himself in history. Special revelation includes not only those acts in history, but also the prophetic-apostolic interpretation of those events, meaning that revelation occurs in deeds and words.[24]

Special revelation is primarily redemptive and personal.[25] God reveals Himself personally as "I am" (Exod. 3:14). He talked with Moses face to face as with a friend (see Exod. 33:11). Like His appearance to Samuel (see 1 Sam. 3:21), His many personal encounters continued in the covenant and throughout the Old Testament.

The ultimate point of God's personal revelation is found in Jesus Christ. In Him the Word became flesh (see John 1:1,14, 18; 14:9). God was decisively confronting people in Jesus Christ. The good tidings that the holy and merciful God promises salvation as a divine gift to people who cannot save themselves has been fulfilled in the gift of His Son. The redemptive revelation of God is that the incarnate Word (Jesus Christ) has borne the sins of fallen humanity, has died in their place, and has been raised to ensure justification. This is the fixed center of special revelation.

Propositional revelation. Likewise, God's self-disclosure is propositional in that it made known truths about God to His people.[26] This assertion has been rejected by much modern theology but it certainly seems plausible that knowledge about someone precedes intimate knowledge of them. The primary purpose of revelation is not necessarily to enlarge the scope of one's knowledge about God. Yet the purpose of knowledge about God is coming to know God. We can thus affirm that special revelation has three stages. First is God's redemptive work in history, which ultimately centers in the work of the Lord Jesus Christ during the time of His incarnation. The second is the written source of God's revelation, the Bible. In Holy Scripture God has provided interpretative records of what He has done for the redemption of men and women. For instance, it is not enough to know that Jesus Christ died. What is necessary is the interpretation of that event: Jesus Christ died for our sins. The third stage is the work of the Holy Spirit in the lives of individuals and in the corporate life of the church. The Spirit applies God's revelation to the minds and hearts of His people by helping them interpret and understand God's written Word (this is sometimes called illumination). As a result, men and women receive Jesus

Christ as Lord and Savior and are enabled to follow Him faithfully in a believing, covenant community until life's end.

The content of special revelation is primarily God Himself. In revelation the veil is removed, the gap is bridged so that God makes Himself known in His self-manifestation. Mystery remains in God's self-revelation (see Eph. 3:2–13). God does not fully reveal Himself to any person. No person could fully understand; and beyond that, the full manifestation of God would result in the death of the recipient (see Exod. 33:20). However, God reveals Himself to persons to the degree they can receive it.

Not only is the mystery of God Himself unveiled, but God's truth is also revealed. Special revelation is the declaration of truth about God, His character, and His actions in relationship with His creation. His self-disclosure is intelligible and meaningful, communicating divine truth for the mind and heart. The purpose of God's gracious manifestation was well stated by the apostle Paul: "He made known to us the mystery of his will according to his good pleasure, which he purposed in Christ, to be put into effect when the times will have reached their fulfillment—to bring all things in heaven and on earth together under one head, even Christ" (Eph. 1:9–10).

The proper setting of special revelation is Christian faith. God makes Himself known to those who receive His revelation in faith. Faith is the instrument by which we receive God's revelation. When faith is present, the things of God become manifest (see Heb. 11:1–6). Faith is the glad recognition of truth, the reception of God's revelation without reservation or hesitation (see Rom. 10:17). God is pleased to reveal Himself and His majestic Word to people of faith. Thus we can conclude that God reveals Himself both personally and propositionally. While there is tension between these two means of revelation, there is no contradiction. Revelation is both knowledge about God and knowledge of God. It is knowledge about God that leads us to know God in a personal and salvific way.[27]

Revelation and Scripture. Today it is evident that the Bible is of crucial importance, for it is through the Bible that the Spirit witnesses to individuals of God's grace and the need for a response of faith. In the Bible we learn of God's redemption of sinners through Christ Jesus. Our response of faith to God's words and acts,

23

recorded and interpreted by the prophets and the apostles, calls for us to embrace with humble teachableness, without finding fault, whatever is taught in Holy Scripture.

It is not enough to say that God has revealed Himself only in words or only in acts.[28] We must say that this revelation has come to us in both words and acts and has been divinely interpreted through the writings of Holy Scripture for us.

God has initiated the revelation of Himself to men and women. This revelation is understandable to humans, making it possible to know God and to grow in relationship with Him.[29] God's self-manifestation provides information about Himself for the purpose of leading men and women into God's presence. For believers today the Bible is the source of God's revelation. Indeed we can go so far as to say the Bible is a written revelation of the nature of God and His will for fallen humankind.

While we can identify Scripture as a mode of special revelation, along with God's words and acts, it must be acknowledged that Scripture and revelation are not identical. There was special revelation that was not preserved for us in the Bible (see John 21:25). On the other hand, not all of what is in the Bible is necessarily special revelation. Some portions of the material found in the Bible were simply matters of public knowledge, such as the list of genealogies. These most likely were matters of public domain, which could have been recorded by the biblical writers without God having to specially reveal them. Yet the Bible, while not identical at every point with special revelation, must be affirmed as God's written Word for His people.[30]

In the written Word we can identify God; know and understand something about Him, His will, and His work; and point others to Him. Special revelation is not generally speculative. The Bible primarily speaks on matters of cosmology and history when these issues touch the nature of faith. God has manifested Himself incarnationally through human language, human thought, and human action as ultimately demonstrated in the incarnation of Jesus Christ Himself. Since the person and work of Jesus Christ are the fixed center of special revelation, we will move to a discussion of Jesus Christ and the Bible.

JESUS CHRIST AND THE BIBLE

The Bible presents a message about God and His purposes. It describes the creation of the universe, including the direct creation of men and women in a paradise on earth. The Bible describes the call of Abraham, the giving of the Law, the establishment of the kingdom, the division of the kingdom, and the captivity and restoration of Israel. Scripture sees humankind as fallen from a sinless condition and separated from God. The promise of a coming Messiah who will redeem men and women and reign as King appears throughout the Old Testament.

The message of Holy Scripture proclaims that believers are restored to favor with God through the sacrifice of Christ. His sacrifice puts an end to the Old Testament sacrificial system in which the blood of animals represented the handling of the sin problem. The New Testament reveals the Christ who brought salvation and describes how these prophecies about Him were minutely fulfilled. This unifying message ties the biblical library together. The Old Testament promises were fulfilled in the person of Jesus Christ, "the son of Abraham" and "the son of David" (Matt. 1:1).[31] As Augustine said more than fifteen hundred years ago, "The New is in the Old contained; the Old is in the New explained." This overarching unity centers in Jesus Christ, who is the primary subject and key to interpretation of Holy Scripture.[32]

Jesus Christ is the central figure of divine revelation and the focus of the Christian faith.[33] The Bible is our primary source of information about Jesus. Yet the Bible's testimony is amply supported by the impact of Jesus Christ on the world of the first century. In this portion of this chapter we will examine how Jesus as the central figure of divine revelation viewed Holy Scripture. We will look both at Scripture's view of Jesus and at Jesus' authentication of Scripture. We will also give attention to the significance of Jesus as both divine and human as a model for the divine-human aspect of Scripture.

JESUS CHRIST AS THE PROMISED MESSIAH

Jesus was born in Bethlehem of Judea, a few miles south of Jerusalem. He was born a Jew. In different ways and at various times God had spoken to His people through His prophets (see Heb.

25

1:1). The purposes of God had been made known through a series of covenants (see Gen. 12; 2 Sam. 7; Jer. 31). In these covenants, God's intent for establishing His kingdom and for redeeming humankind is progressively expressed. God's purposes were to be accomplished through a descendant of David. The people of God in the Old Testament looked forward expectantly to the coming of the promised King, their Messiah. In Jesus Christ these covenant promises found their ultimate fulfillment.

The Old Testament includes two different lines of teaching about the Promised One, sometimes distinct and other times commingled. One line claims that the Messiah would be a Redeemer who would restore humankind to a right relationship with God. This theme is best developed around the idea of a Suffering Servant Messiah in Isaiah 52:13–53:12. Here the Messiah is pictured as one who would become an offering for the sins of men and women.

Another line of Old Testament teaching describes the Messiah as a coming King destined to restore Israel to its rightful place as God's people on earth. The promises portray the restoration as a time of peace and righteousness. Aspects of each purpose can be seen in the covenant promises and the prophetic pictures, though the details of the completion of these teachings remained somewhat unclear.[34]

The New Testament, however, interprets the Old Testament and announces that the promised Messiah had come in Jesus of Nazareth. Through His ministry, teachings, sacrificial death, and resurrection, Jesus fulfilled the messianic promises, accomplished the messianic mission, and provided for the salvation of the lost world. The New Testament also declares that Jesus will come again and reign as King, bringing peace and joy and righteousness.

In identifying Jesus as the Messiah, the New Testament authors affirm an essential unity between the Old Testament and the New Testament. The New Testament, which is rooted in the Old Testament, interprets and amplifies the Old Testament. The life and work of Jesus, therefore, were grounded in the Old Testament, which Jesus acknowledged to be the Word of God (see John 10:35), and on which He based His life.[35]

JESUS CHRIST AND THE OLD TESTAMENT

Jesus was responsible for teaching His followers that His life and ministry fulfilled the Old Testament Scriptures. He interpreted the Old Testament in a manner similar to contemporary Jewish exegetes, but His method and message were novel.[36] The new method was a Christological reading, which means that Jesus read the Old Testament in light of Himself.[37] For example in John 5:39–40 Jesus said, "You diligently study the Scriptures because you think that by them you possess eternal life. These are the Scriptures that testify about me." In John 5:46 Jesus said, "If you believed Moses, you would believe me, for he wrote about me." Also on the Emmaus road with His disciples following the resurrection, Jesus said: "How slow of heart you are to believe all that the Prophets have spoken! Did not the Christ have to suffer these things and then enter his glory? And beginning with Moses and all the prophets, he explained to them what was said in all the Scriptures concerning himself" (Luke 24:25–27).

The method that Jesus used to interpret the Old Testament was entirely Christological.[38] We can see this in places like the temptation narratives (see Matt. 4:1–11; Luke 4:1–13), in which we find Jesus' own estimation of His status and calling, where His answers were taken from Deuteronomy 6–8. In this passage, Moses, following the forty years of wandering in the wilderness, exhorted Israel to wholehearted obedience and continued faith in God's provision for them. It was a time of hunger and testing, preparatory to a special task, in which God disciplined His nation Israel to teach it to worship only the true God (see Deut. 8:5). Israel often failed to carry out the mission and call of God. Jesus, at the end of forty days, accepted afresh His messianic mission and His status as the Son of God. His belief in His forthcoming resurrection seemed to be motivated both by the promises of Israel's resurrection and by seeing the account of Jonah as a picture of His own resurrection (see Jon. 1:17; Matt. 12:40). He observed that His own experience was prefigured in the psalms of vindication and suffering. These psalms were used both by individual Israelites and by corporate Israel (see Pss. 22; 41–43; 118; Matt. 21:42; 23:39; 26:38; 27:46).[39]

In these and other pictures in the Old Testament, Jesus saw foreshadowings of Himself and His work. The result was that Jesus was rejected by the majority of Jews, while the true Israel was now to be found in the new Christian community. The history of Israel had reached its decisive point in the coming of Jesus Christ. The whole of the Old Testament was summed up in Him. He embodied in Himself the redemptive destiny of Israel. That status and destiny are to be fulfilled in the community of those who belong to Him.[40]

Because Jesus is the fulfillment of God's purposes for Israel, words originally spoken of the nation could be rightly applied to Him. Jesus is the key to understanding the Old Testament because everything points to Himself. The New Testament writers, following the pattern of Jesus, interpreted the Old Testament as a whole and in its parts as a witness to Christ. It is not surprising that in providing different pictures of Jesus' life, the biblical writers saw that at almost every point He had fulfilled the Old Testament.[41] This realization provides the key to the way Jesus understood and used the Old Testament. It also provides the framework and groundwork for Jesus' authentication of the New Testament.

JESUS CHRIST AND THE NEW TESTAMENT

In the Gospels we learn that Jesus understood His own life in light of the Scriptures. We learn, too, that He accepted the full authority and divine authorship of the Old Testament and that He claimed truth for His own teaching. We know that the New Testament was written after Jesus' life on earth. What then was His relationship to the New Testament?

During His ministry on earth Jesus trained disciples. Among these, twelve were given special attention and a special commission (see Mark 3:14). It is impossible to speak with certainty about the methods Christ used to teach His disciples. Probably, however, Jesus instructed His followers by methods similar to those used by the rabbis of His day. Fifteen times in the Gospels He is called rabbi. At other times He is referred to as teacher (rabbi and teacher are vitally related ideas). The rabbis thought of themselves as bearers of truth or of the true tradition. It was their task to pass on truth to approved disciples, who memorized their teachings. The disciples of Jesus must have committed themselves to intensive instruction. After they received special commissioning, they gave themselves to the Word of God and to preaching. The church followed the example of the disciples by continuing steadfastly in the apostles' (disciples') teaching (see Acts 2:42; 6:2).

Before and after His resurrection Jesus indicated that His disciples would have authority to teach and build His church in His name (see Matt. 16:16–20; 28:18–20). As the Father had sent Jesus, Jesus sent the apostles (see John 20:21). In Jesus' name, repentance and forgiveness were to be proclaimed (see Luke 24:47). All of these things were fulfilled in the early church because Jesus gave the Holy Spirit to the apostles. The Spirit brought events to their remembrance and led them into all truth (see John 14–17). In this way the Spirit of God led the apostles in ministry and mission. The apostles' words were confirmed by Jesus through the inspiration of the Spirit. Paul's commissioning to preaching and teaching was different from that of the other apostles, but Jesus' affirmation of Paul's work was quite similar (see Acts 9). Therefore, there is good reason to believe that Jesus authenticated the work of the apostles in their work of writing Scripture. Following John W. Wenham, we seem justified in saying: "To Christ, His own teaching and the teaching of His Spirit-taught apostles were true, authoritative, inspired. To Him, what He and they said under the direction of the Spirit, God said. To Him, the God of the New Testament was the living God; and in principle the teaching of the New Testament was the teaching of the living God."[42]

Over the past two hundred years much debate in scholarly circles has wrestled over the question of Jesus Christ. These discussions have led to the "quest for the historical Jesus," "the new quest for the historical Jesus," Christologies "from below," Christologies "from above," and now the so-called Jesus Seminar, which raises suspicion about the entire New Testament.[43] This is not the place to evaluate the relationship between the Jesus of history and the picture presented of Him in the New Testament. But it seems clear to us that Jesus created the church; the church did not create Jesus. So the words of Jesus were not created by the church; the words of Jesus became the foundation and cornerstone for the church and its writings.[44] We need to see what the New Testament writers believed about Jesus. Our purpose in doing so is to help us establish a model for the written Word of God by looking at the living Word of God.

JESUS CHRIST THE GOD-MAN

The apostle John proclaimed, "In the beginning was the Word, and the Word was with God, and the Word was God" (John 1:1). John identified the Word with Jesus (see John 1:14). Jesus has always been because He is eternal. He is God. Before His death He prayed, "Father, glorify me in your presence with the glory I had with you before the world began" (John 17:5). His own prayer affirms His preexistence. These themes are echoed in the epistles (see Phil. 2:5–11; Col. 1:15–16). Claims to Jesus' preexistence are simultaneously claims to His deity. When we point to Jesus, we say that He is God (see Heb. 1:8; Rom. 9:5). Not only does God live through Jesus and with Jesus, but also Jesus Himself is God (see John 1:1).[45]

Yet Jesus is also portrayed as a man. His humanity is taken for granted in the synoptic Gospels. Other points in the Bible seem to witness to His humanity in particular, as if it might have been called into question or its significance neglected. Mark's Gospel focuses on Jesus' humanity. Luke and Matthew present the birth stories and some aspects of His human life. Luke even emphasizes Jesus' human development (see Luke 2:40,52). John, more than any other writer, pictures Jesus' humanity. His humanity was like ours. It was visible for all to see (John 1:14). As we have already noted, He was regarded as a teacher or rabbi (John 1:38; 3:2; 9:2; 11:8). Jesus grew tired (see John 4:6), grew thirsty (see John 4:7), and displayed genuine emotions (see John 11:33–35). These are all traits of genuine humanity.

The New Testament identified Him as "Jesus of Nazareth" (Acts 2:22; 4:10; 22:8). He was seen, heard, and touched by His disciples. To deny Jesus' genuine humanity is viewed as heresy (see 1 John 4:2–3). Because of His humanity Jesus is able "to sympathize with our weaknesses." He "has been tempted in every way, just as we are—yet was without sin" (Heb. 4:15). The early church confessed Jesus as a real man. Yet He was a unique man, as evidenced by His virgin birth and resurrection. His significance as a man is not found in comparison with others but rather in contrast with others.

In His complete humanity Jesus remained sinless. He always did the will of His Father (see John 10:37; 14:10; 15:10; 17:4). Jesus was called "the Righteous One" (1 John 2:1), the "Holy One" (Acts 2:27), "the light of the world" (John 8:12), "the faithful and true one" (Rev. 19:11), for He knew no sin (see 2 Cor. 5:21; 1 Pet. 2:22). The New Testament simultaneously affirms His humanity, His real temptations (see Matt. 4:1–11), and His complete sinlessness. Unquestionably, the New Testament affirms His uniqueness. The total impression it gives is that Jesus was recognized as fully God and fully man.[46]

The tension created by this confession has created intense debate throughout church history. Some have emphasized one or the other—either His deity or His humanity. The result has been the introduction of unorthodox teachings. The deity of Christ has been denied by some (like the Ebionites, the Arians, and their modern day equivalents). Others have denied the reality of His humanity, thinking that He only appeared to be God (like the Docetists).[47] Still others think He was a man who was adopted as divine at His baptism.

Combinations of these faulty views have claimed that Jesus is God, but His humanity is incomplete. Similarly, others have maintained His humanity but have been less than clear about His deity. Classic Christian tradition has always claimed that Jesus Christ is fully God and perfect man. He is one person with two natures. The two natures are united in one person without forming a third nature or two separate persons.[48]

CONCLUSION

We have seen that God has revealed Himself in acts and deeds, as well as in words. These words include the interpretation of the acts and deeds and make up the prophetic-apostolic witness. The prophetic-apostolic witness is for us today the source of God's divine revelation. Thus when we read the Bible we are not just reading a human interpretation of God's work in history but we are reading a divinely inspired, divine interpretation of God's own works. The central figure in God's revelation and the ultimate revelation Himself is Jesus Christ (see Heb. 1:1–2). We have seen that the Old Testament looked forward to Jesus' coming. Jesus understood His life and ministry in light of the Old Testament. He lived in light of the truthfulness and authority of the Old Testament. Jesus Christ, the Son of God incarnate, who claimed divine authority for all that He did and taught, not only affirmed the absolute authority of the Old Testament, but also unreservedly submitted to it. His reading of the Old Testament was shaped by His own messianic mission. At the heart of Jesus' biblical interpretation was a Christocentric perspective. Jesus thus became the direct and primary source for the church's understanding of the Old Testament.

Jesus stamped His authority on the Holy Scriptures by His submission to them and also by His commissioning of the apostolic witness. Jesus discipled and commissioned His followers to pass on His teaching. The Spirit of God was given to enable them to carry out this task. The result was Spirit-directed writings that focused on the life, ministry, death, resurrection, and exaltation of Christ. The New Testament equally affirms the deity and humanity of Jesus. This picture of the living Word serves as a model for rightly viewing the written Word. Our next chapter will develop a Christological model for understanding Holy Scripture as a divine-human book.

The Bible evidences genuine human characteristics and divine superintending. As Jesus was fully human, He remained sinless, even though He genuinely struggled with temptation (see Heb. 2:18; 4:15). Likewise, the Bible is a fully human book yet completely truthful in all its affirmations. Before moving to our next chapter, a reminder will be helpful: Jesus Christ is not merely a model for our view of the Bible or its interpretation. He is the main theme and goal of our study of Scripture. The focus is on Jesus. The Bible is important in illuminating His words in deeds rather than the reverse. Our study of the Bible begins from our belief in Christ and concludes with the building of our faith. Indeed, in all our theological pursuits Jesus is the Alpha and Omega, the author and finisher of our faith.

ENDNOTES

1. William Temple, *Revelation*, eds. John Baille and Hugh Martin (New York: MacMillan, 1937), 83.

2. See Millard J. Erickson, *Christian Theology*, vol. 1 (Grand Rapids: Baker, 1983), 153–98. I follow Erickson's direction throughout this discussion on "Revelation."

3. An affirmation of natural revelation is not an affirmation of natural theology, though we believe that there is a theology of nature. See G. C. Berkouwer, *General Revelation* (Grand Rapids: Eerdmans, 1955), 117–36.

4. See the most recent comprehensive study of general revelation in Bruce A. Demarest, *General Revelation: Historical Views and Contemporary Issues* (Grand Rapids: Zondervan, 1982).

5. See Craig L. Blomberg, *Matthew*, New American Commentary (Nashville: Broadman, 1992).

6. See John B. Polhill, *Acts*, New American Commentary. (Nashville: Broadman, 1992).

7. See C. E. B. Cranfield, *A Critical and Exegetical Commentary on the Epistle to the Romans*, vol. 1 (Edinburgh: T & T Clark, 1975); also Douglas J. Moo, *Romans 1–8* (Chicago: Moody, 1991).

8. See Ericksons, *Theology*, 173–74; also Wolfhart Pannenberg, *Basic Questions in Theology*, vol. 1 , trans. George H. Kelm (Philadelphia: Westminster, 1983), 96–136.

9. See John R. W. Stott, *The Spirit, The Church, and the World: The Message of Acts* (Downers Grove: InterVarsity, 1990).

10. See the detailed discussion in James Leo Garrett, Jr., *Systematic Theology*, vol. 1 (Grand Rapids: Eerdmans, 1990), 45–91.

11. Paul Helm, *Divine Revelation: The Basic Issues* (Westchester: Crossway, 1982), 6; also see Leon Morris, *I Believe in Revelation* (Grand Rapids: Eerdmans, 1976).

12. See the discussion on this matter in Karl Barth, *Church Dogmatics*, II/1, trans. T. H. L. Parker (Edinburgh: T & T Clark, 1957), 119. Barth concludes that not only will people not respond to general revelation, but finally there is no general revelation, only special revelation.

13. Millard Erickson contends that this represents faithfully John Calvin's position; cf. *Theology*, 171; however, Donald G. Bloesch claims that Erickson has misrepresented Calvin; cf. *Holy Scripture*, 315, n. 102. See Calvin's discussion in *Institutes of the Christian Religion*, 1.6.1.; also Kenneth S. Kantzer, "John Calvin's Theory of the Knowledge of God and the Word of God" (Ph.D. dissertation: Harvard University, 1950).

14. See James M. Boice, *Romans*, vol. 1 (Grand Rapids: Zondervan, 1992).

15. See the lengthy discussion in Emil Brunner, *Revelation and Reason*, trans. Olive Wyon (Philadelphia: Westminster, 1946), 221–36.

16. See Helm, *Divine Revelation*.

17. See Moo, *Romans 1–8*.

18. See discussion in John Baillie, *The Idea of Revelation in Recent Thought* (New York: Columbia University Press, 1956), 125–33.

19. See Karl Barth, "No!" in Emil Brunner and Karl Barth, *Natural Theology*, trans. Peter Fraenkel (London: Centenary, 1946).

20. This does not affirm a natural theology as in Thomas Aquinas, *Summa Theologica*, part 1, question 2.

21. There are several evangelicals, however, who do not find salvific value in general revelation, who nevertheless find apologetic value therein. See C. S. Lewis, *Mere Christianity* (New York: Macmillan, 1952); E. J. Carnell, *Christian Commitment: An Apologetic* (Grand Rapids: Eerdmans, 1957); Francis Schaeffer, *The God Who Is There* (Downers Grove: InterVarsity, 1968); R. C. Sproul, John Gerstner, and Arthur Lindsley, *Classical Apologetics* (Grand Rapids: Zondervan, 1984).

22. Bloesch quibbles with this assertion. See *Holy Scripture*, 63–73.

23. See Erickson, *Theology*, 175–98.

24. See Bernard Ramm, *Special Revelation and the Word of God* (Grand Rapids: Eerdmans, 1961).

25. Examples of those who think revelation is only relational or personal are: Karl Barth, William Temple, John Baillie, Emil Brunner, and William Hordern. See the discussion in Garrett, *Theology*, 101.

26. The most significant defense of propositional revelation is Carl F. H. Henry, *God, Revelation, and Authority*, 6 vols. (Waco: Word, 1976–83). Henry presents fifteen theses contending that revelation is rational and conveyed in intelligible ideas and meaningful words.

27. See the insightful contribution in E. J. Carnell, *The Case for Orthodox Theology* (Philadelphia: Westminster, 1959), 173; also Ronald Nash, *The Word of God and the Mind of Man* (Grand Rapids: Zondervan, 1983).

28. G. Ernest Wright, *God Who Acts: Biblical Theology as Recital* (London: SCM, 1952) has argued that God only reveals Himself in acts or events. Gordon H. Clark has come close to seeing revelation totally in the form of words and propositions; see *God's Hammer: The Bible and Its Critics* (Jefferson, Mo.: Trinity Foundation, 1982). Both extremes need to be avoided.

29. See Bloesch, *Holy Scripture*, 49–56.

30. See Erickson, *Theology*, 196–98; idem., "Revelation," *Foundations for Biblical Interpretation* (Nashville: Broadman and Holman, 1994), 13–15.

31. See R. T. France, *Jesus and the Old Testament* (Downers Grove: InterVarsity, 1971).

32. See John W. Wenham, *Christ and the Bible* (Downers Grove: InterVarsity, 1972).

33. See H. D. McDonald, *Jesus—Human and Divine: An Introduction to Christology* (Grand Rapids: Zondervan, 1968); also Carl F. H. Henry, *The Identity of Jesus of Nazareth* (Nashville: Broadman, 1992).

34. See John Rogerson, et al., *The Study and Use of the Bible* (Grand Rapids: Eerdmans, 1988).

35. See C. K. Barrett, "The Old Testament in the New," *Cambridge History of the Bible*, vol. 1 (Cambridge: University Press, 1970), 377–411.

36. See Donald Juel, *Messianic Exegesis: Christological Interpretation of the Old Testament in Early Christianity* (Philadelphia: Fortress, 1988).

37. I am following Richard N. Longenecker, *Biblical Exegesis in the Apostolic Period* (Grand Rapids: Eerdmans, 1975).

38. We will discuss this matter more fully in the section focusing on interpretation.

39. See France, *Jesus and the Old Testament*.

40. Matthew Black, "The Christological Use of the Old Testament in the New," New Testament Studies 18 (1971): 1–14.

41. See E. Earle Ellis, "How the New Testament Uses the Old," *New Testament Interpretation*, ed. I. Howard Marshall (Grand Rapids: Eerdmans, 1975), 199–219.

42. Wenham, *Christ and the Bible*, 123.

43. See David F. Wells, *The Person of Christ* (Westchester, Ill.: Crossway, 1984).

44. Barrett, "Old Testament in the New," 405.

45. See the carefully stated and historically supported defense of this approach in Gerald L. Bray, *Creeds, Councils, and Christ* (Downers Grove: InterVarsity, 1984).

46. See Donald G. Bloesch, *Essentials of Evangelical Theology*, vol. 1 (San Francisco: Harper and Row, 1978), 127–46.

47. Ibid.

48. See Carl F. H. Henry, ed., *Jesus of Nazareth: Savior and Lord* (Grand Rapids: Eerdmans, 1966).

III

THE INSPIRATION OF
CHRISTIAN SCRIPTURE

The Bible is a book written by numerous authors over a period of hundreds of years, and yet at the same time it is the Word of God. The variety of views that will be surveyed in this chapter have attempted to do justice to the mystery of Scripture's divine inspiration and still maintain its human authorship. Clark Pinnock, who followed a survey of several approaches to this subject, acknowledged: "The prime theological issue which became evident in our survey of options on biblical authority is the need to maintain with equal force both the humanity and divinity of the Word of Scripture."[1] The precise relationship between divine revelation and the human writings that comprise the canonical Scripture has been and continues to be a subject of contention.[2]

It is our belief that the divine-human tension is the most crucial issue in contemporary discussions concerning Christian Scripture. The purpose of this chapter is to examine the meaning of the divine inspiration of Scripture including the relation of its divine and human aspects. First, we will investigate the divine authorship of the Bible, then the human authorship. We will attempt to explain how the writings of the human authors are at the same time truly human words and truly God's. We will then survey the various attempts to explain the mystery of the Bible's inspiration. Our concluding section will focus on the result of inspiration, including the questions relating to an inerrant and normative Scripture.

Scripture cannot rightly be understood unless we take into consideration that it has dual-sided authorship. It is not enough to affirm that the Bible is a human witness to divine revelation because the Bible is also God's witness to Himself. An affirmation that Scripture is partly the Word of God and partly the word of humans is inadequate. What must be affirmed is that the Bible is entirely and completely the Word of God and the words of the human authors (Acts 4:25).

It is not entirely appropriate to make a direct correspondence between Scripture and Jesus Christ, but nevertheless there is an observable analogy.[3] Just as the conception of Jesus came by the miraculous overshadowing of the Holy Spirit (Luke 1:35), so Scripture is the product of the Spirit's inspiration (2 Tim. 3:16). Likewise, as Jesus took on human form through a human mother, so the Bible has come to us in human language through human authors. The result is that Jesus is the living Word of God, the God-man, and the Bible is the written Word of God, the divine-human Scripture.

An affirmation that Scripture is completely the Word of God and the very words of humans also points to its dual-sided nature. Because it is the Word of the infinite, all-knowing, eternal God, it speaks eternal truth that is applicable to readers of all time, beyond the original recipients. Yet, at the same time, it is the word from godly men to specific communities addressing problems and situations within certain contexts and cultures.

Some have contended that the Bible is primarily, if not entirely, a human product of an illumined religious consciousness.[4] Such a view maintains the possibility that the Bible could lead its readers to divine truth though it would deny that the Bible is a revelation of divine truth. By comparison with the heretical views in the early Christological statements, we could classify this position as ebionitic, a view that stresses the humanity while losing sight of the essential deity.[5] On the other hand, the divine aspect of Scripture has been emphasized so prominently by many that the human element is only an outward appearance of the divine. Such an approach denies the Bible's genuine humanity as well as its historicity. Again, parallel to the unorthodox views of the person of Christ, the latter view has tendencies toward a docetic view of Scripture.[6]

We can see the importance of affirming a balanced view of Scripture. But how does the Christian community maintain such a balance? How can it be affirmed that Scripture is the inspired Word of God when it is a collection of books by human authors? Can the words of the Bible be identified with the Word of God? Is some of the Bible God's Word? Or can this be affirmed for all of the Bible? How is it possible that the Bible can simultaneously be the Word of God and a human composition? It is to these questions that this chapter is addressed.

THE DIVINE AUTHORSHIP
OF INSPIRED SCRIPTURE

In the history of the church, the divine character of Scripture has been the great presupposition for the whole of Christian preaching and theology. This is readily apparent in the way the New Testament speaks about the Old Testament. That which appears in the Old Testament is cited in the New Testament with formulas like "God says" and "the Holy Spirit says" (Acts 4:24,25; 13:47; 2 Cor. 6:16). Scripture and God are so closely joined together in the minds of the New Testament authors that they naturally could speak of Scripture doing what it records God as doing (Gal. 3:8; Rom. 9:17). The introductory phrase "It is [stands] written" (*gegraptai*) is also used of New Testament writings (John 20:31). The New Testament concept of faith is in accord with the divine character of the apostolic word (Rom. 1:5; 10:3; 16:26). The reference to the divine character of the apostolic word in its written and oral form deserves unconditional faith and obedience.

Because of the apostolic word's divine origin and content, Scripture can be described as "sure" (2 Pet. 1:19), "trustworthy" (1 Tim. 1:15; 2 Tim. 2:11; Titus 3:8), "confirmed" (Heb. 2:3), and "eternal"

(1 Pet. 1:24,25). As a result, those who build their lives on Scripture "will not be disappointed" (Rom. 9:33; 1 Pet. 2:6). The Word was written for "instruction and encouragement" (Rom. 15:4), to lead to saving faith (2 Tim. 3:15), to guide people toward godliness (2 Tim. 3:16b), and to equip believers for good works (2 Tim. 3:17).

The purpose of Scripture is to place men and women in a right standing before God and to enable believers to seek God's glory in all of life's activities and efforts. But Scripture is not concerned solely with a person's religious needs. On the contrary, the divine character, origin, and content of Scripture teaches us to understand everything *sub specie Dei*—"humanity, the world, nature, history, their origin and their destination, their past and their future."[7] The Bible is not only a book of conversion but also a book of creation and history. It is a book of redemptive history, and it is this perspective that best represents and defines the divine character of Scripture.

We must recognize that central to Scripture is the unifying history of God's redeeming words and acts, of which the advent and work of Jesus Christ is the ultimate focus. Jesus Christ is the center to which everything in Scripture is united and bound together—the beginning and the end, creation and redemption, humanity, the world, the fall, history, and the future.[8] If this overriding unity is ignored, Scripture is denatured and can lose its "theological-Christological definition" and become "abstracted from the peculiar nature and content of Scripture."[9]

As we have noted, we cannot construct dualistic operations of Scripture that stress only its religious or pietistic sense.[10] This could lead to distinguishing between what is and what is not inspired Scripture, what is and what is not from God. We must resist relating divine inspiration merely to content and not to form, to the Bible's purpose and not to its essence, or to its thoughts and not to its words. The entirety of Scripture is divinely inspired and is God's light upon our path and God's lamp for our feet. We now turn our attention to the nature of inspiration and the Bible's witness to itself.

THE BIBLE'S WITNESS TO ITSELF

In addition to those passages mentioned in the previous section, there are many other verses that address the divine aspect of Scripture (Ps. 119; Luke 24:25–27; John 10:34–35; Heb. 1:1–2; 2 Pet. 3:16), but the primary witness of the Bible to its own inspiration is found in 2 Timothy 3:16–17, "All Scripture is God-breathed and is useful for teaching, rebuking, correcting, and training in righteousness, so that the man of God may be thoroughly equipped for every good work."[11]

The term *inspiration*, a translation of *theopneustos*, has a long heritage in the theological literature, but it is always used with further explanation and disclaimers. This is because *theopneustos* means "God-breathed."[12] In contemporary usage, the term inspiration suggests the idea of "breathing into." Secular emphasis is generally synonymous with illumination or human genius. But the New Testament emphasis is that God "breathed out" what the sacred writers communicated in the biblical writings. A preferable term might be spiration, rather than inspiration in order to emphasize the divine source and initiative, rather than human genius or creativity. "In short, the Bible's life-breath as a literary deposit is divine."[13] Recognizing the shortcomings in the term inspiration, we shall continue to use the word, primarily because of its long-term standing in theological literature. The point that must be stressed when using this term is that it points to God as the source of Scripture.

It has been suggested that 2 Timothy 3:16 does not refer to all of Scripture, because of the possible translation "Every Scripture inspired of God is also useful."[14] I. Howard Marshall has noted that this suggestion can be confidently rejected, since no New Testament author would have conceived of the possibility of a book being classified as Scripture, and yet not being inspired by God.[15] We realize that some disagree with Marshall and affirm a limited inspiration for the so-called salvific parts. The problem with this approach is its difficulty in distinguishing the salvific parts from the nonsalvific. Thus, one cannot tell precisely what parts of the Bible are inspired. It must be acknowledged that 2 Timothy 3:16 refers primarily to the Old Testament writings (*graphe*). There are fifty occurrences of *graphe* ("Scripture") in the New Testament, all of which primarily refer to the Old Testament, though the entirety of canonical Scripture is not ruled out. Furthermore, it is not too much to affirm that the construction used in verse sixteen has a broader meaning that allows for the inclusion of the New Testament writings, as well. The anarthrous construction, *pas graphe* ("all Scripture"), can have a characteristic idea, so that the phrase can mean "all that have characteristics of canonical Scripture."[16] In addition, it needs to be observed that *graphe* includes references to New Testament writings in 1 Timothy 5:18 and 2 Peter 3:18.

THE INCLUSIVENESS OF INSPIRATION

The passage in 2 Timothy 3 focuses primarily on the product of inspiration, while it includes the secondary aspects of purpose and process. What is being asserted is the activity of God throughout the entire process, so that the completed, final product ultimately comes from Him. It is a mistake, however, to think of inspiration only in terms of the time when the Spirit moves the human author to write. The biblical concept of inspiration allows for the activity in special ways within the process without requiring that we understand all of the Spirit's working in one and the same way. Just as in the processes of creation and preservation of the universe, God providentially intervened in special ways for specific purposes; so too we can say that, alongside and within this superintending action of the Spirit to inspire human writings in the biblical books, we can posit a special work of the Spirit in bringing God's revelation to the apostles and prophets.[17]

God's Spirit is involved both in revealing specific messages to the prophets (Jer. 1:1–9) and in guiding the authors of the historical sections in their research (Luke 1:1–4). It is not outside the view of inspiration, then, to include the literary processes that take place on the human level behind Scripture. Summarizing the inclusiveness of inspiration, we can say that it encompasses ". . . the collection of information from witnesses, the use of written sources, the writing of and editing of such information, the composition of spontaneous letters, the committing to writing of prophetic messages, the collecting of the various documents together, and so on. At the same time, however, on the divine level we can assert that the Spirit, who moved on the face of the waters at creation (Gen. 1:2), was active in the whole process, so that the Bible can be regarded as both the words of men and the Word of God."[18]

CONCURSIVE INSPIRATION

This approach to inspiration attempts to take seriously the human factors in the composition of the Bible. Theologians have described the activity of the Spirit with the activities of the human writers through which the Bible was written as a concursive work. While this perspective of inspiration is consistent with a plenary view of inspiration, it avoids any hint that God mechanically dictated the words of Scripture to the human authors so that they had no real part in the Scripture's composition.[19] Our approach to inspiration attempts to take seriously the circumstances of the human authors.

This concursive approach allows for a viewpoint that gladly confesses that God's purpose is accomplished through the writer, but the emphasis of the Spirit's work is on the product of inspiration (the inscripturated Word). We can assert that inspiration extends to the choice of words based upon a comprehensive encompassing approach.[20]

This is accomplished by the Spirit's leading the human author in points of research, reflection, and subsequent writing or editing. It is possible that revelation and inspiration take place simultaneously at certain points in Scripture, such as the Ten Commandments and, perhaps, apocalyptic works like Daniel and Revelation.[21]

THE SCOPE OF INSPIRATION

It might be contended that we have contradicted ourselves by allowing for such direct inspiration at certain points or by asserting that inspiration extends even to the very words of Scripture, while simultaneously allowing for the genuine human authorship. We think not, however. We believe the answer is found in the spiritual characteristics of the biblical writers. These men of God had known God, learned from Him, and walked with Him in their spiritual pilgrimage for many years. God had prepared them through their familial, social, educational, and spiritual backgrounds for the task of inscripturating His word. The experiences of Moses, David, Jeremiah, Paul, Luke, John, and Peter differ, yet throughout their lives God was working to prepare and shape them, even their own vocabulary, to pen the Scriptures. Beyond this, we dare not say much regarding the how of inspiration, except to affirm God's providential oversight in the entire process of inspiration.[22] We think it quite plausible to suggest that just as revelation came in various ways (Heb. 1:1–2), so the process of inspiration differed with each author.

The ability to detect marks of inspiration may differ within passages and genres, but the quality and nature of inspiration is the same throughout. God is the source of Scripture and His purposes are accomplished efficaciously.[23] This means that the Sermon on the Mount or the epistle to the Romans may be more readily recognized as inspired Scripture than the books of Esther or Chronicles. Yet, this is due in part to the subject matter. The inspiration in such historical passages assures the general characteristic of reliability that is brought to these records. Even if inspiration differs and is somehow less recognizable to the reader in some places, the entire Bible (*pas graphe*, that is, "all canonical Scripture") can be characterized as inspired (*theopneustos*). The previous section, which focused on the Bible's teaching about itself, provides for us a framework in which to operate. Now, our focus must shift to the vantage point of the phenomena of Scripture, that is, to its humanness and historicity.[24]

THE HUMAN AUTHORSHIP OF INSPIRED SCRIPTURE

The biblical writers employed the linguistic resources available to them as they wrote to specific people with particular needs at particular times. The human authors were not lifted out of their culture or removed from their contexts. They were not autonomous, but functioning members in communities of faith, aware of God's presence and leadership in their lives. Whether or not they were fully aware that they were writing inspired Scripture, they did demonstrate a God-consciousness.[25] Obviously, the writers were not unbiased historical observers; they were people of faith. Thus, the concursive action of the Holy Spirit and human authorship is informed by the spiritual commitments of the writers.

IMAGE OF GOD AND CULTURAL-TEMPORAL DISTANCE

It is quite true that the biblical writers were limited to their own contexts, yet they shared similarities that spanned time and place.

The primary similarity was one the writers shared with all human beings, since all men and women have been created in God's image (Gen. 1:26–27), and as a result, share certain common characteristics.[26] As theologians since the time of Augustine have observed, human beings created in the image of God can have memories of the past, considerations of the present, and expectations of the future. To the extent that these potential capacities are employed, persons—contrary to objects—are neither temporally nor culturally bound. The writers are certainly time-related, but not necessarily time-bound. Moses and Paul, among others, demonstrated cross-cultural influences and experiences. The writers were certainly not entirely culturally or behaviorally conditioned. Even though they were obviously influenced by the time and culture in which they wrote, it can be observed that the writers freely rejected some concepts of their culture and freely endorsed others.[27]

Eugene Nida has observed that humans created in God's image can develop the ability to think and communicate in linguistic symbols. Because of this, communication is a possibility among the diverse linguistic cultures of the world for three reasons: (1) The processes of human reasoning are essentially the same, irrespective of cultural diversity. (2) All people have a common range of experience. (3) All peoples possess the capacity for at least some adjustment of the symbolic "grids" of others.[28]

We do not want to press these assertions beyond their limits. Nevertheless, it can be granted that a revelation written through a human author in a particular language (Hebrew, Aramaic, or Greek) can be intelligible to those who know other languages. God can communicate with humanity, those who have been created in His image. Likewise, humans can communicate with other humans cross-culturally and cross-temporally. By maintaining these observations about humanity, we can affirm the genuine humanness of Scripture without denying that God can speak through a divine-human Scripture.

D. E. Nineham draws attention to the cultural and temporal distance that exists between the biblical writers and our world and has concluded that the Bible is basically unusable today.[29] Because of the commonality discussed above, however, we disagree with Nineham and affirm that God's revelation can be communicated through human authors who lived two thousand years ago in various cultures. The biblical text is, indeed, the words of human authors in temporal-cultural context, but that does not limit the plausibility that God's eternal revelation can be communicated through their writings through contemporary men and women. We fully recognize the humanness and historicity of the biblical text, but simultaneously acknowledge that God's Word can be communicated through this situation. The fact that the biblical authors were men of faith informed the issue of concursive inspiration; in the same way, recognition that every person bears the image of God has implications for the possibility of communication across cultures and ages.

UNITY AND VARIETY IN THE BIBLICAL MESSAGE

The stress upon human authorship in contemporary theological literature reveals the diversity of beliefs and theologies among biblical writers.[30] The concept of overall unity, characteristic of evangelical theology, merges from a full-orbed concept of biblical inspiration. As we observed, the overriding themes of redemptive history and the Bible's inspiration form the basis for recognizing the theological unity in the Bible. Yet, this theological unity must be carefully examined in light of the genuine variety brought about by the unique theological emphases of the different authors and the diverse human and historical situations in the writings. It is readily obvious that the Bible is composed of different types of literature. Likewise, the forms in which the teaching is expressed is influenced by the literary genre. Each genre (whether legal, prophetic, poetic, gospel, epistolary, historical, or apocalyptic) has distinctive characteristics, as we will observe later in this volume. It is from the varied collection of writings that the basic prophetic-apocalyptic message is discovered.

Not only is there a variety of genres, but there is often variety within a particular genre. For instance, the different theological emphases among the synoptic writers demonstrate the variety even within the genre of gospel. Matthew's kingdom theology differs from Mark's servant theology, and they are each different from Luke's stress upon Jesus as Savior of the world. Yet, the central unity of Jesus Christ and the developing history of redemption cannot be ignored.[31]

Beyond this matter is the possibility of theological development within the Old and New Testaments and even within the individual authors themselves.[32] Donald Guthrie's succinct comments on this difficult issue are extremely appropriate:

> The idea of progressive revelation is familiar in Old Testament interpretation and, also in the area of the relation of the Old Testament to the New Testament . . . . With Christ, the Old Testament ritual symbol became obsolete, as the epistle to the Hebrews makes clear . . . . One obvious area where this is undeniable (development in the New Testament) is the difference between the gospels and the rest of the New Testament. Before the death and resurrection of Christ, the revelation given to the disciples was limited. In the nature of the case, Jesus could not give a full explanation of his own death to his disciples until they had grasped the fact of it. But after the resurrection, the apostolic preachers were guided into an understanding of it, although again not in any stereotyped way, but with rich variety.[33]

We can see that the differences between the writers themselves and the development (progressive revelation) occurring within the Testaments and even some of the writers themselves (e.g., Isaiah, Paul) point to the genuine humanness of the biblical text. There is diversity, or variety in the sense of variations, within the expression of the central message of the gospel. The basis of unity is located in the oneness of the gospel. Therefore, diversity works within the limits of the gospel and the overall canonical message.[34]

Diversity does not imply contradiction. The different writers, with their own emphases, vary their expression according to their unique purposes and settings. However, within this very real and rich variety that evidences the humanness of Scripture, there is a genuine unity that is the result of the divine superintending work of inspiration.

IMPROPER DEDUCTIONS

Sometimes people reach improper conclusions from the data that has been presented related to the human authorship of Scripture. Five common, yet improper, deductions are often reached about the human authorship of Scripture. Let us briefly examine these issues.

THE PHENOMENA OF SCRIPTURE

The Bible generally represents things as they appear (phenomena). For example, the Bible refers to a sunrise when, in fact, we all know that the earth rotates on its axis; the sun does not rise. Yet, the weather report tells us what time we can expect tomorrow's sunrise. Why do we speak this way? Because we are describing things as they appear. It is no mistake or error in Scripture when the biblical writers do the same. The Bible is a book of events and communication from common, everyday people. It is not a technical treatise of weather or other areas of science. The great Baptist theologian, A. H. Strong asked, "Would it be preferable, in the Old Testament, if we should read: 'When the revolution of the earth upon its axis caused the rays of the solar luminary to impinge horizontally upon the retina, Isaac went out to meditate' (Gen. 24:63)?"[35]

It is illogical to assume that the Bible contains errors because the human authors reported things in a way contrary to reality. If the Bible taught that things appear one way, but they did not appear that way, we would probably agree that that could be considered an error. If the Bible taught that things are one way, but they were not that way, that too could be considered an error. But, for the Bible to teach that things appear one way, when they actually are another way, is hardly an error. It reflects the genuine humanness of Scripture, for the authors are reporting things as they actually appear.

THE ACCOMMODATION OF SCRIPTURE

John Calvin used expressions like "God must speak baby-talk for humans to understand his Word." He meant that God accommodated Himself to the level and culture of the Bible's original recipients. It is true that the Bible represents God as accommodating Himself to human language. But this recognition does not lead to the conclusion that accommodation to human language must involve accommodation to human error and, thus, the further conclusion that the Bible contains or teaches error. An example concerns the biblical phrase "God repents." Some say that this must be an error, since God is unchangeable. The Bible presents God as changing His actions to be consistent with His overall will or purpose, because His will or purpose does not change. The Bible pictures God as repenting, because that is how it appears to the human authors. This does not suggest contradiction or error in Scripture when it is rightly understood as accommodation to human language.

THE SALVATION EMPHASIS

As we have seen in the previous chapter, special revelation is primarily redemptive. Second Timothy 3:15 says that the Holy Scriptures make us wise for salvation. Obviously, the salvation message is the focal point of Scripture. But it does not follow that because the Bible stresses one thing, it errs in lesser emphases. For example, it is not proper to conclude that because the Bible emphasizes salvation, it can be trusted on that matter, but that since it does not stress history, it may err in historical details. What the Bible says about history and other similar matters serves to support the truthful redemptive message of the Bible. When the Bible reports matters as history, they are intended to be understood as historical—though not necessarily with the kind of precisions required of modern historiography.

TEXTUAL CRITICISM

Textual criticism is the science of determining the truest reading of a biblical passage by comparing one historical text with another historical text. Often textual critics decide that a certain verse or group of verses is not a faithful reading—that is, they doubt that it was a part of the oldest manuscripts. Examples of these kinds of passages include John 7:53–8:11; Mark 16:9–20; Romans 8:1; 1 John 5:7; and Matthew 6:13. Because scholars examine a text and decide that it does not belong to the original text of the Bible, some conclude that the Bible has errors. Questioning the ending of Mark's gospel or the concluding doxology to the Lord's Prayer does not imply that the gospel writers are in error. Textual criticism points us to the truthfulness of the genuine or authentic text. Such great scholars as A. T. Robertson affirmed that textual criticism is a necessary exercise in order to determine what is the original inerrant text.

SINFUL HUMANITY

We have seen that the Bible was written by men. Even though these men were faithful believers, they were not sinless. Yet it does not follow that since God inspired these humans to write Scripture, He would be incapable of keeping them free of human error in their writing. We know that King David was an adulterer, but we cannot infer that the Psalms, therefore, contain error. The same applies for the apostle Paul, who described his own struggle with sin in Romans 7:14–25. The same could be said for the rest of the biblical authors. God's Spirit could certainly keep these writings free from human error.

These common misconceptions or objections are really improper deductions or conclusions that develop from an imbalanced view of Scripture. We cannot in any way ignore the human authorship of Scripture. But, neither can we stress only the humanness of Scripture and ignore its divine inspiration. A proper understanding of the Bible demands a balanced view of the divine-human authorship. The Bible as a divine-human book is indeed special. But that means that it must be treated as equal to, and yet more than, an ordinary book. We must study the Bible through the use of literary and critical methodologies. To deny that kind of study would treat the Bible as less than human, less than historical, and less than literature. The Bible is a literary work that is both human and historical, yet, simultaneously the very Word of God. We will now turn our attention to the inspiration and dependability of Scripture, including various explanations of the divine-human authorship of Scripture.

EXPLANATIONS OF INSPIRATION

We would not naively maintain that the Bible fell from heaven on a parachute, inscribed with a particular heavenly language that uniquely suited it as an instrument for divine revelation. Nor would we claim that the Bible was dictated directly and immediately by God without reference to any local style or perspective. The presence of a multiplicity of historical, contextual, linguistic, and cultural factors must be maintained and accounted for.[36]

A number of views have arisen in recent years attempting to account for the divine-human character of Scripture.[37] A brief survey of these attempts will prove helpful for our discussion. Many of the contemporary theories are attempts to deal seriously with the two-sided character of the Scripture and also to explain how a book penned two thousand years ago should be understood in a post-Enlightenment era.

The Enlightenment era was a watershed in the history of Western civilization. It was then that the Christian consensus was broken by a radical, secular spirit. The Enlightenment philosophies stressed the primacy of nature, a high view of reason and a low view of sin, an anti-supernatural bias, and it encouraged revolt against the traditional understanding of authority. This philosophy was foundational for much of the liberal theology that dominated nineteenth-century European and early twentieth-century American thought. It was initiated by Friedrich Schleiermacher's *On Religion: Speeches to Its Cultured Despisers* at the turn of the nineteenth century. The modern assaults upon classic formulations of scriptural inspiration and authority can be traced to attacks upon the Bible initiated during the early period of the Enlightenment. The positive element that has resulted from the questions raised by modern and postmodern scholars has been a more careful consideration of the human authorship and historical context of Scripture. In the following survey, the dictation view has basically ignored modernity, the illumination view has surrendered to modernity, and in assorted ways, the encounter, dynamic, and plenary views have attempted to respond to the modern mindset and still maintain the church's confession that the Bible is the Word of God. Yes, we face new challenges in a postmodern world, but many of the issues remain the same.

DICTATION VIEW

The dictation theory places the emphasis upon God's actual dictation of His Word to the human writers. The theory is developed from certain prophetic passages, primarily found in the Old Testament prophets, where the Spirit is pictured as telling the human writer what to communicate. What is a proper assessment of particular aspects of Scripture ("thus says the Lord . . .") is applied to the whole Bible. This approach fails to consider seriously the distinctive styles of the different authors or the particular contexts to which they were addressed.

While it is true that the prophets claimed to hear God addressing them before they proclaimed His Word, this is not always parallel with the way the other writers depict themselves. For example, Luke tells his readers that other people before him had attempted to write the story of Jesus and that he consulted these works and did additional research before compiling his Gospel (see Luke 1:1–4). Thus, it can be seen that the dictation theory cannot account for all aspects of Scripture. The dictation approach is without doubt confessed (perhaps unconsciously) by numerous faithful believers. Because of this, it is often assumed that advocates of a plenary view of inspiration hold to the dictation view, but adherents of the plenary view take great pains to dissociate themselves from the dictation theorists. It is right to judge the dictation theory as docetic and, therefore, less than orthodox.

ILLUMINATION VIEW

This view maintains little more than some kind of recognition of the Spirit's working within the human authors to raise their religious insight. This approach claims that the human authors were enabled to express themselves with eloquent language to produce a certain emotional response from the readers or hearers. In this view, inspiration is the illumination of the authors beyond their normal abilities to express themselves creatively as men of human genius. Inspiration is very limited when understood in this manner, not only in relation to the nature of inspiration, but also as to the extent of inspiration. Portions of Scripture such as poetry, proverbs, and parables best exemplify this type of literary or religious insight. Thus, it is easily seen that this approach fails to explain the inspiration of the entire Bible. The illumination view emphasizes the freedom and creativity of the human author, but fails to account for the Spirit's guidance of the writers in the communication of divine truth; there is only a mere increase in sensitivity regarding spiritual matters. This view of inspiration can be characterized by the Ebionite error we noted earlier, and is a failure as far as accounting for the divine character of Scripture.[38] Nevertheless, it needs to be observed that this view is more akin to the English term *inspiring* than the biblical concepts of a God-breathed Scripture (*theopneustos*). Fortunately, there are better options than these first two extreme positions, neither of which accounts for the two-sided character of Scripture.

ENCOUNTER VIEW

A more complex approach developed by Karl Barth can be classified as an encounter view of inspiration.[39] This view states that in regard to its composition, the Bible differs little from other books. Yet, the Bible is unique because of the Spirit's ability to use it as a means of revelation to specific individuals or communities. Through the on-going work of inspiration, the Bible becomes revelation. The Bible is correlated as a witness to God's original act of revelation.

Inspiration brings the Bible to the contemporary human situation as a source of God's revelation. It is in this way that Barth seeks to take seriously the human authorship of Scripture and the Bible as the Word of God. He attempts to avoid a concept of inspiration that in some way confines the Holy Spirit in the Bible. It is a misunderstanding on his part, however, to assume that those who hold that the Bible was Spirit-inspired in its original composition ignore the Spirit's illumination of the text, thereby bringing it to life for present-day readers. Barth's stress upon ongoing inspiration seems to ignore inspiration at the time of the Bible's composition.

Barth, however, seeks to make it possible for God's Word to be encountered through Scripture. In evaluating Barth's contention, I. Howard Marshall states that "it is doubtful whether Barth's view does justice to that very character of the Bible as inspired Scripture which makes it possible for the Spirit to continue to witness through its words to the Word of God which it embodies."[40] The encounter view is inadequate in accounting for the human and divine aspects of inscripturation. In comparison to the illumination theory, it has many strengths, yet it does not fully explain why we should trust the text as Barth himself did. Barth preached the errancy of the text; however, as Clark Pinnock has observed, he "treated it with reverence and practiced its inerrancy."[41] However, Colin Brown's note is an appropriate concluding evaluation: "It is impossible to maintain high doctrines of revelation and inspiration without at the same time being willing to defend in detail the veracity and historicity of the biblical writings."[42]

DYNAMIC VIEW

This broadly held approach endeavors to be a via media, in contradistinction to the liberal and fundamentalist camps, which seek to emphasize a combination of divine and human elements in the process of inspiration. A. H. Strong and E. Y. Mullins are Baptist representatives of this view, while Donald Bloesch represents more contemporary evangelical approaches to the dynamic viewpoint.[43] Also, contemporary advocates with nuanced approaches include G. C. Berkouwer (1975), Paul J. Achtemeier (1980), and William J. Abraham (1981).[44]

In many ways this approach originated as a reaction to the dictation theory. It sees the work of the Spirit in directing the writer to the concepts he should have and then allowing great freedom for the human author to express this idea in his own style, through his own personality, in a way consistent with and characteristic of his own situation and context.

More contemporary approaches have expanded the view beyond the human author to see the place of the community in the Scripture's composition. The complexity of this position sees the Bible arising out of several traditions that confess what God has done within the situation of the community, recognizing the respondents or authors who take up the traditions and reformulate them in specific situations. Inspiration is then generally limited to God's initiating impulse, and thus the stress of inspiration falls not upon the product—Scripture itself—but upon the purpose and process.

The dynamic view's strength is its attempt to maintain the two-sided character of Scripture. Its stress upon the creativity of the human author and his community is quite commendable. Inspiration, however, refers to the entire process, not just the momentary event of initiation. In some ways, similar to Barth's view, inspiration and illumination are conflated and confused. The theory properly stresses the relation of inspiration to ideas and concepts, but it fails to account for the relationship between ideas and words. In emphasizing the process of inspiration, it does not place the emphasis where Scripture itself places it—on the product of inspiration. The real shortcoming of this approach, with its various nuances, is its imbalanced stress upon God's initiating impulse rather than His superintending work over the entire process and product. Finally, it must be seen that in this approach the emphasis is more upon the biblical writers (who, granted, are referred to in 2 Pet. 1:19–21) than upon the writings (which are referred to in 2 Tim. 3:16).

PLENARY VIEW

The last theory we shall examine is that which is put forward in this book as the most acceptable model of inspiration based on the Scripture's own testimony and consensus within the history of the church. This approach is careful to see the Spirit's influence both upon the writers and, primarily, upon the writings. It also seeks to view inspiration as extending to all (thus, the adjective plenary) portions of Holy Scripture, even beyond the direction of thoughts to the selection of words. Even though the writers expressed this message in a way that evidences the situation of the writing and the author's unique style, background, and personality, we must recognize the element of mystery involved in this process, which does not fully explain the how of inspiration.[45] The plenary view seeks to do justice to the human factors in the Bible's composition and avoids any attempt to suggest that the entire books of the Bible were dictated. We believe that this model for understanding biblical inspiration best accounts for the design and character of Scripture and the human circumstances of the Bible's composition.

CONCLUSION

Our approach to the doctrine of inspiration might appear circular but it is a viable, not a viscous, circle. We have explored the Bible's message to affirm its own inspiration and divine character. The plenary model of inspiration was seen to account best for the Bible's own claim and to balance the divine-human authorship of Scripture.

The Bible's inspiration preserves divine revelation for God's people. We acknowledge Scripture's literary diversity and affirm that it is more than a historical accident or decorative device. This recognition of literary diversity brings a healthy realization of the divine-human authorship of the Bible. Inspiration is thus concursive and plenary, meaning that all Scripture is inspired. We affirm verbal inspiration, meaning that the Spirit's work influences even the choice of words by the human authors, while remaining cognizant of contemporary linguistic theory that suggests that meaning is located at the sentence level and beyond. The corollary of inspiration is its truthfulness and authority. It is to this issue that we now turn our attention.

ENDNOTES

1. Clark Pinnock, "Three Views of the Bible in Contemporary Theology," in *Biblical Authority*, ed. Jack B. Rogers (Waco: Word, 1977), 71.

2. Cf. Donald G. Bloesch, *Essentials of Evangelical Theology*, 2 vols. (San Francisco: Harper and Row, 1978–79), 1:51–56.

3. We recognize that diverse conclusions have been drawn from the analogy between the divine and human in Jesus and in Scripture by scholars with differing theological positions. It is not absolutely clear whether the analogy can be applied to the human authors through whom God was active in the composition of Scripture or to the actual result of inspiration. The doctrine of the incarnation does account for the true activity of God in the human dimension, thus allowing for at least the possibility that God could work in human beings to communicate His Word in human words. More important to the theology of Scripture than the analogy described above is Jesus Christ's own view of Scripture.

4. Gene M. Tucker and Douglas A. Knight, ed., *Humanizing America's Iconoclastic Book* (Chico, Calif.: Scholars, 1982).

5. See Bloesch, *Evangelical Theology*, 1:134.

6. Ibid., 134–35; see also the discussion of the docetic view of Scripture in John Gerstner, "The Church's Doctrine of Biblical Inspiration," in *The Foundation of Biblical Authority*, ed. James Montgomery Boice (Grand Rapids: Zondervan, 1978), 12; Klaas Runia and Karl Barth, *Doctrine of Holy Scripture* (Grand Rapids: Eerdmans, 1962); James Tunstead Burtchaell, *Catholic Theories of Biblical Inspiration Since 1810: A Review and Critique* (London: Cambridge, 1969), 290–91.

7. Herman Ridderbos, *Studies in Scripture and Its Authority* (St. Catherines, Ontario: Paideia, 1978), 24.

8. See D. L. Baker, *Two Testaments: One Bible* (1976; Grand Rapids: Baker, rev. 1993).

9. Ridderbos, *Studies in Scripture*, 25.

10. See James E. White, *What is Truth?* (Nashville: Broadman, 1994); Anthony Thiselton, "Truth," *New International Dictionary of New Testament Theology*, vol. 3, ed. Colin Brown (Grand Rapids: Zondervan, 1979); Roger Nicole, "The Biblical Concept of Truth," in *Scripture and Truth*, eds. D. A. Carson and John D. Woodbridge, 287–98. For a different perspective, see Frank Stagg, "What Is Truth?" in *Science, Faith and Revelation*, ed. Robert E. Patterson (Nashville: Broadman, 1979), 239–60. There are hints of this

dualism in E. Y. Mullins, *The Christian Religion in its Doctrinal Expression* (Philadelphia: Judson, 1917), although his purpose was to affirm the religious and soteriological nature and purpose of Scripture.

11. See Wayne A. Grudem, "Scripture's Self-Attestation and the Problem of Formulating a Doctrine of Scripture," in *Scripture and Truth*, eds. D. A. Carson and John D. Woodbridge, 19–59; also James M. Grier, "The Self-Witness of the Bible," *Grace Theological Journal* 1 (1979):71–76; Edwin A. Blum, "The Apostle's View of Scripture," in *Inerrancy*, ed. Norman L. Geisler (Grand Rapids: Zondervan, 1979), 39–53. The approach of self-attestation is sometimes rejected on the grounds of circular reasoning. But the dilemma involved in this approach is apparent: either the Bible has its starting point upon itself or upon some other foundation, in which case it would be guilty of inconsistency. We can allow for additional testimony, but surely the Scripture's own claim must be given prior consideration. As with all points of theology, a consistent method would call for a theological statement in Scripture about itself to be considered prior to an examination of the phenomena in Scripture. Yet Beegle (*Scripture, Tradition and Infallibility*, 175-97) seeks to develop a theology of inspiration based upon the phenomena of Scripture. His approach and conclusions differ from those in this book.

12. See Carl F. H. Henry, "The Authority and Inspiration of the Bible," *The Expositor's Bible Commentary*, ed. F. E. Gaebelein, 12 vols. (Grand Rapids: Zondervan, 1979), 1:13.

13. Ibid. Cf. J. N. D. Kelly, *A Commentary on the Pastoral Epistles* (New York: Harper and Row, 1963), 203.

14. For an example of this approach, see especially Martin Dibelius and Hans Conzelmann, *The Pastoral Epistles*, trans. Philip Buttolph and Adela Yarbro (Philadelphia: Fortress, 1962), 120. However, such a translation is highly unlikely because it makes the *kai* ("also") quite awkward. It is doubtful that the apostle would affirm that Scripture has a second characteristic ("also") before describing its initial characteristic. The passage evidences a predicate construction and calls for the more straightforward translation: "The whole of Scripture is inspired . . ." (e.g. KJV, NASB, NIV). Cf. C. F. D. Moule, *An Idiom Book of New Testament Greek* (Cambridge: University Press, 1953), 95. Also Gottlob Schrenk, *grapho* Theological Dictionary of the New Testament, ed. G. Kittel and trans. Geoffrey Bromiley (Grand Rapids: Eerdmans, 1964), 1:759, who comments, "This obviously means every passage of Scripture." The extent of inspiration is discussed adequately by Millard J. Erickson, *Christian Theology* (Grand Rapids: Baker, 1983), 210–12.Herman Ridderbos (*Studies in Scripture*, 27) says that "the predicative significance of *theopneustos* is not in my opinion disputable."

15. Marshall, *Biblical Inspiration*, 25.

16. It is highly probable that the author is not making a distinction in his mind between the LXX and the MT in making this assertion. See Homer A. Kent, Jr., *The Pastoral Epistles* (Chicago: Moody, 1982), 281; also see Nigel Turner, *Syntax*, vol. 3 of *A Grammar of New Testament Greek* (Edinburgh: T & T Clark, 1963), 199. Though Turner's comments are ambiguous, it seems best to take *pas* in an inclusive manner. We could then translate as "Everything that takes on the character of Scripture," and thus the entire canon, even the New Testament, is included by inference. Yet, we must note that the Old Testament is what is primarily in view as the term *graphe* indicates. Note the reference to the Holy Scriptures in verse 15.

17. Marshall, *Biblical Inspiration*, 43.

18. Ibid., 42.

19. Even though John R. Rice, *Our God-Breathed Book* (Murfreesboro, Tenn.: Sword of the Lord, 1969), 192–287, accepts the term "dictation," he denies the idea of mechanical dictation. Some have wrongly characterized inerrantists as advocates of mechanical dictation (e.g. Dale Moody, *The Word of Truth*, [Grand Rapids: Eerdmans, 1981], 46–47), but this is not the case. Rice is perhaps one of the few fundamentalists who used the term "dictation," but he denies mechanical dictation (see p. 287); see especially the discussion of the fundamentalist approach to Scripture in Donald K. McKim, *What Christians Believe About the Bible* (Nashville: Nelson, 1985), 56–57. Even Harold Lindsell (in *The Battle for the Bible*, [Grand Rapids: Zondervan, 1976], 33) claimed he did not know any scholar who believes in biblical inerrancy who holds that the Scriptures were received by dictation. Many wrongly attribute the dictation approach to John Calvin. Calvin used the word dictation in *The Second Epistle of Paul to the Corinthians and the Epistles to Timothy, Titus, and Philemon*, trans. T. A. Small and eds. D. W. Torrance and T. F. Torrance (Grand Rapids: Eerdmans, 1964), 329–31. While he obviously employed the term dictation, numerous Calvin scholars, such as John Gerstner, W. Robert Godfrey, Kenneth Kantzer, and J. I. Packer have shown that Calvin did not have a developed concept of mechanical dictation. His view of inspiration could be characterized as a "plenary" approach; see J. I. Packer, "Calvin's View of Scripture," *God's Inerrant Word*, ed. J. W. Montgomery (Minneapolis: Bethany, 1974), 102–104.

20. Donald G. Bloesch, *Holy Scripture* (Downers Grove, Ill.: InterVarsity, 1994), 117–30.

21. It is possible that at these points, and perhaps at others where the prophet confesses "Thus says the Lord . . ." that dictation may be possible, though not probable. The Ten Commandments quite likely can be con-

sidered dictation material, but we cannot know for sure about this or other portions of Scripture.

22. Erickson, *Christian Theology*, 215–20; also see B. B. Warfield's classic work, *The Inspiration and Authority of the Bible* (Philadelphia: Presbyterian and Reformed, reprint 1948), 155-56.

23. See Pinnock, *Scripture Principle*, 1–82. This is not to affirm that some parts are more inspired than others, but that characteristics of inspiration are evidenced differently between Luke's gospel, Proverbs, the Apocalypse, and the Ten Commandments. The biblical writers themselves either acknowledge or give indication of such differences.

24. For a full treatment of the human dimension, see Pinnock, *Scripture Principle*, 106–29; Gordon R. Lewis, "The Human Authorship of Inspired Scripture," *Inerrancy*, 229–64. If we take the human situation seriously, it demands that we study Scripture not only theologically and devotionally, but also grammatically, historically, contextually, and critically. See David S. Dockery, et al., eds., *Foundations for Biblical Interpretation* (Nashville: Broadman and Holman, 1994) and David A. Black and David S. Dockery, *New Testament Criticism and Interpretation* (Grand Rapids: Zondervan, 1991).

25. Erickson, *Christian Theology*, 204–06.

26. See Anthony A. Hoekema, *Created in God's Image* (Grand Rapids: Eerdmans, 1986).

27. Lewis, "Human Authorship," 244–46.

28. Eugene Nida, *Message and Mission* (New York: Harper, 1960), 90.

29. See D. E. Nineham, *The Use and Abuse of the Bible* (London: SCM, 1976), who has presented useful insights regarding cultural and temporal distance. Yet his work is basically negative in its approach, although he does not deny entirely the possibility that God can speak through the Bible. We agree with Pinnock, (*Scripture Principle*, 110) that "we must resist a misuse of cultural relatedness as a cloak to evade what the Scriptures really want to teach. . . . God's Word comes to us in human language, it is true, and there are features in it incidental to its teaching purposes. But 'in all things necessary' that the Bible wishes to teach us it is true and coherent and possesses the wisdom of God" (p. 115).

30. See Robert Sloan, "Canonical Theology of the New Testament," *Foundations for Biblical Interpretation*, 565–94.

31. Craig L. Blomberg, "The Diversity of Literary Genres in the New Testament," *New Testament Criticism and Interpretation*, 507–32; also Robert H. Stein, *Playing by the Rules* (Grand Rapids: Baker, 1994).

32. See Richard N. Longenecker, "On the Concept of Development in Pauline Thought," *Perspectives in Evangelical Theology*, eds. Kenneth Kantzer and Stanley N. Gundry (Grand Rapids: Baker, 1979), 195–200.

33. Donald Guthrie, *New Testament Theology* (Downers Grove: InterVarsity, 1981), 51.

34. Ibid., 59.

35. A. H. Strong, *Systematic Theology* (Old Tappan, NJ: Revell, 1907), 223.

36. R. C. Sproul, "Controversy at Culture Gap," *Eternity* 27 (May 1975):13.

37. See J. I. Packer, "Encountering Present-Day Views of Scripture," *Foundations of Biblical Authority*, ed. James M. Boice (Grand Rapids: Zondervan, 1978); Robert K. Johnston, ed., *The Use of the Bible in Theology: Evangelical Options* (Atlanta: John Knox, 1985); McKim, *What Christians Believe About the Bible*; D. A. Carson, "Recent Developments in the Doctrine of Scripture," *Hermenuetics, Authority, and Canon* (Grand Rapids: Zondervan, 1986), 10–48.

38. See L. H. DeWolf, *A Theology of the Living Church* (New York: Harper and Brothers, revised 1960), 48–75.

39. In some ways Karl Barth shares this view with Emil Brunner, Reinhold Niebuhr, and, to a much lesser extent, Rudolf Bultmann. We focus on Barth because he was not only the first, but also in many ways, the greatest and most brilliant of neo-orthodox theologians. J. I. Packer ("Present-Day Views") comments that Barth is likely to have more long-term influence than other theologians of this type; both because neo-orthodoxy appears at its strongest intellectually and noblest spiritually in the writings of Barth, and because his weaknesses, however great, are comparatively less than the corresponding defects of others on the same trail. It should, however, be realized that Barth stands at the extreme right of the neo-orthodox spectrum. See also Colin Brown, *Karl Barth and the Christian Message* (London: InterVarsity, 1967), 99–140; Karl Barth, *Church Dogmatics*, trans. G. W. Bromiley and T. F. Torrance (Edinburgh: T & T Clark, 1956), 1:1, 51–335.

40. Marshall, *Biblical Inspiration*, 36.

41. Pinnock, "Three Views of the Bible," *Biblical Authority*, 37.

42. Brown, *Karl Barth and the Christian Message*, 146.

43. See Strong, *Systematic Theology*, 211; also Bloesch, *Holy Scripture*.

44. See Achtemeier, *The Inspiration of Scripture*; Abraham, *The Divine Inspiration of Holy Scripture*; Berkouwer, *Holy Scripture*.

45. See David S. Dockery, *The Doctrine of the Bible* (Nashville: Convention, 1991); Carl F. H. Henry, "Authority and Inspiration," *Expositor's Bible Commentary*, ed. Frank E. Gaebelein (Grand Rapids: Zondervan, 1979), 1:13–35; idem., *God, Revelation, and Authority*, vol. 4; and Erickson, *Christian Theology*, 199–220.

IV

THE TRUTHFULNESS AND AUTHORITY OF SCRIPTURE

Building on a plenary model of inspiration we must ask, "In what sense can we confess that Scripture, which evidences genuine human authorship written in a time-related context, is normative?" Or must we conclude that Scripture is wholly descriptive and the student of Scripture is little more than a historian or an antique keeper, who displays the exhibits in the best possible way? We think such a descriptive approach is unacceptable and lacks all the dynamic of the experience of the biblical authors and their communities of faith.[1]

THE TRUTHFULNESS OF SCRIPTURE

Perhaps we should rephrase the question. Does any Bible student accept a descriptive approach completely? Is not the real issue to what extent is the Bible normative for the contemporary church? Even Rudolf Bultmann, while maintaining that first-century cultural patterns cannot be considered normative, nevertheless, sought to reinterpret these patterns for the contemporary church.[2]

THE SCRIPTURE AS NORMATIVE

Although the cultural background and environment have radically changed since the biblical writings were penned, the human condition has not changed. It is to the human condition, men and women created in the image of God, yet fallen, that the unity of the biblical message speaks in a normative manner. We can maintain this confession for the following reasons: (1) The Scriptures are the result of divine inspiration. (2) They proclaim the saving acts of God. (3) They are historically proximate to the saving acts of God. (4) They are based on the prophetic-apostolic authority.[3]

Even with cultural advancements and scientific progress, the need of men and women for a right standing and a right relationship with God remains unchanged. The reason is that even the advancing wisdom and knowledge of the world cannot help humanity in the ultimate aspects of life (see 1 Cor. 1–4). The basic problem of how sinful humans are to approach a holy God and how these persons are to live in relationship to the life-giving Spirit of God is the same for all ages.

It is our belief, therefore, that divinely inspired teaching concerning God and matters relating to God and His creation (*sub specie Dei*) are normative for the contemporary church. When such matters are proclaimed and confessed in the twentieth century, however, mere repetition of early Christian beliefs may not be sufficient; a contextualized application that awakens modern readers to an awareness that the Bible speaks in relevant ways to contemporary issues in church and society is also necessary.[4] When Scripture is approached from this perspective, it will be necessary to determine underlying principles for all portions of Scripture that address the contemporary situation, even if the direct teaching of Scripture is somehow limited by cultural-temporal factors (see 1 Tim. 5:23; 1 Cor. 16:20; Eph. 6:5). Believers will recognize that this is the case because of the two-sided character of Scripture. Because it is authored by humans in specific contexts, certain teachings may be contextually limited, but because Scripture is divinely inspired, the underlying principles are normative and applicable for the church in every age. When approaching the Bible, recognizing its authoritative and normative character, we can discover truth[5] and its ramifications for the answers to life's ultimate questions as well as guidelines and principles for godly living as we move toward the twenty-first-century world.[6]

THE SCRIPTURE AS TRUTHFUL

Having affirmed the possibility of a normative Scripture, we must probe further and ask if we can also confess the complete truthfulness and reliability of Scripture. This issue must be addressed because of the ongoing misunderstanding in contemporary discussions about the Bible and because inerrancy is the corollary and result of our affirmations about a plenary view of inspiration. While the term *inerrancy* continues to be a "red-flag" word among many and subject to misunderstanding among others, it remains, when properly defined, a helpful and informative theological term to describe the results of inspiration.

These misunderstandings have resulted from false associations with a literalistic hermeneutic and dictation theories of inspiration. Additional problems have developed from careless statements on the part of advocates who have been overzealous in their defense of the doctrine (even denying the use of textual criticism) or who have concentrated unduly upon issues of preciseness and "errors" when the focus should instead be placed upon the issues of truthfulness and reliability. Others have attempted to prove that inerrancy is a direct teaching of Scripture instead of acknowledging that it is the proper implication of inspiration. Still others have attempted to defend the issue from a "slippery-slope" standpoint and have unintentionally moved the primary focus of the issue away from theological concerns to historical concerns (this is not to say the historical concerns are unimportant).

One additional matter that we should consider is related to the importance of inerrancy. This teaching is important primarily for theological and epistemological reasons, and shifting the argument to the secondary realm of soteriological concerns has only confused the issue. Individual salvation is not dependent upon one's confession of inerrancy, but consistent theological method and instruction needs the base of inerrancy in order to continue to maintain an orthodox confession in salvific matters. Thus we see that inerrancy, as a corollary of inspiration, is a foundational issue upon which other theological building blocks are laid.

With these warnings behind us and an awareness of the complexity of the issue, let us suggest a definition of inerrancy. Inerrancy means that "when all the facts are known, the Bible (in its original writings) properly interpreted in light of which culture and communication means had developed by the time of its composition will be shown to be completely true (and therefore not false) in all that it affirms, to the degree of precision intended by the author, in all matters relating to God and his creation."[7]

No doubt some will say that with the carefulness of the definition, which attempts to recognize the complexity of the issues, it is futile to carry on further discussion. But hopefully the exact opposite is true! We trust that the careful manner in which the definition is stated will help many who have misunderstood the doctrine to come to grips with what inerrancy is and what it is not. The definition seeks to be faithful to the phenomena of Scripture as well as theological affirmations in Scripture about the veracity of God. It will be helpful at this point to offer some brief comment about our definition.

1. *When all the facts are known:* The statement begins from the vantage point of faith, recognizing that we may not have all the data necessary on this side of the eschaton to bear on the Bible. It is also likely that our sinful, finite minds may misinterpret some facts that we do have. Thus, we should exercise caution with things we might not understand until all the facts are known.

2. *The Bible (in its original writings):* Inerrancy applies to all aspects of the Bible as originally written. A claim to complete inerrancy is limited to the original words of the biblical text. A reference to these original writings is not restricted to some lost codex but is an affirmation relating to the original words that were written by the prophetic-apostolic messengers. Thus, our confession of inerrancy and inspiration applies to translations to the degree that they represent accurately the original words. It is our belief that we can express great confidence in our present translations. Therefore, the qualifying

statement regarding the original writings is not intended as an apologetic sidestep but is a theological appeal to the providential oversight and the veracity of God in His superintending work of inspiration.[8] Such a statement is never intended to remove trust from our present-day translations (whether KJV, NIV, NASB, NRSV, etc.), but to ensure and confirm faith in these translations because they rest upon a sure foundation.

3. *Properly interpreted:* The definition recognizes that statements concerning the nature of the biblical text cannot be separated completely from hermeneutical issues. While these issues must be distinguished they cannot be separated.[9] Other chapters in this volume underscore this assertion. Before falsehood can be recognized, it is necessary to know if a text has been interpreted properly. The author's intention must be recognized, and matters of precision and accuracy must be judged in light of the culture and means of communication that had developed by the time of the text's composition. The text, as a guideline, should be interpreted normally, grammatically, historically, contextually, and theologically. The context, background, genre, and purpose of the writing must be considered in interpretational matters.

4. *Is completely true (and therefore not false):* A very important aspect of the definition is the evaluation of whether or not the Bible is inerrant in terms of truthfulness and falseness rather than in terms of error or lack of error. This removes the discussion away from grammatical mistakes or lack of precision in reports. Inerrancy, on the other hand, must not be associated with strict tests of precision in which careless harmonization attempts to bring about a precision uncommon to the text itself.[10] On the other hand, we cannot shift the emphasis to such general and meaningless definitions as willful deceit for inerrancy and infallibility.[11] Recognizing that the issue is truthfulness may confirm what many have inferred when declaring *inerrancy* an improper term to describe Scripture. But inerrancy, like inspiration, has become imbedded in the theological literature, and it is best to emphasize careful definitions rather than to attempt to change terms, especially in

the midst of the ongoing controversy over the nature and meaning of Scripture.

5. *In all areas:* The definition states that inerrancy is not limited merely to "religious" matters, thus creating, or at least providing the framework for, an improper dualism. We want to affirm that inerrancy applies to all areas of knowledge, since all truth is God's truth. Yet issues of history and science must be evaluated in light of the communication means at the time of inscripturation. Modern canons of science and historiography and their concern for exactness are not proper standards for first-century (and earlier) authors. These matters must be analyzed in light of the author's intended level of precision, which most likely should be seen in terms of phenomenological observation.[12]

In light of this brief commentary on our definition, we can maintain that inerrancy primarily points to theological and epistemological matters. In providing a statement about an inerrant Bible, we must be careful with "slippery-slope" theories or avoid them altogether, though it is important to recognize that missions, evangelism, and zeal for ethical application of Scripture have declined where a high view of Scripture has likewise declined! Yet we know that God can, and certainly does, overrule departure from orthodoxy, as church history bears testimony.

We must avoid unnecessary associations with a literalistic, stilted, hermeneutic, but we do not care to dissociate the issue from hermeneutics. It must be recognized that inerrancy is not a direct teaching in Scripture (though Matt. 5:18 and John 10:35 may point in that direction) but is a direct implication and important corollary of the direct teaching about Scripture's inspiration, which can be described as plenary, verbal, and concursive.

We must seek a view of inerrancy that is consistent with the divine-human nature of Scripture. This means that the phenomena must be accounted for and Scripture's witness to itself and its divine character must be satisfied. Such an approach is not primarily dependent upon a correspondence view of truth, although many of the affirmations of Scripture can be verified. Most, if not all, of the theological and ethical statements in Scripture lie outside the realm of current verification, and thus a coherence view of truth is more encompassing and applicable for all of Scripture. We can work from a correspondence view of truth only in light of eschatological realities. Realizing these issues, we can gladly confess that the Bible is a dependable, truthful, trustworthy, faithful, and thus inerrant Word of God to humanity.[13]

Nevertheless, the term inerrancy may not go far enough. The Bible, like other forms of human communication, is certainly more than true assertions. Communication involves emotions, aesthetic and affective abilities, and the will, in addition to propositional statements. Certainly praise is more than a proposition. While a Psalm may include a declaration of God's faithfulness, it is true even if it is not principally a proposition. The same can be said for ethical commands. So although we affirm the inerrancy of the Bible, the idea of total trustworthiness better describes the whole of the Bible and its uniqueness. It is important for us to say more than just propositions are true; in fact all aspects of Holy Scripture are totally reliable.

While truth is more than propositional, this certainly does not imply that it is less than propositional. Biblical truth is not just some mystical encounter or vague experience that we have as a result of reading Scripture. The fact that truth is more than doctrine should never be used to imply that doctrine is not necessary or important. Truth would be unknowable and incommunicable without the doctrinal framework and propositional grounding that we find in Holy Scripture.

Thus we can affirm the Bible's total truthfulness, its coherence, and its perspicuity (made possible by the witness of the Holy Spirit). The Bible focuses on Christ, is applicable for the church, and is affirmed to us by the testimony of the Holy Spirit in our hearts. Without these presuppositions we cannot move forward in understanding how the Bible should be rightly interpreted or applied to our lives.

We can summarize this portion of our discussion by saying that the Bible has a two-sided divine-human character. Equally, we have observed that the Bible testifies to its own divine nature and inspiration. Divine inspiration should be understood primarily as referring to the final product (the written text), although we desire to avoid a conflict between the inspiration of the human authors of the text and the written text itself. But it is our conclusion that a view of inspiration limited to the human authors alone is quite insufficient.

While focusing on the product of inspiration—the inscripturated text—we do not want to ignore the purpose and process of inspiration. The purpose of inspiration is ultimately for salvific purposes, which in its full understanding, includes teaching, reproof, correction, and training in righteousness, so that believers can be equipped for service and good works. The process of inspiration is inclusive in the training and preparation of the authors, their research, and their use of witnesses. As a result we can posit that the Bible is simultaneously the Word of God and the words of men.

Having surveyed several approaches to the issue of inspiration, we noted that inspiration does not mean that God dictated all of Scripture, for this fails to account for the human activity. Neither can it be affirmed that the Bible is merely a human book, whose authors, due to special spiritual sensitivity, produced inspiring works of literature. Not only must inspiration recognize the human authorship and the divine character of Scripture, but it must not divorce God's deeds from His words. Neither must we create dichotomies between thoughts and words, processes and product, writers and written word, God's initiating impulse and His complete superintending work. A comprehensive, plenary view of inspiration is essential.

This understanding of biblical inspiration applies to all of canonical Scripture (including the process, the purpose, and ultimately the product) and asserts that by the concursive action of God the Scriptures are, in their entirety, both the work of the Spirit and the work of human authors. Such a view of inspiration is not only plausible, but necessarily important for affirmations of truth. We believe that a plenary, verbal, inclusive view of inspiration alone does justice to the theological teachings and the phenomena within the text.

We examined these temporary conclusions in light of the human authorship of the Bible. We recognized that a concursive view of inspiration accounted for the style, personality, background, and context of the human authors. We noted the possibility of confessing a concursive view because the human authors were not autonomous but were men of faith, functioning in communities of faith with an awareness of God's direction in their lives. Consistent with our view of the genuine humanness of the biblical text is the need to notice the cultural-temporal factors involved in this issue. But recognition that the writers were bearers of the image of God opens up the possibility of qualifying historical and cultural distance. This is due to the belief that they, along with their readers and hearers, had memories of the past, consideration of the present, and expectations of the future. This allows for the possibility of cross-cultural and cross-temporal communication. The reality of human authorship is evidenced by the variety of emphases in Scripture, the different writing styles, and the development within the Testaments and the writers themselves. It is our conclusion that this variety is complementary and not contradictory. The variety of Scripture has a genuine unity that is not forced upon the text but is present as a result of divine inspiration.

We have already noted the very real plausibility of maintaining the normative character of Scripture, while simultaneously affirming the historical situation of the human authors and the time-relatedness of the text. Because of the basic needs shared by men and women of all ages and races in all times and cultures, the central message of Scripture can speak in a normative and authoritative way. Beyond this, we acknowledged that Scripture speaks not only to pietistic and religious needs but to the truth of and about God, and to the ramifications affecting all matters related to life and godliness. We believe that such a normative Scripture can be described as inerrant when inerrancy is carefully defined to avoid overstatement or improper association with a dictation view of inspiration. We believe, therefore, that it is quite important, even epistemologically necessary, that as the church moves into the twenty-first century it carefully articulates a statement concerning Scripture that maintains with equal force both the humanity and deity of the Bible. Thus we can have confidence in the Bible as a trustworthy and authoritative guide. Now let us turn our attention to the issue of biblical authority.

The Authority of Scripture

The ultimate concern in a discussion of Christian Scripture is its authority. We confess the authority of the Bible and its rightful role in commanding obedience for the people of God. We recognize that the Bible is authoritative for contemporary cultural issues, as well as for ethics and decision making.

A view of the Bible that affirms its divine inspiration and total truthfulness is of little value if it is not accompanied by an enthusiastic commitment to the Bible's complete and absolute authority. An approach to the subject of biblical authority must begin with God Himself, for in God all authority is ultimately located. God is His own authority. There is nothing outside Him on which His authority is established. When God made His promise to Abraham, He pledged His own name because there was nothing or no one greater by whom He could swear (see Heb. 6:13). God's authority is the authority of who and what God is. As we learned in earlier chapters, who God is has been made known in His self-manifestation, since God can be known only in His own self-revelation. The key to God's authority is His revelation. In this manner, revelation and authority are seen as two sides of the same reality. God thus declares His authority through His revelation, and He alone is the ultimate source of authority for all other lesser authorities.

Authority is the right or power to command obedience or belief. God's sovereign, universal, and eternal reign over the entire universe evidences His authority (see Exod. 15:18; Job 26:12; Isa. 52). He establishes His purposes in time and does all things according to His will (see Dan. 4:34–35; Eph. 1:11). All authority on earth and in heaven comes from God alone. His providential direction over the events of history demonstrates His authority.

Men and women are creatures of the self-revealing, eternal God. Since He has created humankind, life's meaning is found in dependence on and relationship with Him. God exercises authority over His creation; and God's people respond to His authority in obedience and worship, as well as in confession and repentance. God's authority is communicated in the church and its tradition, in human reason, in conscience and experience, in nature and history, in Christ and the Bible. Of course, as noted in chapters 1 and 2,

God has ultimately revealed Himself in the person of Jesus Christ (see John 1:1–18; Heb. 1:1–3).

God reveals Himself in all of the ways mentioned above; yet the Bible is the primary means of God's authoritative self-disclosure for people today. The Bible pictures Jesus' authority in terms of acting for God the Father. Jesus exercises all the rightful authority of God. He forgives sin (see Mark 2:5–8), casts out demons (see Mark 1:27), teaches with authority (see Matt. 5:21–48; 7:28–29), and raises the dead (see Luke 7:11–17; John 11:38–44). As the obedient Son of God, He follows the Word of God revealed in the Scriptures and acknowledges and appeals to the Scripture's authority (see Matt. 4:1–11; John 10:33–36). Jesus' death and resurrection provided victory over sin, evil, and death (see Col. 2:15; 1 John 3:8). All authority in heaven and on earth has been given to Him (see Matt. 28:18–20).

Jesus' authority is exercised over the church (see Eph. 1:20–23) and is uniquely expressed through His personal ambassadors, the apostles (see Mark 3:14; John 17:18; Acts 1:8; 2 Cor. 5:20; Gal. 1:1–2:9). In this way the apostles served as the foundation of the church (see Eph. 2:20–3:5). In fulfillment of Christ's promises (see John 14:26; 16:13), the apostles' authority has been placed permanently in their writings. Thus, the Spirit of God has inspired the prophetic-apostolic writings, and the Scriptures become the recognized authority that communicates God's truth, which is to be taught, believed, and obeyed. The Bible, then, is the Book of God's truth. Because the Bible is completely truthful, it must be wholly trustworthy in its affirmations. Because it is truthful and trustworthy, it is our final authority in all things that pertain to life and godliness.[14]

The Bible is to be seen as the ultimate standard of authority for God's people. The Bible derives its authority from the self-revealing and self-authenticating God. The Bible's authority can and does communicate across cultural, geographical, and temporal differences between the biblical world and our setting. Scripture is authoritative as it is rightly and faithfully interpreted in its historical setting. The Holy Spirit illumines our minds and hearts to understand the biblical message. Likewise, the Spirit leads us to recognize the authority of Scripture and to respond and obey its message today.[15]

The Bible calls for an obedience to the authority of God revealed in His Word, not in reaction to authority nor in an authoritarian sense but from a true freedom that belongs to the children of God. We must avoid a concept of freedom that loses a sense of "oughtness" and responsibility. At the same time, we must avoid a swing toward authoritarianism, where our commitment to Scripture's authority is misplaced in a church leader or in a societal or cultural trend.

Many people confuse a desire to obey Scripture's authority with a personal insecurity that calls for a leader to tell them constantly what to do or think. More troubling is that some leaders encourage this confusion by commingling a commitment to biblical authority with a type of authority associated with certain positions of church leadership. What is needed more than ever is a clear-cut distinction between human and divine authority so that the authority of the Bible is not undercut or lost through a false equation with human structures.[16]

We demonstrate our concern for biblical authority not only by careful biblical interpretation but also by repentance and prayer. A commitment to the complete truthfulness and trustworthiness (or inerrancy) of Scripture is important because it is the foundation that establishes the full extent of Scripture's authority.[17]

Living with a Holy Spirit-prompted desire to respond to the message and authority of the Bible brings reproof and correction (see 2 Tim. 3:16), which results in contrition, discipleship, and enablement for worship and service (see 2 Tim. 3:17). It results in training in righteousness that bears on Christian business people and the integrity of their practice. It bears on Christians, who must speak to matters of injustice in society and in the church. Biblical authority addresses families and their commitments to one another. It tells preachers and teachers to handle carefully the Word of God (see 2 Tim. 2:15). The authority of the Bible calls on us to recognize God's desire for unity (through variety) in the church (see Eph. 4:1–16; John 17; 1 Cor. 12) and the need to love one another (see John 13:34–35), even when we disagree over the interpretation of Scripture itself. Thus, we need a renewed commitment to biblical authority that enables us to relate to one another in love and humility, bringing about true fellowship and community and resulting in not only right doctrine, but also right practice before a watching, unbelieving world. We need a renewed commitment to biblical authority that will transform our performance-oriented church meetings into authentic worship and praise, that will turn our church programs into service that is pleasing to God. The Holy Spirit, through the Scriptures, illuminates our appreciation of grace and motivates us toward faithful evangelism, discipleship, social engagement, and worldwide missions.[18]

We confess that God has revealed Himself to us. His revelation has been preserved for us in Holy Scripture by the Holy Spirit's work of inspiration. We confess our belief in the divine inspiration, total truthfulness, and supreme authority of the Bible. Even beyond this affirmation, with willing spirits and open minds and hearts, we must dedicate ourselves anew to the authority of Holy Scripture, assured that we can place our complete confidence in God's truthful and reliable Word.[19]

As we have seen in the concluding section of this chapter, a close relationship exists between biblical authority and biblical interpretation. It is to the important matter of biblical interpretation that our discussion turns after we examine the important issue of canonization.

ENDNOTES

1. Donald Guthrie, *New Testament Theology* (Downers Grove, Ill.: Inter-Varsity, 1981), 953–82.

2. See Rudolf Bultmann, *New Testament Theology* (New York: Scribners, 1955).

3. See R. P. C. Hanson, *The Bible as a Norm of Faith* (Durham, N.C.: University Press, 1963), 7; idem., *Tradition in the Early Church* (London: SCM, 1962), 213–24; H. E. W. Turner, *The Pattern of Christian Truth* (London: Maybrays, 1954); and Edward J. Carnell, *The Case for Orthodox Theology* (Philadelphia: Fortress, 1959).

4. John Jefferson Davis, "Contextualization and the Nature of Theology," *The Necessity of Systematic Theology*, ed. John Jefferson Davis (Grand Rapids: Baker, 1980), 169–85; Clark Pinnock, *Scripture Principle* (San Francisco: Harper and Row, 1984), 210–21; David Hesselgrave, "Contextualization and Revelation Epistemology," *Inerrancy and Hermenuetics*, eds. Earl D. Radmacher and Robert D. Preus (Grand Rapids: Zondervan, 1986), 693–764.

5. Anthony C. Thiselton, "Truth," *Dictionary of New Testament Theology*, ed. Colin Brown (Grand Rapids: Zondervan, 1979), 3:874–902.

6. Anthony C. Thiselton, *The Two Horizons* (Grand Rapids: Eerdmans, 1980), 432–38.

7. Similar careful statements on the subject can be found in Millard J. Erickson, *Christian Theology* (Grand Rapids: Baker, 1983), 221–40. Paul D. Feinberg has written several informative and helpful articles; e.g. "The Meaning of Inerrancy," *Inerrancy*, ed. Norman L. Geisler (Grand Rapids: Zondervan, 1979), 267–304; "Bible, Inerrancy and Infallibility of," *Evangelical Dictionary of Theology*, ed. W. A. Elwell (Grand Rapids: Baker, 1984), 141–45. Two extremely significant volumes are D. A. Carson and John D. Woodbridge, eds., *Scripture and Truth*; and Roger Nicole and J. Ramsey Michaels, eds., *Inerrancy and Common Sense*.

8. See Greg L. Bahnsen, "The Inerrancy of the Autographa," *Inerrancy*, 172–89. The issue of the autographa is one of the most misunderstood aspects of the doctrine of inerrancy.

9. This is one of the real strengths of Clark Pinnock's work, *Scripture Principle*, 197–202. Pinnock's earlier work, *Biblical Revelation* (Chicago: Moody, 1971), is, in our opinion, a more consistent explanation of the doctrine of Scripture, but his discussion of the relationship of inspiration to interpretation in the latter work is a major advance. See also E. Radmacher and R. Preus, eds., *Inerrancy and Hermeneutic* (Grand Rapids: Zondervan, 1984); D. A. Carson and J. Woodbridge, eds., *Hermeneutics, Authority, and Canon* (Grand Rapids: Zondervan, 1986). It is because discussions of the full truthfulness of the Bible, while certainly distinguishable, are inseparable from hermeneutical issues that so much attention is given to the subject in the second part of this book.

10. It seems to me that the kind of undue concern for excessive harmonization, as exhibited in Harold Lindsell, *Battle for the Bible* (Grand Rapids: Zondervan, 1976), 174–76, is more confusing than helpful in demonstrating the full truthfulness of the Bible. Even though Lindsell does not include precision or preciseness as an aspect of his definition of inerrancy, he nevertheless confuses the issue with his focus on excessive harmonization. A more constructive approach to the matter of harmonization can be found in Craig L. Blomberg, "The Limits of Harmonization," *Hermeneutics, Authority, and Canon*.

11. Rogers and McKim, *Authority and Interpretation*, 3, while not affirming of inerrancy, but acknowledging infallibility, nevertheless define their confession about the nature of Scripture in terms of a lack of willful deception. This is hardly an acceptable definition, for it says nothing about the essence of Scripture, but is only a very general statement about Scripture's intent. The same misunderstanding is advanced by Russell Dil-

day, *The Doctrine of Biblical Authority* (Nashville: Convention Press, 1982). The weaknesses of the definition and the historiography behind it are ably discussed in John D. Woodbridge, *Biblical Authority* (Grand Rapids: Zondervan, 1983) and Richard Muller, *The Study of Theology: From Biblical Interpretation to Contemporary Formulation* (Grand Rapids: Zondervan, 1991).

12. For further discussion and clarification of this matter see David S. Dockery, "The Inerrancy and Authority of Scripture: Affirmation and Clarifications," *Theological Educator* 37 (1988): 15–36.

13. John Jefferson Davis, *Theology Primer* (Grand Rapids: Baker, 1981), 20–21.

14. See Bernard Ramm, *The Pattern of Authority* (Grand Rapids: Eerdmans, 1957).

15. James Leo Garrett, Jr., *Systematic Theology*, vol. 1 (Grand Rapids: Eerdmans, 1990), 181–82.

16. See John R. W. Stott, *Decisive Issues Facing Christians Today* (Old Tappan, N.J.: Revell, 1990).

17. Helpful insights on the relationship of truthfulness and authority can be found in Kenneth S. Kantzer, ed., *Applying the Scriptures* (Grand Rapids: Zondervan, 1987).

18. See Geoffrey W. Bromiley, "Authority," *International Standard Bible Encyclopedia*, ed. G. W. Bromiley, 4 vols. (Grand Rapids: Eerdmans, 1979), 1:346–71.

19. D. A. Carson, "Recent Developments in the Doctrine of Scripture," *Hermeneutics, Authority, and Canon*, 46–48.

V

THE TRANSMISSION AND CANONICITY OF THE BIBLE

What was the process for determining what books could be in the Bible? Why is it the case that Protestants have sixty-six books and other traditions have more? What criteria has been used in making these decisions? How does inspiration relate to canonicity? How does the issue of canon relate to the unity and diversity of the Bible? This chapter will address these issues while including a short history of the discussion of these matters.

THE TRANSMISSION OF THE BIBLE

We are briefly informed of the transmission of the preexilic parts of the Old Testament. Deuteronomy 31:9–26 commands that "the book of the wall" be placed by the side of the ark of the covenant and read publicly every seventh year at the Feast of Tabernacles. This directive points to an early form of preservation and transmission. The oracles of some of the prophets were committed to writing and entrusted for safekeeping until the prophecies should be fulfilled and the prophets vindicated (see Isa. 8:16; Jer. 36).

It is testimony to the providence of God that so much Old Testament material survived the Babylonian exile. Psalms that figured prominently in preexilic worship remained unsung for two generations while the temple lay in ruin. Although the people could not sing the Lord's song in a foreign land (see Ps. 137:4), they did not forget the familiar words, which were later reincorporated into the postexilic psalter and celebrated in the Second Temple.

Important examples of the transmission of the writings in the postexilic period are Ezra's mission to Jerusalem with the law of God in his hand (see Ezra 7:14) and the public reading of "the books of Moses" in Jerusalem during the Feast of Tabernacles in what was probably the initial year of Nehemiah's governorship (see Neh. 8:1–18). A critical threat to the transmission of the Scriptures came with the persecution under Antiochus IV (ca. 167 B.C.), when the officials burned "the books of the law" that were found. Jews who possessed these books were executed (see 1 Macc. 1:56). The persecution lasted three years. But when it was over, copies of the Scriptures could be procured from Jewish communities outside Judea.[1]

The New Testament documents were all written in Greek in the first century. Transmission of individual documents began prior to their corporate collection. Early in the second century the four Gospels and the Pauline Letters were circulated as two collections. From that time on, collections, rather than individual documents, were transmitted. Acts and the General Epistles were generally associated together. The Book of Revelation, for the most part, was transmitted by itself.[2]

The Western canon has generally followed the pattern of Gospels, Acts, Pauline Letters, Hebrews and the General Epistles, and Revelation. The Eastern canon has followed a different pattern. The Gospels are first followed by Acts, then the General Epistles without Hebrews, the Pauline Letters with Hebrews, and then Revelation. The Eastern church has continued to accept the Pauline authorship of the Book of Hebrews while it has been generally rejected in the West. Thus, we see that the transmission of the collections has taken different routes.[3]

EARLY ATTESTATIONS AND TRANSLATIONS

The early copies of the Old Testament were written on leather or papyrus from the time of Moses to the time of Malachi. The Jews' mystical reverence for the sacred books prompted them to bury copies that had become too old for use. Providentially, these scrolls, known as the Dead Sea Scrolls, were discovered in 1947. Until that discovery, we did not possess copies of the Old Testament dated earlier than A.D. 895.

The well-known Masoretic text was preserved by traditionalists, known as Masoretes. The Masoretes added accents and vowel points to the Hebrew text. They also devised extremely complex methods to safeguard the making of copies (ca. A.D. 600–950). They checked each copy carefully by counting the middle letter of pages, books, and sections. Everything countable was counted by the Masoretes. When the Dead Sea Scrolls were discovered, they provided us an earlier Hebrew text dating from the second century B.C. This was true for all Old Testament books except Esther. These discoveries have confirmed the reliability of the older Masoretic text.[4]

Historical research and archeological findings have led to the discovery of other important copies of translations of the Old Testament. These include the Samaritan Pentateuch, the Aramaic Targums; the Syriac version, called the Peshitta; and the Latin translation of Jerome (ca. A.D. 400), called the Vulgate. The most important of all the transmissions of the Old Testament is the pre-Christian Greek version called the Septuagint (LXX). Tradition claims that this version was produced by seventy-two Jewish elders at the request of Ptolemy II, king of Egypt, for the use of the Greek-speaking Jewish community in Alexandria, Egypt.

With rare exceptions, the Septuagint manuscripts that have been passed down were copied and preserved by Christians, not by Jews. The translation is of unequal quality. The Pentateuch, as we would expect, was treated with special care. The Septuagint is frequently quoted in the New Testament, since it served as the Bible of Greek-speaking Christians in the apostolic period. Many of the important theological terms in the New Testament derived their meanings from the Septuagint. While the Septuagint is not considered a completely trustworthy rendering of the Hebrew text, it still permits us to compare the Greek with our Hebrew versions. The same can be said of Targums, which are Aramaic paraphrases of Scripture, and of the Talmud, which records the comments of rabbis on the written text. All of these ensure us of having a faithful text of the Old Testament.

Early translations of the New Testament include Latin, Syriac, and Coptic (an Egyptian translation). Transmission and translation of the New Testament text present different issues than we face with the Old Testament. There are more than five thousand manuscripts of the New Testament, making the New Testament the best-attested document among all ancient writings. New Testament scholar F. F. Bruce has written:

> Perhaps we can appreciate how wealthy the New Testament is in manuscript attestation if we compare the textual manuscript for other ancient historical works. For Caesar's Gallic War (composed between 58 and 56 B.C.) there are several extant MSS (manuscripts), but only nine or ten are good, and the oldest is some 900 years later than Caesar's day. Of the 142 books of the Roman History of Livy (59 B.C.–A.D. 17), only thirty-five survived; these are known to us from not more than 20 MSS of any consequence, only one of which, and that contains fragments of Books III–VI, is as old as the fourth century. Of the fourteen books of the Histories of Tacitus (c. A.D. 100) only four-and-a-half survived. Of the sixteen books of his Annals, ten survived in full and two in part. The text of these extant portions of his two great historical works depends entirely on two MSS, one of the ninth century and one of the eleventh . . . . The History of Thucydides (c. 460–400 B.C.) is known to us from eight MSS, the earliest belong to c. A.D. 900, and a few papyrus scraps, belonging to about the beginning of the Christian era. The same is true of The History of Herotodus (c. 480–425 B.C.). Yet, no classical scholar would listen to an argument that the authenticity of Herodotus or Thucydides is in doubt because the earliest MSS of their works which are of any use are over 1,300 years later than the original.[5]

Not only are there many more copies of the New Testament, but many of them are also quite early. Approximately seventy-five papyri fragments can be dated from the early second to the mid-eighth century, covering twenty-five of the twenty-seven New Testament books. In addition, hundreds of parchment copies survived, two thousand church worship books contain many Scripture passages, and over eighty thousand New Testament quotations or allusions in writings of the church fathers.[6]

From these early copies and translations, scholars have tried to recapture the original Greek text. The work has been successful, and today we possess a very accurate and reliable New Testament text. It is true that we do not have the first written text of either the Old or the New Testaments. But sufficient evidence exists that our English versions are trustworthy translations of reliable Hebrew and Greek texts, which faithfully represent the originals.[7]

TRANSLATION IN LANGUAGE OF THE PEOPLE

All ancient translations were called forth by practical needs. In addition to the Septuagint, there were other Greek versions of the Old Testament. Origen (ca. A.D. 185–254) produced a remarkable work called the Hexapla, in which he compared the Hebrew Bible with the Greek version and his own revisions. The whole Bible existed in at least seven versions (Latin, Syriac, Coptic, Armenian, Georgian, Gothic, and Ethiopic) by the sixth century A.D.

The movement to translate the Bible into the language of the people found very little support during the Middle Ages. The Latin translation, known as the Vulgate, became the churches' standard translation. At the time of the Reformation, through the impetus of Martin Luther, the needs of the people again brought about new translations. These movements occurred not only in Germany but also in France and England. Modern Bible societies have translated the Bible into the vernacular of people around the world, even Third World and tribal languages.[8]

Today many versions of the Bible are available in English. These versions can be classified in various ways.[9]

The King James Version (1611) is the most well-known of all English versions, but several English translations were completed prior to it. Two of the most important, in the last decade of the fourteenth century, were associated with the name of John Wy- cliffe. In 1534, William Tyndale completed what was then the definitive English translation. Miles Coverdale published several editions of the English Bible, called the Great Bible. Some months after James VI of Scotland became king of England as James I in 1603, he con-

Translation	Year	Translator
The Holy Bible	1833	Noah Webster
Literal Translation	1863	Robert Young
English Revised Version	1881–85	54 scholars
The Holy Scriptures	1871–90	John Nelson Darby
Twentieth Century New Testament	1898	3 scholars, 32 laypersons
American Standard Version	1901	30 American scholars
The Emphasized Bible	1872–	
	1902	Joseph B. Rotherham
New Testament in Modern Speech	1903	Richard E. Weymouth
The Bible: A New Translation	1913–24	James Moffatt
The Complete Bible, an American Translation	1923–35	E. J. Goodspeed and others
The New Testament: A Private Translation in the Language of the People	1937	Charles Williams
Revised Standard Version of the Bible	1949–52	32 scholars
The New Testament in Modern English	1958	J. B. Phillips
The Holy Bible: The Berkeley Version in Modern English	1959	Gemtt Verkuyl and others
The New World Translation of the Holy Scriptures	1950–60	New World Translation Committee
The New Testament: An Expanded Translation	1956–61	Kenneth S. Wuest
The New English Bible	1961	C. H. Dodd and others
The Amplified Bible	1958–65	Francis Siemert and others
The Jerusalem Bible	1966	28 Roman Catholic scholars
The Modern Language Bible	1969	3 scholars
The Barclay New Testament	1961–70	C. H. Dodd and 50 others
The New American Bible	1970	50 Roman Catholic scholars
New American Standard Bible	1963–71	58 scholars
The Living Bible, Paraphrased	1962–71	Kenneth Taylor
Good News Bible, The Bible in Today's English Version	1966–76	Robert G. Bratcher and others
The Holy Bible in the Language of Today: An American Translation	1976	William F. Beck
New International Version	1973–78	115 scholars
New King James Version	1979–82	130 scholars
The Reader's Digest Bible	1982	Bruce Metzger and others
The Word: New Century Version, New Testament	1983–86	21 scholars
New Revised Standard Version	1990	Bruce Metzger and others
The Message	1993	Eugene Peterson

vened a conference to deal with various controversial issues in the church. From that meeting came the proposal to produce a fresh English translation from the Greek and Hebrew texts. Because of the kings' sponsorship, the translation was named the King James Version. Several significant translations have appeared in the nineteenth and twentieth centuries, most of which are included in the preceding list. Comments on the most important of these will follow. In the middle column the first date indicates the year of publication of the first portion of the project; the second date indicates the year the project was completed.[10] Several translations are attempts at literal, word-for-word equivalents. Examples are the American Standard Version and the New American Standard Bible. Increasingly, translators have felt the need to express the meaning of the original in the language of their times. Translators have therefore employed idiomatic English, seeking words or phrases that would communicate the range of meanings of words in the original sources.[11] This approach, referred to as dynamic equivalence, is best seen in The New English Bible, The New Revised Standard Version, and the New International Version. Some translations are really paraphrases, which actually interpret the original source for the reader. The best examples of this expanded approach are the Living Bible, The Amplified Bible, the New Testament in Modern English, and The Message. Paraphrases are generally less reliable than translations, which seek to express the meaning of the original through more literal or dynamic-equivalent methods, though the paraphrases are generally much more readable for the average person. For devotional purposes, paraphrases are excellent; but for serious study of the Bible, translations that faithfully represent the original sources are necessary.[12] How do we know which books to study or which books should be included in a Bible translation? It is to these questions that we now turn our attention in the discussion of the biblical canon.

THE CANONICAL BOOKS

What do we mean by the term *canon? Canon* (from the Greek *kanon*) means a standard by which something is measured. Designating a carpenter's rule, the word was possibly borrowed from a Hebrew term (*qaneh*) referring to a measuring reed six cubits long.

COMPARISON OF LISTS OF THE OLD TESTAMENT BOOKS

RABBINIC CANON 24 BOOKS	SEPTUAGINT 53 BOOKS	ROMAN CATHOLIC OLD TESTAMENT 46 BOOKS
The Law	*Law*	*Law*
Genesis	Genesis	Genesis
Exodus	Exodus	Exodus
Leviticus	Leviticus	Leviticus
Numbers	Numbers	Numbers
Deuteronomy	Deuteronomy	Deuteronomy
The Prophets	*History*	*History*
The Former Prophets		
Joshua	Joshua	Joshua
Judges	Judges	Judges
1-2 Samuel	Ruth	Ruth
1-2 Kings	1 Kingdoms (1 Samuel)	1 Samuel (1 Kingdoms)
The Latter Prophets	2 Kingdoms (2 Samuel)	2 Samuel (2 Kingdoms)
Isaiah	3 Kingdoms (1 Kings)	1 Kings (3 Kingdoms)
Jeremiah	4 Kingdoms (2 Kings)	2 Kings (4 Kingdoms)
Ezekiel	1 Paralipomena (1 Chronicles)	1 Chronicles (1 Paralipomena)
The Twelve	2 Paralipomena (2 Chronicles)	2 Chronicles (2 Paralipomena)
Hosea	1 Esdras (Apocryphal Ezra)	Ezra (1 Esdras)
Joel	2 Esdras (Ezra-Nehemiah)	Nehemiah (2 Esdras)
Amos	Esther (with Apocryphal additions)	Tobit
Obadiah	Judith	Judith
Jonah	Tobit	Esther
Micah	1 Maccabees	1 Maccabees
Nahum	2 Maccabees	2 Maccabees
Habakkuk	3 Maccabees	
Zephaniah	4 Maccabees	*Poetry*
Haggai		Job
Zechariah	*Poetry*	Psalms
Malachi	Psalms	Proverbs
	Odes (including the prayer of Manasseh)	Ecclesiastes
The Writings	Proverbs	Song of Songs
Poetry	Ecclesiastes	Wisdom of Solomon
Psalms	Song of Songs	Ecclesiasticus (The Wisdom of
Proverbs	Job	Jesus the son of Sirach)
Job	Wisdom (of Solomon)	
Rolls—"the Festival Scrolls"	Sirach (Ecclesiasticus or The Wisdom	*Prophecy*
Song of Songs	of Jesus the son of Sirach)	Isaiah
Ruth	Psalms of Solomon	Jeremiah
Lamentations		Lamentations
Ecclesiastes	*Prophecy*	Baruch (including the Letter
Esther	The Twelve Prophets	of Jeremiah)
Others (History)	Hosea	Ezekiel
Daniel	Amos	Daniel
Ezra-Nehemiah	Micah	Hosea
1–2 Chronicles	Joel	Joel
	Obadiah	Amos
	Jonah	Obadiah
	Nahum	Jonah
	Habakkuk	Micah
	Zephaniah	Nahum
	Haggai	Habakkuk
	Zechariah	Zephaniah
	Malachi	Haggai
	Isaiah	Zechariah
	Jeremiah	Malachi
	Baruch	
	Lamentations	*Appendix*
	Letter of Jeremiah	The Prayer of Manasseh
	Ezekiel	The two apocryphal books of
	Daniel (with apocryphal additions, including the Prayer of Azariah and the Song of the Three Children, Susanna, and Bel and the Dragon)	Esdras

Thus, we refer to Scripture as canonical, meaning that it serves as a rule, a measure, or a standard for God's people.[13]

We must not think that the church determined or defined the books in the church's canon. In reality, the church did not create the canon, but received the canon that God created for His people. The church recognized the canonical books as spiritually superlative writings by which all other books were measured and found to be of secondary value in general church use. The church then did not decide which books belonged in the canon, but only affirmed those books that God had inspired.[14]

THE OLD TESTAMENT CANON

Most of the Old Testament canon, especially the Law and Prophets, was established long before the time of Christ. The details of the process by which the Old Testament writings were recognized as authoritative and distinguished from other Jewish works remain largely unknown. Later, Judiasm believed that the Word of God came in twenty-four books. The Talmudic treatise Baba Bathra (ca. A.D. 200) contains a list of books that is virtually the same as our present canon. Books are listed in tripartite form: the five books of Moses, eight books of the Prophets, and eleven Writings.

It is likely that Jesus and the apostles shared this view of the Old Testament (see Luke 24:44). The implications of Jesus' words in Matthew 23:35 (also see Luke 11:51) are most informative. He speaks of "all the righteous blood that has been shed on earth, from the blood of righteous Abel to the blood of Zechariah son of Berekiah." Abel was obviously the first righteous person to suffer at the hands of the wicked, but why include Zechariah? Zechariah, son of Jehoiada (see 2 Chron. 24:20–22), is not chronologically the Old Testament's last martyr. He is mentioned because, probably, by the time of Jesus, Chronicles was recognized as the last book in the Hebrew.[15]

Josephus, the Jewish historian (ca. A.D. 37–100), followed the tripartite grouping but included only twenty-two books. The reason is that he included only nine Writings, since Judges-Ruth was considered one book, as was Jeremiah-Lamentations. The Dead Sea Scrolls indicate that the Qumran covenant community had commentaries on most Old Testament books. These commentaries point to the high regard the convenanters had for the Scriptures. These writings make clear a marked difference between the canonical Scriptures and the numerous other books in the Qumran library.[16]

Much debate surrounds the details of the recognition of the Old Testament canon. Tradition has it that Ezra was primarily responsible for collecting the material into a recognized canon. Critical scholars challenge this tradition, since they date several Old Testament books after Ezra. They instead point to a council of Jewish elders held at Jamnia (ca. A.D. 90) as the important time for establishing the Old Testament canon. But the supposed role of the council of Jamnia has been severely attacked by recent scholarship, as have other crucial assumptions of the nonevangelical reconstruction. R. T. Beckwith contends that the closing of the Old Testament canon was settled by the time of Judas Maccabaeus, around 165 B.C. It is probable that the Old Testament canon was settled by the time of Jesus. In the absence of enough evidence on the origin of the Old Testament canon, it is impossible to be certain.[17] As men of the old were moved by the Spirit to write the Holy books (see 2 Pet. 1:21), God providentially led His people to preserve, recognize, and treasure these writings.

THE NEW TESTAMENT CANON

The New Testament writings functioned authoritatively from their beginning; yet, as with the Old Testament, their collection and distinction from other literature of the time was a gradual process spanning several centuries.

Authority was inherent in Jesus' commission to the apostles (see Matt. 28:18), but it was not accepted without question by all (see 1 Cor. 9:1–3). Not all books written by apostles were included in the canon (see 1 Cor. 5:9; Col. 4:16). But by the late second century, Irenaeus considered apostolicity the fundamental test of canonical authenticity. Nonapostolic authors, like Mark, Luke, and James, were considered to have equal authority because of their association and sanction by the apostles.[18]

When the apostolic writings were initially gathered is not known for sure. By the time of the writing of 2 Peter, several letters of Paul were known (see 2 Pet. 3:16). Letters were expensive to produce.

STAGES IN THE DEVELOPMENT OF THE NEW TESTAMENT CANON

BOOKS OF THE CANON

MATTHEW, MARK, LUKE, JOHN, ACTS, ROMANS, 1 CORINTHIANS, 2 CORINTHIANS, GALATIANS, EPHESIANS, PHILIPPIANS, COLOSSIANS, 1 THESSALONIANS, 2 THESSALONIANS, 1 TIMOTHY, 2 TIMOTHY, TITUS, PHILEMON, HEBREWS, JAMES, 1 PETER, 2 PETER, 1 JOHN, 2 JOHN, 3 JOHN, JUDE, REVELATION

Quoted by Irenaeus
(ca. A.D. 130–200), Bishop of Lyons, in his
work *Against Heresies*

Listed in the *Muratorian Canon*
(ca. A.D. 170–210) –a Latin manuscript

Listed by Eusebius
(ca. A.D. 260–340), in his work *Ecclesiastical History*, 3.25

Listed by Athanasius
Bishop of Alexandria, Egypt, in his thirty-ninth
Paschal Letter (A.D. 367)

List is "closed" by Council of Carthage
(A.D. 397)

GOSPELS

BOOK OF HISTORY
OF THE EARLY CHURCH

LETTERS OF PAUL
(probably collected before the end of the first century)

LETTER BY UNKNOWN AUTHOR

GENERAL, OR "CATHOLIC," LETTERS

BOOK OF PROPHECY

✱ "Disputed Books"
(not yet universally
accepted)—according
to Eusebius

Certainly, letters from apostles would have been welcome blessings for the young churches during a time when no official New Testament existed. The churches' leadership was provided by the Spirit's ministry through gifted people (see 1 Chron. 14; Eph. 4:11–16). The apostles' letters were to be read in the struggling churches during their worship meetings (Col. 4:16). They would have been received as valuable directives. The letters of Paul were widely circulated and read by the beginning of the second century (see 1 Clement 47:1–3).[19]

Tradition has held that the decisive period in the history of the New Testament canon was A.D. 140–200, during which time the basic form of the canon developed.[20] The reason for the canon's fixture came largely as a result of the church's need to counter the heresies of Marcionism and Montanism. The New Testament canon, in the majority, was accepted by growing consensus around the end of the second century.

The general acceptance and use in the first two centuries A.D. of all twenty-seven New Testament books was followed in the third and fourth centuries by a period of intense debate regarding the "apostles" portion of the canon as well as some of the commonly valued writings like the Apocalypse of Peter and the Shepherd of Hermas. Yet, it was these very debates that led to an increasingly more precise definition of what constituted a "canonical" writing and to a clearer determination of the limits of the canon. The Muratorian Canon (ca. A.D. 200) is of considerable value in understanding the kinds of distinctions that were increasingly employed by those wrestling with the issue of canon in the early church. A distinction was made between those books that were authorized for public reading, such as Jude, 2 John, 3 John, and those recommended only for private devotional edification such as the Shepherd of Hermas. The Muratorian fragment is viewed as the earliest datable list in the history of the New Testament canon. The text is in Latin and most likely was translated from Greek. The list includes four gospels, Acts, Pauline Letters, 1 Peter, 1 John, and the Book of Revelation. As mentioned above, it distinguished between which books should and which books should not be used in public church worship. Hippolytus of Rome (ca. A.D. 236) has been widely suggested as the author of this list, but this cannot be proven.

By the fourth century, Eusebius, the early church historian, delineated several categories of books: (1) accepted, (2) disputed, (3) rejected, and (4) heretical. The accepted books contain most of our present New Testament books. The disputed books contain James, Jude, 2 Peter, and 2 and 3 John. Revelation was accepted by some and rejected by others. Among the spurious books are the Epistle of Barnabas, the Shepherd of Hermas, the Acts of Paul, the Apocalypse of Peter, the Teachings of the Apostles, and the Gospel of the Hebrews. Category of disputed included those books which were put forward under the name of the apostles including the writings of the Gospels of Peter, Thomas, and Mathias, and the Acts of Peter, Andrew, and John.[21]

Eusebius also included a list of heretical books which he considered to be out of harmony with the orthodox teachings of the apostles. Eusebius exhorted his readers not to refer to these writings since they were impious and "beyond the pale."[22]

Growing consensus and use of the term canon became solidified by the fourth century. From the common notion of a rule of faith, the term was used from the second century. It was easy to see how in the fourth century the term rule or canon came to be applied to a list of books whose content was viewed as inspired and authoritative for all matters of faith and practice. Athanasius, bishop of Alexandria (ca. A.D. 353), who stated that the Shepherd of Hermas did not belong to the canon, was the first church father to employ the word in this technical sense while the Synod of Laodicea (ca. A.D. 363) was the first church council to employ the term to distinguish canonical writings from noncanonical writings. The term canon had become a widely accepted reference by the end of the fourth century.

The emergence of a churchwide consensus was primarily the result of a series of councils that tackled the question of canon in the context of wider discussions related to the Trinity and Christology. As the church attempted to define orthodoxy and to protect books of the church in order to transmit the faith from one generation to the next, it was natural for the church leaders to seek a consensus regarding the orthodox writings that would provide the foundation for the church's belief. It is important to say again that these councils did not create the canon, but they merely acknowledged those inspired writings that were already recognized by the churches.[23]

The first list of canonical books that contains the twenty-seven books currently accepted appears in bishop Athanasius' festal letter of A.D. 367. The order, however, is different. The first church council to list all twenty-seven books of the New Testament was the Council of Carthage in A.D. 397. The selection of the canonical books stabilized after each book proved its worth by generally passing the criteria or tests of canonicity. The consensus was more widespread in the West than in the East, where the limits of the New Testament canon remained elusive.

We have referred to these tests, but now we need to pursue this issue in more detail. It is somewhat debated as to how the tests were employed and which ones were used at which time and in what places. But following the work of F. F. Bruce, we will suggest five general questions that helped the church recognize what was already true: that these twenty-seven books are inspired and authoritative.[24]

Neither the church councils nor the application of these tests made any book authoritative or authentic. The book was inspired, authoritative, and therefore genuine when it was written. The councils recognized and verified certain books as the written Word of God, and eventually those so recognized were collected in what we call the Bible. The tests involved the following issues:

1. Was the book authored or sanctioned by an apostle or a prophet?

2. Was the book widely circulated?

3. Was the book Christologically centered?

4. Was the book Orthodox, that is, faithful to the teachings of the apostles?

5. Did the book give internal evidence of its unique character as inspired and authoritative?

The bottom line for each of these questions was the relationship of inspiration to canonicity. The books were included in the canon because they were believed to be inspired.[25] Likewise, the books were known to be inspired because they were in the canon. How far was this the case in the early church? Ellen Flesseman-Van Leer claims that "apostolicity was the principal token of canonicity for the West, inspiration for the East;not indeed in a mutually exclusive way, since in the West apostolicity to a certain extent includes inspiration, while in the East apostolicity was an attendant feature of inspiration."[26]

Only one of the New Testament writers expressively based the authority of his writings on the prophetic inspiration. The book of Revelation is called "the book of this prophecy" (see Rev. 22:19). John implied that his words were inspired by the same spirit of prophecy that spoke to the prophets of earlier ages; thus, he stands in succession to them (Rev. 22:9). Likewise, he claims "the testimony of Jesus is the spirit of prophecy" (Rev. 19:10). The readers of the book are expected to hear what the "Spirit says to the churches" (see Rev. 2:7). While these passages are unique to the last book of the Bible, it is a clear indication that at the beginning of the Christian era, the inspiration of the prophetic oracles of the Old Testament was believed to extend to the New Testament Scriptures as well; at least in part if not in whole. While the New Testament writers were not always aware of inspiration as in the case of the writing of the Apocalypse, most of the New Testament writers believed they wrote with the "mind of Christ" (1 Cor. 2:14–16). Some have suggested that inspiration was not a criterion of canonicity but a corollary of canonicity. Kaster Stendahl has observed that "It was until the red ribbon of the self-evident had been tied around the twenty-seven books of the New Testament that 'inspiration' could serve theologians as an answer to the question: Why are these books different from all other books?"[27]

Consensus related to the canon was important for two primary reasons. First, it was imperative for the church officials in times of persecution to distinguish between those books that might be handed over to the church's opponents and those which must be preserved. The bottom line was that the church needed to know which books were worth dying for if indeed one's life was put on the line.[28] Secondly, canonicity enabled the theologians of the church to distinguish those books that might be used for settling doctrinal questions from those which were generally helpful for edifying and private reading. Only those books that carried apostolic authority or sanction were to be appealed to for the establishment of the truths to be believed and passed on to other generations.[29]

The early church displayed surprising unanimity about which books belonged to the inspired collection. Although it is true that a few books such as Jude, 2 Peter, and Revelation were the subjects of considerable debate, no book whose authenticity was doubted by a large number of churches was later accepted. The persecution of the church helped distinguish the canonical books from other helpful writings as the people were forced to decide what books should be protected during times of oppression.

THE CONTEMPORARY DEBATE

"Most points of the history of the canon are now so fully clarified that one can almost speak of a *communis opinio*," wrote Wilhelm Schneemelcher in his introduction to the long-awaited 1959 revision of Edgar Hennecke's *Neu Testamentliche Apokryphem.*[30] Likewise, H. von Campenhausen's monumental volume, *The Formation of the Christian Bible* echoed this confidence, as did contributions by such outstanding and confessionally diverse scholars as F. F. Bruce, Wainwright, and Käsemann.[31] Yet, Schneemelcher, in 1980, reopened the question of canon observing that its history is still seen through a glass darkly.[32] In agreement, we find Albert Sundberg's revision of F. W. Beare's work, suggesting a demise of the previous consensus.[33] "What was the older consensus theory?" "What are the new suggestions?" are the matters that concern us at this stage.

Formerly, as we have described above, it was held that the decisive period in the history of the New Testament canon was A.D. 140–200, during which time the basic form of the canon developed. The New Testament canon was basically accepted by the end of the second century. Sundberg, on the other hand, has argued that the development of the canon should be seen as consisting of three stages: (1) the rise of the Christian writings to the status of Scripture; (2) the conscious collection of Christian writings into closed sub-collection; and (3) the formation and standardization of New Testament lists; canonization proper. It is basically the third point of his suggestion that issues in a potential revision. He posits that the Muratorian canon should be dated much later, perhaps as late as the fourth century with Eusebius.

Two major studies in recent years, however, question the validity of Sundberg's thesis and point us to the previously described consensus. David Dunbar and Bruce Metzger have written major works that counter the revisionist authors. Dunbar maintains that, "The revisionist authors simultaneously underestimate the stability of the canon as it has been held by the church during the last fifteen centuries and overestimated the creativity of the Reformation. That was marked indeed by a Protestant rejection of the Old Testament Apocrypha, but no change at all in the New Testament canon."[34] Thus, while giving due consideration to Sundberg, we contend that the traditional thesis is a helpful foundation on which to base our understanding of the canon.

At every point in the transmission, translation, preservation, and canonicity of the Bible, we see God's providential hand at work. The testimony of the church witnesses to this providential guidance and cannot readily be dismissed. The sixty-six books that we have are the Word of God written, inspired, and authoritative. The canon of Scripture is authenticated by the testimony of the Holy Spirit, who inspired the writings, to the individual Christian and to the community as a whole.

When we read our present translations, we can read with the assurance that they faithfully represent the original sources. Also, we believe that they include neither more nor less than the writings God purposed to include in the canonical Scriptures. Since God has nowhere provided a table of contents for the Bible, how do we know that new books should not be added? While this is a complex question, we believe that the canon is closed and includes the inspired books that should be accepted as authoritative. This affirmation is based on the recognition that the church of the second, third, and fourth centuries was much closer to the time of the apostles and thus in a better position to recognize and preserve the written prophetic-apostolic materials. To consider expanding the canon simultaneously underestimates the stability of the canon as it has been held by the church during the past sixteen centuries and overestimates the creativity of the post-Reformation period. Our belief in a closed canon also grows from a confidence that God in His providence not only inspired the authors of Scripture to write those things He wanted to communicate to His people, but also superintended their collection and preservation. These issues direct us to another important question: How should these canonical writings be employed and interpreted? In the following chapters we will wrestle with those questions while surveying the use and interpretation of the Bible throughout the history of the church.[35]

ENDNOTES

1. See Kyle P. McCarter, *Textual Criticism: Recovering the Text of the Hebrew Bible* (Philadelphia: Fortress, 1988).

2. See Michael W. Holmes, "Textual Criticism," *New Testament Criticism and Interpretation*, eds. David A. Black and David S. Dockery (Grand Rapids: Zondervan, 1991), 101–34.

3. See Lee M. McDonald, *The Formation of the Christian Biblical Canon* (Nashville: Abingdon, 1988).

4. See Bruce K. Waltke, "Old Testament Textual Criticism," *Foundations for Biblical Interpretation*, eds. David S. Dockery, K. A. Mathews, and Robert B. Sloan (Nashville: Broadman and Holman, 1994), 156–86.

5. F. F. Bruce, *The New Testament Documents: Are They Reliable?* (Downers Grove, Ill.: InterVarsity, 1960), 16–17.

6. See David Alan Black, "New Testament Textual Criticism," *Foundations for Biblical Interpretation*, 396–413.

7. Much of the material in the previous sections was informed by F. F. Bruce, *The Books and the Parchments* (London: Pickering & Inglis, 1963); Bruce M. Metzger, *The Text of the New Testament* (New York: Oxford, 1968); and P. R. Ackroyd and C. F. Evans, eds., *The Cambridge History of the Bible*, vol. 1 (Cambridge: University Press, 1970).

8. See Philip W. Comfort, *Early Manuscripts and the Modern Translations of the New Testament* (Wheaton: Tyndale, 1990).

9. See John Beekman and John Callow, *Translating the Word of God* (Grand Rapids: Zondervan, 1974).

10. See F. F. Bruce, *The English Bible* (New York: Oxford, 1970).

11. See Eugene Nida, *Toward a Science of Translating* (Leiden: Brill, 1964).

12. The two best surveys are S. Kubo and W. Specht, *So Many Versions?* (Grand Rapids: Zondervan, 1983); and Jack P. Lewis, *The English Bible from KJV to NIV* (Grand Rapids: Baker, 1991). For discussions related to the King James Version see D. A. Carson, *The King James Version Debate* (Grand Rapids: Baker, 1979); for information on the New International

Version, see Kenneth L. Barker, ed., *The NIV: The Making of a Contemporary Translation* (Grand Rapids: Zondervan, 1986); and for insights concerning the New Revised Standard Version, see Bruce M. Metzger, R. C. Dentan, and Walter Harrelson, *The Making of the New Revised Standard Version* (Grand Rapids: Zondervan, 1991).

13. See David Dunbar, "The Biblical Canon," *Hermeneutics, Authority and Canon*, eds. D. A. Carson and J. D. Woodbridge (Grand Rapids: Zondervan, 1986), 299–360.

14. Linda Belleville, "Canon of the New Testament," *Foundations for Biblical Interpretation*, 375–76.

15. Paul House, "Canon of the Old Testament," *Foundations for Biblical Interpretation*, 143–55. For an alternative interpretation see Craig Blomberg, "Matthew," *New American Commentary* (Nashville: Broadman, 1992), 349.

16. Ibid., 151–52.

17. See R. T. Beckwith, *The Old Testament Canon of the New Testament Church and Its Background in Early Judaism* (Grand Rapids: Eerdmans, 1985).

18. F. F. Bruce, *The Canon of Scripture* (Downers Grove, Ill.: InterVarsity, 1988), 117–33.

19. See Bruce M. Metzer, *The Canon of the New Testament: Its Origin, Development and Significance* (Oxford: Clarendon, 1987).

20. Ralph P. Martin, "Muratorian Canon," *New International Dictionary of the Christian Church*, ed. J. D. Douglas (Grand Rapids: Zondervan, 1978), 684–85.

21. See Eusebius, *The History of the Church from Christ to Constantine*, trans. G. A. Williamson (Minneapolis: Augsburg, 1965), 6.25.

22. Ibid., 3.25.

23. Belleville, "New Testament," 392–94.

24. See Bruce, "Canon," 255–69.

25. See Richard B. Gaffin, "New Testament as Canon," *Inerrancy and Hermeneutic* (Grand Rapids: Baker, 1988), 165–83.

26. Ellen Flesseman-VanLeer, "Prinzipien der Sammlung und Ausscheidung bei der Bildung des Kanons," *Zeitschrift for Theologie und Kirche* 61 (1964): 415–16.

27. K. Stendahl, "The Apocalypse of John and the Epistles of Paul in the Muratorian Fragment," *Current Issues in New Testament Interpretation*, eds. W. Klassen and G. F. Snyder (New York: Harper, 1962), 243.

28. I am dependent here on William R. Farmer and Denis M. Farkasfalvy, *The Formation of the New Testament Canon* (New York: Paulist, 1983).

29. See Donald G. Bloesch, *Holy Scripture* (Downers Grove, Ill.: InterVarsity, 1994), 141–60; also James Leo Garrett, Jr., *Systematic Theology* (Grand Rapids: Eerdmans, 1990).

30. Wilhelm Schneemelcher, "General Introduction" to *New Testament Apocrypha*, by Edgar Hennecke, trans. and ed. R. M. Wilson (Philadelphia: Westminster, 1963), 29. The consensus of this time is underscored by the discussions in the standard works of J. N. D. Kelly, *Early Christian Doctrine* (New York: Harper and Row, 1960), 52–60; and F. W. Beare, "Canon of the New Testament," *Interpreter's Dictionary of the Bible* (Nashville: Abingdon, 1962), 334–58.

31. See H. von Campenhausen, *The Formation of the Christian Bible*, trans. J. A. Baker (Philadelphia: Fortress Press, 1973); Bruce, *Canon*; Geoffrey Wainwright, "New Testament as Canon," *Scottish Journal of Theology* 28 (1975): 551–71; Ernst Käsemann, ed. *Das Neue Testament als Kanon* (Gottingen: Vandenhoeck & Ruprecht, 1970), 9.

32. Wilhelm Schneemelcher, "Bibel I/II: Die entstehung des Kanons des Neuen Testaments und der Christlichen Bibel," *Theologische Realenzyklopadic* I, ed. Gerhard Krause and Gerhard Müller (Berlin: deGruyter, 1980) which develops prior concerns of Hans Lietzmann, *Kleine Schriften II: Studien zum Neue Testament, Texte und Untersuchungen* 68, ed. Kurt Aland (Berlin: Akademic-Verlag, 1958).

33. See Albert Sundburg, *The Old Testament of the Early Church* (Cambridge: Harvard, 1964); iden., "Toward a Revised History of the New Testament Canon," *Studia Evangelica* 4 (1968): 452–61; idem, "Canon Muratori: A Fourth Century List," *Harvard Theological Review* 66 (1973): 1–41; idem., "The Bible Canon and the Christian Doctrine of Inspiration," *Interpretation* 29 (1975): 352–71.

34. Dunbar, "Biblical Canon," 299.

35. It is at the point of interpretation that issues of a "canonical center" as well as matters of unity and diversity within the canon are so important. See Robert B. Sloan, "Unity in Diversity," *New Testament Criticism and Interpretation*, 437–69.

VI

PRE-REFORMATION
HERMENEUTICS

The contemporary world of biblical studies is facing not only a crisis in biblical authority, but also a hermeneutical impasse. One of the reasons for this quagmire is the preoccupation solely with contemporary issues. Much contemporary scholarship has seemingly forgotten that valuable biblical interpretation existed before F. D. E. Schleiermacher, the "father of modern hermeneutics." The purpose of this chapter is not necessarily to argue for the superiority of the pre-critical exegesis, but to remind us of the value and insights provided by select influential interpreters in the early church and the medieval period.

Interpreters of the Bible have read the Bible differently and emphasize various parts of Scripture over and against others. Because of this there is some confusion about the nature and task of biblical interpretation. Many Bible teachers have related the story of the student who inquired of his professor as to the meaning of a biblical passage. The teacher answered the student: "It means what it says." The inquiring student raised a follow-up question: "But what does it say?"

All texts require interpretation. As we have seen in our previous chapters the first step toward the interpretation of the Bible is translation. Discovering the meaning of biblical texts is not always easy. Throughout the history of the church there has been disagreement over how to carry out the responsibility of the interpretive task. Before we offer our guidelines for interpretation, it will be helpful to learn how those who have gone before us have handled the issues. At the heart of the discussion have been two paramount questions: (1) How many meanings does a text have? and (2) Where is/are meaning(s) located? There have been other issues of import that we will note in our survey. Let us now look at how the Bible has been understood throughout the history of the church. In this chapter we will examine interpreters prior to the Reformation period. The next chapter will focus on the period from the Reformation to the present.

JESUS AND THE BEGINNING
OF CHRISTIAN HERMENEUTICS

From the beginning of the Christian movement, the early believers shared the Holy Scriptures of the Jews. Following the example of Jesus, these believers held that Scripture was first and foremost the authoritative, inspired Word of God. Indeed, not only did the earliest church inherit its Scriptures from the Jews, it also inherited various methods of interpretation and interpretations themselves. The interpretation of the Jewish Scriptures by the earliest church, however, included an additional factor that stamped a new meaning upon Scripture: the life, death, and resurrection of Jesus. In this opening section, we shall lay the foundation for our survey by examining briefly how Jesus and the apostles interpreted the Old Testament.

The New Testament account of the ministry of Jesus maintains that Jesus Himself instructed His followers to show that His life and ministry fulfilled Scriptures.[1] Although Jesus interpreted the Scriptures in a manner similar to His contemporary Jewish exegetes, there also was novelty in His method and message.

This new method was a christological reading, meaning that Jesus read the Old Testament in light of Himself. For example, in John 5:39–40, it is recorded that Jesus said: "You diligently study the Scriptures because you think that by them you possess eternal life. These are the *Scriptures that testify about me*" (italics added). And in John 5:46: "If you believed Moses, you would believe me, *for he wrote about me*" (italics added). On the Emmaus road Jesus said, "'How foolish you are, and how slow of heart to believe all that the prophets have spoken! Did not the Christ have to suffer these things and then enter his glory?' And beginning with Moses and all the Prophets, he explained to them what was said in all the Scriptures concerning himself" (Luke 24:25–27).

His belief in His own resurrection after three days in the tomb seemed to be motivated both by the promises of Israel's resurrection (cf. Hos. 6:2) and by seeing Himself in light of the Jonah story (cf. Jon. 1:17; Matt. 12:40). He observed His own experiences prefigured in the psalms of vindication and suffering, used both by individual Israelites and by corporate Israel (Pss. 22, 41, 42, 43, 118).[2]

R. T. France sums up the evidence of the synoptic Gospels in these words:

> He uses persons in the Old Testament as types of himself (David, Solomon, Elijah, Elisha, Isaiah, Jonah) or of John the Baptist (Elijah); he refers to Old Testament institutions as types of himself and his work (the priesthood and the covenant); he sees in the experiences of Israel foreshadowings of his own; he finds the hopes of Israel fulfilled in himself and his disciples and sees his disciples as assuming the status of Israel; in deliverance by God he sees a type of the gathering of men into his church, while the disasters of Israel are foreshadowings of the imminent punishment of those who reject him, whose unbelief is prefigured in that of the wicked in Israel and even, in two instances, in the arrogance of the Gentile nations.[3]

In all these aspects of the Old Testament people of God, Jesus saw foreshadowings of Himself and His work. This resulted in opposition from and rejection by the majority of the Jews, while the promises concerning Israel were partially fulfilled in the new Christian community. The history of Israel had reached its decisive point in the coming of Jesus. The whole of the Old Testament pointed to Him. He embodied the redemptive destiny of Israel, and in the community of those who belong to Him that status and destiny are to be fulfilled.[4] The New Testament writers, following the pattern of Jesus, interpreted the Old Testament as a whole and in its parts as a witness to Christ.[5]

It is not surprising that in providing different pictures of Jesus' life, the biblical writers saw that at almost every point His life had fulfilled the Old Testament. His birth had been foretold (Isa. 7:14; Matt. 1:24; Mic. 5:2; Matt. 2:6); as had the flight to Egypt (Hos. 11:1; Matt. 2:15); the slaughter of the innocent children by Herod (Jer. 31:15; Matt. 2:18); and His upbringing in Nazareth (cf. Matt. 2:23). The overall impact of His ministry had been described (Isa. 42:1–4; Matt. 12:17–21), as well as His use of parables in His teaching (Isa. 6:9–10; Ps. 78:2; Matt. 13:14–15,35). The message of Jesus' passion is filled with allusions to the Old Testament, including accounts of the triumphal entry into Jerusalem (Zech. 9:9; Matt. 21:5); the cleansing of the temple (Isa. 56:7; Ps. 69:9; Matt 21:13), and the events surrounding the cross (John 19:24,28,36–37).[6]

What is emphasized throughout the New Testament is that numerous themes, images, and motifs of revelation and response are fulfilled in Jesus Christ. The note of Phillip's jubilant words, "We have found him" (John 1:45), was echoed by the Gospel writers as the way to interpret the Old Testament events, pictures, and ideas. It was not so much one fulfillment idea, but a harmony of notes presented in a variety of ways by different hermeneutical methods.[7] The teaching of Jesus and His hermeneutical practices became the direct source for much of the early church's understanding of the Old Testament. The church appears to have taken Jesus' own interpretation of Scripture and its themes as paradigmatic for their continued exegetical endeavor.

The new paradigm developed because the prior paradigm lacked the christological focus. What was needed was a hermeneutical perspective that could transform the Torah into the messianic Torah.[8] Thus, through the pattern that Jesus had set and His exalted lordship expressed through the Spirit, Jesus served as the ongoing source of the early church's hermeneutical approach to the Scriptures. The christological perspective of the earliest Christians, therefore, enabled them to adopt Jesus' own usage of the Scriptures as normative and look to Him for guidance in their hermeneutical task. We will now move to the second century to see how this pattern continued among the apostolic fathers.

SECOND-CENTURY HERMENEUTICS

While the apostolic fathers were on the whole more wildly fanciful than the New Testament writers, they followed the New Testament exegetical pattern and remained christocentric in their interpretation.[9] At the close of the apostolic age, some marked changes began to occur; primarily, the New Testament was in the process of being recognized as Scripture. The relation of the New Testament to the Old Testament was the issue raised by the Gnostics and the issue confronting the second-century church. Marcion and the Gnostics abandoned the Old Testament as a Christian book, and recreated the New Testament texts to suit themselves. The motivating factor that raised the issue among orthodox Christians was the Gnostic view that the God of the Old Testament was incompatible with the God revealed in Christ in the New Testament. As texts were challenged, altered, and even abandoned, the church had to demonstrate on biblical grounds that the same God was revealed in both Testaments and that, therefore, the church should not abandon the Old Testament. The apostolic fathers continued the New Testament hermeneutical practices and modified those practices so that the emphasis was placed on the moral usage of Scripture.[10] This approach can be identified as a "functional hermeneutic." That is, the readers applied the text to their own context and situation without attention to its original context or situation. Meaning was bound up in Scripture's functional application. Thus, Scripture explained to the church, primarily on the basis of the words of Jesus, what it was to do. Similarly, the Gnostics turned to the words of Jesus for their authority, yet they were considered heretics. The church was faced with new problems. Which approach to the words of Jesus was correct? By what authority could this be known?

FUNCTIONAL HERMENEUTICS

Clement of Rome. The Epistle of Clement, a letter from the church at Rome to the troubled church in Corinth, has been traditionally ascribed to Clement of Rome near the end of the first century (A.D. 90–100). The letter began with a common epistolary salutation, *he ekklesia tou Theou he paroikousa Romen tei ekklesiai tou Theou tei parakousei korinthon* (The church of God which sojourns in Rome to the Church of God which sojourns in Corinth).

Regarding the use of the Old Testament, 1 Clement included one hundred sixty-six quotations or allusions.[11] He interpreted Scripture in a christological fashion, not unlike his predecessors. Yet he did not so much seek to discover the Old Testament's message concerning the work of Christ, but offered the pictures of Christ as basis for moral obedience.[12]

Ignatius. Seven letters by Ignatius, bishop of Antioch (A.D. 35–107), are generally accepted as authentic: (1) the Ephesians, (2) the Magnesians, (3) the Trallians, (4) the Romans, (5) the Philadelphians, (6) the Smyrnaeans, and (7) Polycarp. These letters, from the beginning of the second century A.D., were apparently written by Ignatius as he traveled on his way to his anticipated martyrdom in Rome. They were written to churches whose messengers Ignatius had met, churches in cities in Asia Minor where he stopped on his journey to Rome, to the church at his intended destination, and to Polycarp, bishop of Smyrna.

Ignatius was highly influenced by the Pauline letters and seems to have had 1 Corinthians memorized. There are almost fifty references to this one book alone in his writings. He could take Pauline expressions from their contexts and use them in his own contexts. This functional usage hardly surprises us. In fact, Ignatius could not have used Pauline expressions in Pauline contexts. This indicates that exegesis was not yet the art form it would become with the Alexandrian school, nor a science as it would become with the Antioch school.

Ignatius served as a transitional figure.[13] As has generally been the case in theology, a paradigm shift brings something new while maintaining much of what has preceded it. With Ignatius, who was perhaps fifteen years later than Clement, we have an initial movement toward an authoritative or apologetical hermeneutic, where Scripture could be used to show the false beliefs of the heretics. This was done by establishing the correct theological meaning of Scripture, with the guidance of the bishop. He warned the congregations against heretics and urged them to close unity in submission to the hierarchy of the church, especially the bishop. As the church faced conflicts, the rise of heretics, docetics, and Judaizers, Ignatius appealed to the authority of the bishop as the exemplar of orthodoxy. Thus it was the need to address the rise of heresy and the equal need for church unity that initially pushed the church in the direction of authoritative hermeneutics.

AUTHORITATIVE HERMENEUTICS

In the latter part of the second century the church had to demonstrate that the God of Israel was also the God of the church. The challenge involved confirming for the Gnostics the continuity between the Testaments; demonstrating to the Montanists the development, as well as the cessation, of revelation; and convincing the Judaizers within Christianity as well as Judaism in general of the discontinuity of the two Testaments. Two responses arose: (1) the typological hermeneutics of Justin Martyr, and (2) the authoritative approach of Irenaeus and Tertullian.

Justin Martyr. For Justin, (A.D. 100–165) both general and special revelation were the outgrowth of the Logos. Pagan philosophers possessed the Logos, Jesus was and is the Logos, and the Bible contains the written residue of the Logos. His view of biblical revelation allowed little room for development of the message from the Old Testament period to the New. This formed the basis of his views concerning the authority of biblical inspiration, resulting in a non-contradicting Bible.[14] He seemingly had little concern for Scripture's original context or the meaning of Scripture for its original readers. His typological exegesis was characteristically christocentric; the Old Testament in its entirety pointed to Jesus. In demonstrating the christocentric nature of Scripture, Justin used terms such as "mystery, announcement, signs, parable, symbol, and type." All six of these terms were essentially synonymous, indicating a representative or inner meaning of an act or a person representative of a later act or incident. At times it is difficult to distinguish between an allegorical interpretation and a typological one because Justin seemed to delight in finding esoteric meaning in cryptic passages. Any person or event in the Old Testament that foreshadows an episode in either the life or work of Christ was gladly employed.[15]

Willis A. Shotwell has analyzed and compared the hermeneutical approach of Justin with that of Jesus, Paul, and other New Testament writers. Justin shared a christocentric use of the Old Testament with Jesus and the apostles. He, like the New Testament writers, used midrashic methods to argue for the relationship of Judaism with Christianity while emphasizing the superiority of the latter. Justin argued from minor to major, from general to particular, and from analogy in the New Testament. It has been pointed out that there were at least forty Justinian parallels with rabbinic exegesis.[16]

Justin used rabbinic methods to his advantage so that his arguments and counter arguments could spring from this approach. Trypho used the Haggada, but Justin also employed haggadic material to further his apology. Upon examination there appears substantial agreement between the hermeneutical principles of Justin and those of Hillel regarding some of his basic principles in the exegesis of Scripture.[17]

In following the christocentric hermeneutics of the New Testament writers and employing the principles from Hillel, Justin linked the Old Testament to the New, the very antithesis of both Judaism and Marcionite Gnosticism. Marcion's total rejection of the Old Testament was the exact opposite of Justin's typological viewpoint. Drawing on real or supposed messianic prophecies from the Jewish tradition, he argued that Jesus clearly was the expected Messiah who fulfilled all of the Old Testament Scriptures literally or typically. Thus Justin established his apologetic method on proof from prophecy. His writings, primarily the *Dialogue*, served as a gold mine of information on second-century Christian typology. In line with the developing Christian creed, the rule of faith, Justin found all the major features of the creed prefigured in the message of the Old Testament text, as summarized by Froehlich: "Christ's virgin birth; his healing ministry, suffering, death, and resurrection; Christian baptism; the church. Types of the cross were of particular interest: Justin found them not only in the figure of Moses praying in the battle against Amalek (Exod. 17:10–11) or in the horns of the wild ox (Deut. 33:17) but in every stick, wood, and tree mentioned in the Bible."[18]

The immense range of types illustrates Justin's christocentric-typological exegetical method. The usage of the creed paved the way for the forthcoming authoritative exegesis used to respond to the challenges of the heretics.

Irenaeus. The church's estimate of its theological norms underwent certain adjustments in the final decades of the second century. While the Old Testament was being challenged by the Gnostics, the established church was promoting the apostolic Scripture to a position of supreme authority. This developing perspective was assisted and indeed made possible by the recognition of the New Testament as fully canonical and entitled to equal status alongside the Old as God-inspired Scripture.

Equally important historically and more significant hermeneutically, the distinction between Scripture and the church's living tradition, as coordinate instruments in conveying the apostolic testimony, became more clearly appreciated, and a growing importance, if not a primary one, began to be attached to the latter. This development resulted from the great struggle between orthodoxy and the Gnostic heretics previously described. Irenaeus claimed that not only did the Gnostics exploit Scripture to their own ends, but one of their successful techniques was to appeal, in support of their positions, to an alleged secret apostolic tradition (the *gnosis*) to which they alone had access.

This developing, more mature position is exemplified, with minor differences, in the writings of Irenaeus and Tertullian. J. N. D. Kelly comments, "For both of them Christ Himself was the ultimate source of Christian doctrine, being the truth, the Word by Whom the Father had been revealed; but He had entrusted this revelation to His apostles, and it was through them alone that knowledge of it could be obtained."[19]

The task faced by these two important thinkers was to demonstrate the unity of the Testaments and the validity of the complete New Testament in light of the challenges from Marcion and the Gnostics. The rise of a specifically Christian literature solved some problems, for the main outlines of the gospel were now fairly well fixed, not to say preserved, but the diversity within the New Testament raised new issues.[20] As we have noted earlier, Marcion solved the problem rather neatly, by merely rejecting much of the Christian tradition and what was to be the Christian Scripture. According to Irenaeus, it was characteristic of heretics that they took only a part of the evidence: "The Ebionites or Jewish Christians used only Matthew; Marcion took Luke; Docetists who separated 'Christ' from Jesus, used only Mark; Valentinian theosophists like John."[21] Also, the followers of Marcion claimed that Paul alone knew the truth of revelation. What was to be done under such circumstances? Obviously the former functional usage of Scripture was in need of an expanded paradigm.

Irenaeus (A.D. 130–200) presented the view accepted by most. He maintained that the true interpretation of the Scripture was to be found among those who had received the apostolic tradition along with the apostolic succession, and who possessed the charismatic gift of truth. Irenaeus contended:

> True "gnosis" is the teaching of the apostles, and the ancient structure of the church throughout the world, and the form of the body of Christ in accordance with the successions of bishops to whom the apostles delivered the church which is in each place; this teaching has come down to us, preserved without any use of forged writings, by being handled in its complete fullness, neither receiving addition nor suffering curtailment; and reading without falsification, and honest and steady exposition of the scriptures without either danger or blasphemy; and the special gift of life.[22]

As can be observed, Irenaeus's rule of faith[23] was not exactly a law, yet by this time it had become an external authority that would permanently fix the meaning of Scripture. This produced a hermeneutical method in which church tradition determined the meaning of Scripture. By this, a hermeneutical circle was enacted: church tradition was created by the interpretation of Scripture and the interpretation of Scripture was then governed by the church's tradition in the rule of faith.

The rule of faith preserved the apostolic tradition in the church and functioned as the normative guide for interpretation. In this connection, we can better understand the meaning and function of the rule of faith. While defined in several ways, the rule of faith could be best expressed as the church's belief "in one God, the Father Almighty, Maker of heaven and earth, and the sea, and all things that are in them; and in one Christ Jesus, the Son of God, who became incarnate for our salvation; and in the Holy Spirit."[24] This contained, in summary form, the fundamentals of the apostolic preaching which were preserved, one and the same, by the succession of bishops in the whole church. It did not add to the content of Scriptures, since the same teaching was found in both; actually it could be unfolded in detail. It could and did function, however, as a criterion against the misinterpretations of the Scriptures by the heretics. Irenaeus's classic illustration is worth noting. The heretics were like those who take apart an artful mosaic of precious stones representing the image of the king and compose with the same pieces an inferior picture of a fox. Extending this comparison beyond its explicit use by Irenaeus, it can be said that the rule of faith provided the essential Christian message transmitted by the apostolic preaching and writings, enabling the church to recognize any heretical distortion for what it was.[25]

Tertullian. In dealing with the heretics who were using the Bible to defend their position, Tertullian (died A.D. 212) forced them to take their stand on two questions: (1) Whose are the Scriptures? (2) How should they be understood? The Scriptures belonged to the church, not the heretics; the heretics could not use them. He commented, "Only the churches which stand in the succession of the apostles possess the teaching of Christ."[26]

Certainly Irenaeus was the father of authoritative exegesis, but as can be seen from Tertullian's *Against Marcion* and *On Prescription Against Heretics,* Tertullian shifted the issue from a right understanding of Scripture to the more sharply stated issue of whether the Gnostics could even use Scripture. According to Tertullian, arguing with Gnostics about Scripture interpretation was useless. He reached this conclusion after realizing that functional exegesis produced ambiguity at best and opened the door for heretical interpretations to dictate the theological agenda. He moved the issue away from interpretation to questioning the heretics' very right to use Scripture at all. Apostolic Scriptures, he argued, belong to the apostolic church, as did the apostolic tradition contained in the rule of faith.[27] As Froehlich summarized, "For both Irenaeus and Tertullian, illicit curiosity is the true danger of a Gnostic hermeneutics of inquiry."[28]

ALLEGORICAL INTERPRETATION

While several Christian writers of the second and third centuries engaged in biblical interpretation, the first important scholarly commentator was Origen of Alexandria. He brought the touch of a master to what had "been nothing much more than the exercise of amateurs."[29] Along with Clement, he was the greatest of the interpreters associated with the Alexandrian school of interpretation, those Christian scholars who understood biblical inspiration in the Platonic sense of utterance in a state of ecstatic possession.

CLEMENT OF ALEXANDRIA

Titus Flavius Clement (A.D. 150–215), considered by many to be the first Christian scholar, became the leader of the Alexandrian school in A.D. 190, a position he held until after the turn of the century. His principal literary works produced during this time were the trilogy of *Protrepticux (Exhortations to Conversion)*, the *Paidagogus (The Tutor)* and *Stromateis (Miscellanies)*. The Logos, according to Clement, first of all converts us, then disciplines us, and finally instructs us.

Clement, Origen's predecessor at Alexandria, found a solution to the tension faced by the church by seeing the literal meaning as a "starting point," suitable for the mass of Christians, and as something that piques the curiosity of the more spiritually advanced. He suggested that "finding the deeper meaning is thus the process by which God gradually, by means of parable and metaphor, leads those to whom God would reveal Himself from the sensible to the intelligible world."[30] It is clear that the Alexandrians lived in a complex hermeneutical environment. Out of this environment Clement began to forge a hermeneutical methodology. He believed that in every text there was always one or more additional or deeper meanings beyond and above its primary or immediate sense. These deeper meanings were to be uncovered through allegorical interpretation. This method insisted that the literal senses, particularly of historical passages, did not exhaust the divinely purposed meaning of such passages, but that they also included a deeper, higher, spiritual and mystical sense. The literal sense indicated what was said or done, while the allegorical showed what should be believed. The allegorical approach, then, was adopted for apologetical and theological purposes.

Clement believed that this method should be used because God's bountifulness was such that it would be folly to believe that there could only be one teaching in a particular text. He maintained that God is so loving and merciful that in the same text He can reveal Himself from the wise to the ignorant, speaking to them at whatever level of perception each group of believers possessed. The first of his hermeneutical principles, then, included two levels: first, the literal sense must be observed, and then, the allegorical sense must be discovered. Yet, this allegorical interpretation must not discard the primary meaning of the text unless such meaning violated what was previously known of God's character or dignity. Neither was this first principle one which was a boundless allegorism, for the rule of faith still provided a framework for interpretation.[31]

Clement's hermeneutical approach has been evaluated differently by scholars of various traditions. For some, he was a praiseworthy pioneer breaking free from a hampering authoritative traditionalism, boldly putting the meaning of Scripture in contemporary forms and making significant breakthroughs into educational circles. For others, he was a man of compromise, wedding Scripture with forms of Platonic philosophy and Gnosticism. A better evaluation is that Clement's approach had ultimately a strategic rather than a material character. It is important to see how Origen implemented this strategy to raise allegorical interpretation to new heights.

ORIGEN

Origen (A.D. 185–254) was undoubtedly the prince of Christian allegorical interpreters, its most extensive practitioner, and its most adequate exponent. Most of the information about the life of Origen can be located in the sixth book of Eusebius's *Ecclesiastical History*. Origen, born in Egypt, studied under Clement in the school of Alexandria. He followed Clement as the leader and primary teacher in this school, a position he held for twenty-eight years while pursuing an ascetic and extremely pious life. In his early manhood, he sought literally to obey the teachings of Matthew 19:12: "For some are eunuchs because they were born that way; others were made that way by men; and others have renounced marriage because of the kingdom of heaven. The one who can accept this should accept it." In order to obey this teaching, he castrated himself, probably so that he could instruct his female students without fear of a scandal. Thousands came to hear him. According to tradition, a wealthy convert hired secretaries to write down his lectures and then published them. This accounts for his prolific literary accomplishments (more than two thousand different works). Having studied with the father of neo-Platonic thought, Ammonius Saccus, his work was greatly influenced by this approach.

Although Origen was far from being literalistic in his interpretation of the sacred text, he strongly affirmed the literal inspiration of every word of Scripture. The most obviously determinative, explicit assumption Origen made regarding the biblical text was that it is of divine origin. In *Contra Celsum (Against Celsus)*, Origen maintained, "For it was fitting that the creator of the whole world should have appointed laws for the whole world and given a power to the words that was able to overcome men everywhere."[32] And in another passage he said, "The Logos of God arranged the scriptures and spoke them."[33]

The literal sense of Scripture, however, was not necessarily the primary sense. Like Clement, Origen thought it absurd that a God-inspired Scripture should not be interpreted in a spiritual manner, which meant finding the deeper meaning in the text. From this supposition Origen developed a threefold hermeneutical approach. He thought that Scripture had three different, yet complementary, meanings: (1) a literal or physical sense, (2) a moral or psychical sense, and (3) an allegorical or intellectual sense. The threefold sense was based upon his belief in a corresponding threefold division of humankind: (1) the physical, (2) the emotional or psychical, and (3) the spiritual or intellectual.[34] In classifying the different senses, he followed Clement and Philo, though he adopted three senses instead of the prior two. Yet in his spiritualization of Scripture, he often "out-Philos Philo." Rarely did he develop his exegesis in a systematic manner based upon the threefold meanings of the text. Generally, he worked with just two meanings: the literal and the spiritual. Moreover, there are places where he found numerous spiritual meanings in a single text, thus creating an entire scale of allegorical interpretations.[35]

We can enumerate the principles behind Origen's hermeneutical procedure. First, every text is pregnant with profound mysteries and should be discovered through allegory. Second, nothing should be said of God which was unworthy of Him. Third, each text was to be interpreted in the light of the rest of Scripture. Finally, nothing contrary to the rule of faith was to be affirmed. While some in the history of the church have regarded Origen's approach as heretical, his brilliance and ground-breaking work cannot be ignored. It should also be noted that Origen affirmed the primary doctrines of the Christian tradition and felt no freedom to deny the essence of the rule of faith. Therefore, the rule of faith served to keep his interpretation—at least in part—within the sphere of the traditional doctrine of the church.

The ultimate purpose in Origen's biblical interpretation was his love for and nurture of the individual Christians under his care. He was deeply concerned with the formation of spiritual life. Two other purposes need to be mentioned briefly. One is that allegorical interpretation served as a source for inspired illustrations of doctrine.[36] The second purpose was to explain difficulties in Scripture or the doctrine of God. Above all, biblical interpretation was to show that all Scripture, even the seemingly irrelevant parts, communicated a contemporary sense and had something to teach the church. Allegorical hermeneutics was ultimately an effective way to interpret ancient writings to communicate their contemporary relevance.[37]

Origen was ultimately a churchman, and while he advanced over the authoritative exegesis of the second century with his creative hermeneutical procedure, there was some degree of tension between Origen's allegorical interpretation and the priority of the rule of faith. With Origen's followers, Athanasius, the Cappadocian fathers, and later with Augustine, there was a removal of the tension as a moderating theological exegesis began to dominate.

Because of the christological debates in the fourth and fifth centuries, the followers of Origen became more theologically oriented in their exegesis. The consistent articulation of the church's orthodox faith, coupled with pastoral concerns for the edification of the faithful, provided parameters and norms for the implementation of allegorical exegesis. Allegorical hermeneutics tended to give way to analogical hermeneutics. Their purpose in exegesis was primarily practical and their exegesis cannot be understood until this is realized. The successors of Origen were challenged by the school of Antioch with its emphasis on a literal interpretation. The Antiochenes were reacting to the fanciful hermeneutics of the Alexandrians. New issues were raised which we must examine closely in the next section.

LITERAL-HISTORICAL AND TYPOLOGICAL

In order to describe the exegetical school of Antioch, we will concentrate on John Chrysostom and Theodore of Mopsuestia, particularly the influence of Aristotelian thought and the place of typological exegesis in their overall hermeneutical scheme.

The two great Antiochene exegetes, Theodore and Chrysostom, belonged to a later period of the Antioch school. Theodore of Mopsuestia, whom later generations venerated as "the interpreter *par excellence*," distinguished between the pure exegete and the preacher: the exegete's task was to communicate the plain teaching of the gospel. If we maintain this distinction, Theodore was the pure exegete while Chrysostom was the expository preacher.

THEODORE OF MOPSUESTIA

Theodore (A.D. 350–428), the greatest interpreter of the Antiochenes, was also the most individualistic, while remaining the most consistent in emphasizing historical exegesis. It is certainly true that all Christian theology during this period was based on Scripture, yet this was especially true for Theodore. That this was the case can be traced to Theodore's hermeneutical method. Theodore, moreover, seems to have employed a more Jewish exegesis than many of his contemporaries.[38]

In order to understand Theodore's method, it is necessary to recognize his distinction between typological, allegorical, and prophetical material. Perhaps, as Rowan A. Greer has suggested, it is better to think of typological exegesis as the normative method of Antiochene exegesis. Allegorical exegesis, if legitimate at all, and distinct from Alexandrian allegorical practices, represented "left wing typology," while fulfillment of prophecy represented "right wing typology."[39]

Theodore's exegesis was the purest representation of Antiochene hermeneutics.[40] Theodore was first to treat the Psalms historically and systematically, while treating the Gospel narrative factually, paying attention to the particles of transition and to the minutiae of grammar and punctuation. His approach can be described as "anti-allegorical," rejecting interpretations that denied the historical reality of what the scriptural text affirmed. Even where allegorical interpretation could have possibly served to his advantage to bring unity to the overall biblical message, he failed to use it or see its value. For instance, he chose to reject Job and the Song from the biblical canon.[41]

The great value of allegorical interpretation for the Alexandrians was that it made possible a theologically unified interpretation of the Bible as a whole. Theodore, attempting to present unified theological exposition, viewed the Bible as a record of the historical development of the divine redemptive plan. Ultimately, this history must be understood from the perspective of God's purpose in providing the setting of His gracious act in Christ Jesus, by which the new age of salvation was realized. The law and the prophets were to be interpreted typologically as types of Christ. This emphasis, plus the stress on historical development, was the strength of Theodore's creative interpretation. We must now examine the hermeneutical practices and contributions of Theodore's fellow disciple, John Chrysostom.

JOHN CHRYSOSTOM

Chrysostom (A.D. 354–407) gave primary attention to the critical, literal, grammatical, and historical interpretation of Scripture. Like others in the Antiochene tradition, he was influenced by Aristotelian philosophy. Aristotle seemed more down-to-earth compared to Plato's more other-worldly views. Chrysostom, more than his Alexandrian predecessors, was aware of the human factor in Scripture and sought to do justice to the dual authorship of biblical revelation. Yet, he maintained that the Bible spoke with a unified voice.

The Antiochene homilitician insisted that the main reason the Bible existed was for Christians to read it, read it again, meditate over it, and thereby escape the snares of sin. Chrysostom, while a hermit in his ascetic days, memorized the *Testamentum Christi* by heart.[42] His printed treatises and six hundred sermons contain about eighteen thousand Scripture references, about seven thousand from the Old Testament and eleven thousand from the New.

The Bible, according to Chrysostom, represented a supreme act of God's accommodation or condescension *(sunkatabasis)* to humankind. He considered the Scripture to be by Christ and his commentaries to be not a scientific inquiry but a tool to enable the reader to hear the Scripture more clearly and thereby enable the Bible to do its work more effectively.

The ultimate issue in biblical interpretation for John Chrysostom was whether the Bible, being spiritual in nature, was to be treated as a collection of suprahistorical sayings and ciphers which all, by virtue of Christ's being the center of revelation, spoke of Him and His church, or whether it should be interpreted as revelation in history addressed to historical communities, which of course did not exclude Christ from being the center of revelation. As we have seen, many patristic interpreters, and especially those associated with the Alexandrian school, showed by their allegorization that they preferred the former solution. Chrysostom, however, preferred to interpret the text literally and historically.

The crucial proof-text for advocates of allegorical interpretation was, of course, Galatians 4:22–24. Like Theodore, Chrysostom distinguished between the genre of allegory and allegorical hermeneutics. Concerning Paul's usage of *allegoreo*, Chrysostom explained "By a misuse of language he—Paul—called the type allegory. What he means is this: The history itself not only has the apparent meaning but also proclaims other matters; therefore, it is called allegory. But what did it proclaim? Nothing other than everything that now is."[43] Here Chrysostom reflected the Antiochene concept of *theoria*. Elsewhere he explained the relation of two meanings of Scripture by a parallel from art, "The type is given the name of the truth until the truth is about to come; but when the truth has come, the name is no longer used. Similarly in painting: an artist sketches a king, but until the colors are applied he is not called a king; and when they are put on the type is hidden by the truth and is not visible; and then we say, 'Behold the King.'"[44]

The outline can be discovered in the historical meaning, but the final form of the portrait was only available in the typological meaning. When the nature of the text required more than a mere historical exposition, Chrysostom preferred typological methodology that was consistent with the historical event and distinct from allegorization.

Chrysostom rejected out of hand any allegorical interpretation of a passage that failed to agree with Scripture's interpretation of itself. Thus, the rule that Scripture interpreted Scripture took precedence over all others. The details of a passage were not to be separated from the overall context and should not be given allegorical meanings distinct from the text's context. John Chrysostom avoided treating the Old Testament passages as allegories of Christ and the church; instead he sought typological meanings when the text allowed for it.

G. W. H. Lampe has correctly asserted that some form of typological interpretation of the Old Testament was necessary for Christians who believed that the Bible was controlled by a single series of images, that the Bible's explicit or implicit theme throughout is the people of the covenant, and that Christ is the unifying center point of biblical history. Typology, rightly conceived, asserts that since Christ is the culmination of the line of Abraham and of David and is the fulfillment of the hope of Israel, the Old Testament description of Israel's history, institutions, worship, and prophetic message often anticipate the life and work of Christ.[45] Chrysostom and the Antiochene school distinguished allegorical interpretation from typological in two primary ways. Typological interpretation attempted to seek out patterns in the Old Testament to which Christ corresponded, while allegorical exegesis depended on accidental similarity of language between two passages. Second, typological interpretation depended on a historical interpretation of the text. The passage, according to the Antiochenes, had only one meaning, the literal, and not two as suggested by the allegorists. In the typological approach, the things narrated by the text had to be placed in relationship to things which were not in the text, but which were still to come.

Chrysostom, like Theodore of Mopsuestia and the other Antiochene representatives, emphasized the literal and historical meaning of the text. While rejecting fanciful interpretation, he was nevertheless sensitive to figures of speech in Scripture. His sensitivity to biblical language generally helped him to avoid a wooden literalism. Chrysostom rejected crudely literal interpretations of the Bible from both the Antiochene laity and the criticisms of the Alexandrians. He was cautious that no figurative expression in the Bible be misunderstood either from a too literal or a too fanciful interpretation.

For Chrysostom, theology and hermeneutics were not theoretical exercises, but practical and pastoral. He believed the biblical message made changes in people's lives. He declared that the Scriptures' divine message prepared people for good works. It is generally true that the Alexandrians saw a literal and allegorical meaning in Scripture and the Antiochenes found a historical and typological sense. The Alexandrians looked to the rule of faith, mystical interpretation, and authority as sources of dogma. On the other hand, the Antiochenes looked to reason and historical development of Scripture as the focus of theology. The Antiochenes were more aware of the human factor in Scripture and sought to do justice to the dual authorship of the biblical revelation.

TOWARD CANONICAL AND CATHOLIC HERMENEUTICS

The emphasis on literal and historical interpretation was important not only for the Antiochenes, but also for the greatest doctors of the church, Jerome and Augustine. Yet neither was so extreme a literalist as Theodore of Mopsuestia. Instead, they stood closer to Chrysostom, who because of his concern for preaching as opposed to Theodore's pure exegesis, had more spiritualizing tendencies. Jerome and Augustine moved toward a moderate literalism from a different direction. The main lines of their exegesis moved further and further away from the allegorization that they originally admired. We shall examine the hermeneutical practices of these two significant exegetes to observe the developments toward canonical and catholic hermeneutics in the late fourth and the fifth centuries.

JEROME

During his years in Bethlehem, Jerome (A.D. 341–420) became convinced that translations of the Old Testament must be based on Hebrew and not Greek. He professed to be more literal in theory than he was in practice, opting more for a sense-for-sense rather than a word-for-word translation.[46]

As a biblical interpreter, Jerome was strongly influenced by Didymus the Blind (A.D. 313–398), a follower of Origen whom Jerome visited in Alexandria in 385–386 before settling in Bethlehem. From Didymus, Jerome developed his early love for the spiritual sense of Scripture. Yet, in his later days he became suspicious of allegorical interpretation. While accepting Origen's three senses of Scripture, he deemed that recourse to the spiritual meaning was made necessary by the anthropomorphisms and incongruities that seemingly abounded in the Bible. He therefore attempted to combine attention to the literal sense of Scripture learned from Hebrew scholarship with a christological and spiritual interpretation. John Rogerson observes that Jerome referred many psalms to Christ, as well as David:

> In Psalm 3, the "holy hill" from which God answers the psalmist can refer both to the Son of God and to the church. In Psalm 4, the references can only be to Christ, since the psalmist possesses a righteousness not appropriate even to David. In Psalm 5:2 the phrase "my king and my God" refers to Christ, who is king and God of the church. Again the whole of Psalm 17 pertains to Christ in the person of David.[47]

At Antioch, however, Jerome came under the influence of the literal-historical method, taught to him by Apollinaris of Laodicea. The influence of the school of Antioch, along with the Jewish influence, caused Jerome to devalue the allegorical method, even as presented in its modified form by Gregory of Nazianzus. Robert M. Grant aptly summarizes,

> No matter how ingenious the allegorization, Jerome had to insist upon the reality of the literal meaning. The deeper meaning of scripture was built on the literal, not opposed to it. Everything written in scripture took place and at the same time has a meaning more than historical. This meaning is based on the *Hebraica veritas*, the truth expressed in Hebrew. We must have a *spiritualis intelligenta*, a spiritual understanding of scripture, which goes beyond the *carneus sensus*, the fleshly sense, but will not be opposed to it.[48]

Through Jerome's influence, a modified Antiochene literalism was mediated to the later church.

AUGUSTINE

For Protestants, Augustine (A.D. 354–430) serves as the dominant figure in the history of Christian thought and biblical interpretation between the time of the apostles and the sixteenth-century Reformation. For Roman Catholics, Augustine's influence during this period is rivaled only by that of Thomas Aquinas (A.D. 1225–1274). In the history of philosophy, Augustine is only slightly less important; he was the most influential philosopher between Plontius, in the third century, and Aquinas.

Many of Augustine's commentaries, like those of Chrysostom, were expository sermons preached to his congregation at Hippo; therefore they were more practical than grammatical and critical. After covering the first five verses of the first chapter of Romans, Augustine found his comments so elaborate that he withdrew from his task. Augustine's other writings abound in quotations, and his polemical works evidence his knowledge of the Bible and his skill in its use. This was especially so in his theological treatises *On Christian Doctrine* and *The City of God*.

The City of God, whose title was taken by Augustine from the Psalms, was designed, from book 11 onwards, to indicate how the whole Bible was the story of two cities: the heavenly and the earthly. Augustine's approach downplayed the division between the Old and New Testaments. The Old Testament was not considered a preparation for the establishment of the heavenly kingdom of Christ, though Augustine recognized that Christ's coming brought significant changes. The Old Testament was not about blessings in the present earthly world as opposed to the New Testament's offering of heavenly blessings. Instead, both Testaments simultaneously described both cities from their inception to their end. The City of God was equally present in the Israel of the Old Testament as it was with the church in the New.[49] Thus Augustine presented a unified and canonical approach to the Bible that still allowed for the significance of the coming of Jesus Christ, while maintaining the essential unity of the two Testaments.[50]

Literal interpretation. In this approach, Augustine was able to interpret both literally and symbolically. After tracing the establishment of the two cities from their heavenly and earthly points of view in books 11–15 of *The City of God*, he traced their history up to and through the flood account (Gen. 6–9) and on into Israelite history (Gen. 12–50). When dealing with the history of Israel, Augustine demonstrated most clearly what he meant when he said that biblical history was primarily prophetic rather than simply an inspired and correct record of past events. Also, Augustine contextualized his view of the relation between the historical and spiritual interpretation, and between prophecy that had both heavenly and earthly aspects.[51] In books 15 and 16 Augustine made it clear that the primary function of Old Testament history was to point to the existence of the City of God by anticipating the coming of Christ, who made possible for all humanity the reversal of the curse of the disobedience of Adam (Rom. 5:12–21).[52]

Augustine accepted the historical account of the creation story and the flood story in Genesis. On common sense grounds, Augustine argued that the days and years referred to in the genealogy (Gen. 5) should be no different from the days and years for the flood narrative, and it was clear that ordinary days and years were meant in the flood story. There was no reason to suggest that Methuselah's 969 years (Gen. 5:27) were anything other than normal years. While arguing for a literal interpretation, he acknowledged the difficulty of explaining the fact that some patriarchs in Genesis 5 did not father children until they were over one hundred years old.[53]

Symbolic interpretation. Yet, Augustine did offer spiritual meanings of many of the events reported in Genesis. He commented that the door of Noah's ark (Gen. 8:13) was representative of the wound made in the side of Christ at His crucifixion.[54] He maintained that Abraham, in fathering a son through Hagar, his wife's servant (Gen. 16), was not to be blamed because this action was not accomplished with lust. His marriage to Keturah, his second wife (Gen. 25), was also not the result of fleshly lusts, but a foreshadowing of "the carnal people" who thought that they belonged to the New Covenant (Jer. 31; 2 Cor. 3). He contended that Jacob did not act fraudulently when he deprived Esau of his blessing (Gen. 27), since his action enabled Christ to be proclaimed to the nations when Isaac blessed him. One additional example demonstrates Augustine's spiritualizing tendency. Augustine claimed that when Jacob anointed the stone after his heavenly vision (Gen. 28), he was not practicing idolatry but was foreshadowing Christ.[55] This spiritualizing methodology was closer to Chrysostom's typological exegesis than Origen's allegorizing.

Augustine recognized the importance of one's presuppositions when interpreting Holy Scripture. He was perhaps the greatest of the Christian Platonists.[56] The integration of biblical data and Platonic philosophy can be seen in Augustine's famous maxim: *Credo ut intelligam* (I believe in order that I may understand). Augustine derived the biblical foundation of this principle from the Latin version of the Septuagint translation of Isaiah 7:9, *nisi credideritis* (unless you believe, you shall not understand). The philosophical foundation came from the Platonic notion of innate first principles, which enabled persons to understand particulars in this world. In Augustine's work *On Free Will*, he declared:

> You remember the position we adopted at the beginning of our former discussion. We cannot deny that believing and knowing are different things, and that in matters of great importance, pertaining to divinity, we must first believe before we seek to know. Otherwise the words of the prophet would be vain, where he says: "Except ye believe ye shall not understand" (Isa. 7:9 LXX). Our Lord himself, both in his words and by his deeds, exhorted those whom he called to salvation first of all to believe. And no one is fit to find God who does not first believe what he will afterwards learn to know.[57]

Long before the insights of contemporary semiotics or semantics, Augustine recognized that things in the created world could function as "signs" or "symbols" through which God was understood. Understanding is possible because of the illumination afforded by the uncreated light of God. Augustine believed that for the mind to see God it must be illumined by God, and this results in: (1) a faith that believes that what we look for, when seen, ought to make us blessed; (2) a hope that is assured that vision will follow right looking; (3) and a love which longs to see and to enjoy.[58]

Bernard Ramm has noted that Augustine spoke of natural objects that were precepts but not signs, such as pieces of metal or wood. He next spoke of things which signified other things. A tree could signify forestry service, a shoe a shoemaker, and an anvil the blacksmith guild. Then, there were things whose primary, if not sole, function was to signify other things, such as words.[59] Augustine defined a sign as "a thing which apart from the impression that it presents to the sense, causes of itself some other thing to enter our thoughts."[60] These signs are conventional or natural. Smoke is an obvious sign of fire. Conventional signs, according to Augustine, are those which "living creatures give to one another."[61] From this he proceeded to discuss sounds and speech. This included God's method of communication to humans through speech, and speech incarnate in the written Scriptures. Such insight was typical of the genius of Augustine, concerning a subject that was not developed until over one thousand years after his time.

The goal of all biblical interpretation should prioritize the love of God and neighbor (Matt. 22:37–39), the ordering of the Christian life toward its heavenly home. Augustine emphasized the entire biblical canon, the priority of faith, the significance of signs, the biblical text, and the goal of love. Lastly, we must briefly examine the place of allegorical interpretation in Augustine.

Allegorical interpretation. Augustine commended the method of interpreting obscure passages by the light of passages already understood, and as we might expect, this was preferred before the interpretation by reason. Also, he stressed the spirit of the text more than verbal accuracy or critical acumen. Even the mistakes of an exegete, properly disposed, suggested Augustine, may confirm religious faith and establish character.

Augustine did not hesitate to put more than one interpretation upon a text, especially the Psalms, and no one was more elaborate in comparing Scripture with Scripture than was he.

We have noted that the goal of biblical interpretation for Augustine was to increase love for God and for one's neighbor. Augustine asserted that what is read should be subjected to diligent scrutiny until an interpretation that contributes to the reign of charity is produced.[62] It was this hermeneutical theme that determined when Augustine used spiritual or figurative interpretation. He recommended this guideline: "Whatever there is in the word of God that cannot when taken literally be referred to purity of life or soundness of doctrine, you may set down as figurative."[63] Thus Augustine did not limit the Scripture to just one sense. When he approached the Bible, he first asked theological rather than historical questions.[64] As Augustine explained, it was his spiritual father, Bishop Ambrose, who opened the method of allegorical exegesis for him, "I listened with delight to Ambrose, in his sermons to the people, often recommending this text most diligently as a rule: "The letter kills, but the spirit gives life" (2 Cor. 3:6), while at the same time he drew aside the mystic veil and opened to view the spiritual meaning of what seemed to teach perverse doctrine if it were taken according to the letter.[65]

This proof-text for 2 Corinthians 3:6 was a misreading of that text. Nevertheless, despite Augustine's dislike for crude literalism, he did not ignore the historical sense of the text. He was concerned with the historical meaning in biblical texts, but he did not disavow the historical sense even as he simultaneously offered an allegorical one. His approach to this dual sense was described and defended by explaining: "There is no prohibition against such exegesis, provided that we also believe in the truth of the story as a faithful record of historical fact."[66] In reality Augustine suggested not a twofold sense of Scripture but a fourfold sense that would be adopted later by medieval theologians. These four senses were (1) literal, (2) allegorical, (3) tropological or moral, and (4) anagogical. Augustine worked with a different list for the Old Testament, based on the Greek technical terms of a rhetorical analysis of language: (1) historical (*historia*), (2) aetiological (*aetiologia*), (3) analogical (*analogia*), and (4) allegorical (*allegoria*).[67]

The great mind of Augustine, however, could not rest in a simple allegorism. He successfully offered some guidelines for the use of allegorical exegesis, yet, like those before him, he was unable to develop an all-inclusive system to determine what was to be interpreted allegorically and what was not. Like Jerome, in the course of his theological development, he began to emphasize more strongly the literal and historical sense of Scripture, though for Augustine, the theological was always primary. Augustine was no simple traditionalist, but he gladly upheld the authority of the rule of faith. He suggested that if interpreters were troubled and could not distinguish between a literal and figurative interpretation, they should consult the rule of faith. Excesses in Augustine's interpretation were thereby modified by his concern for a catholic interpretation faithful to the authority of the church and creed. He went so far as to acknowledge, "I should not believe the gospel except as moved by the authority of the Catholic Church."[68]

The goal of scriptural exegesis for Augustine was to induce love for God and neighbor, but he felt that these were found in their true form only in the church in interpreting the Bible. Thus, Augustine's genius could hold together creativity and creed; author, text, and interpreter; the historical and figurative; faith and intellect. What Augustine always stressed was that the entire canonical text should produce love for God and for neighbor in the lives of those in the church.

MEDIEVAL HERMENEUTICS

From the time of Augustine, the church, following the lead of John Cassian (died 433), subscribed to a theory of the fourfold sense of Scripture.[69] The literal sense of Scripture could and usually did nurture the virtues of faith, hope, and love, but when it did not, the interpreter could appeal to three additional virtues, each sense corresponding to one of the virtues. The allegorical sense referred to the church and its faith—what it should believe. The tropological sense referred to individuals and what they should do—corresponding to love. The anagogical sense pointed to the church's future expectation—corresponding to hope. Bernard of Clairvaux (1090–1153), in the twelfth century, clearly explicated and practiced this fourfold approach. In the fourteenth century Nicholas of Lyra (1265–1349) summarized this medieval hermeneutical theory in a much-quoted rhyme:

Littera gesta docet,
(The letter teaches facts)
Quid credas allegoria,
(allegory what one should believe)
Moralis quid agas,
(tropology what one should do)
Quo tendas anagogia
(anagogy where one should aspire).

For example, the city of Jerusalem, in all of its appearances in Scripture, was understood literally as a Jewish city, allegorically as the church of Christ, tropologically as the souls of women and men, and anagogically as the heavenly city.[70]

Thomas Aquinas (1224–1274) wanted to establish the spiritual sense more securely in the literal sense than had been the case in earlier medieval thought. He returned to the distinction between things and signs as in Augustine, but because of his Aristotelianism preferred "things" and "words." In Scripture, the things designated by words can themselves have the character of a sign. He maintained the literal sense and derived meaning from it.[71] Thomas also equated the literal sense with the meaning of the text intended by the author. The medieval exegetes and theologians admitted that the words of Scripture contained a meaning in the historical situation in which they were first uttered, but overall these scholars denied that the final and full meaning of those words were restricted to what the first audience thought or heard.

CONCLUSION

The preoccupation with modern and postmodern interpretations has caused many biblical scholars to ignore and neglect the insightful interpretations in the pre-Reformation era. Granted numerous illuminating advances have taken place since the introduction of contemporary critical scholarship. Yet, these advances have been matched by many wrongheaded approaches that have questioned the message of Holy Scripture and removed its authority from the church. A healthy re-examination of the work of biblical interpreters in the early church, the medieval period, and among the reformers can help to restore a healthy balance to some of these questionable trends. Certainly the presuppositions and purposes of biblical interpretation from this period need to be sounded again in the contemporary church. We will now turn our attention to a survey of biblical interpretation in the reformation and post-reformation periods.

ENDNOTES

1. John Rogerson, Christopher Rowland, and Barnabas Lindars, *The History of Christian Theology*, vol. 2, *The Study and Use of the Bible*, ed. Paul Avis, 3 vols. (Grand Rapids: Eerdmans, 1988), 3–5; Donald Guthrie, *New Testament Theology* (Downers Grove, Ill.: InterVarsity, 1981), 955–57.

2. Cf. Matthew 21:42; 23:39; 26:38; 27:46; Mark 12:10; 14:18; 34; 15:34; Luke 13:35; 20:17.

3. R. T. France, *Jesus and the Old Testament: His Application of Old Testament Passages to Himself and His Message* (London: Tyndale, 1971), 75.

4. Ibid., 76; cf. Matthew Black, "The Christological Use of the Old Testament in the New Testament," New Testament Studies 18 (1971): 1–14; Morna D. Hooker, *Studying the New Testament* (Minneapolis: Augsburg, 1979), 70–92.

5. The literature on the way the New Testament writers use the Old Testament is numerous and varied in its approach, but the overall christological emphasis is generally accepted. See D. L. Baker, *Two Testaments, One Bible: A Study of Some Modern Solutions to the Theological Problem of the Relationship Between the Old and New Testament* (Downers Grove, Ill.: InterVarsity, 1976); E. Earle Ellis, "How the New Testament Uses the Old," in *New Testament Interpretation*, ed. I. Howard Marshall (Grand Rapids: Eerdmans, 1975), 199–219; Darrell L. Bock, "Evangelicals and the Use of the Old Testament in the New: Part 1," *Bibliotheca Sacra* 142 (1985): 209–23; idem, "Evangelicals and the Use of the Old Testament in the New: Part 2," *Bibliotheca Sacra* 142 (1985): 306–19; D. A. Carson and H. G. M. Williamson, eds., *It is Written: Scripture Citing Scripture* (Cambridge: Cambridge University Press, 1988); Klyne Snodgrass, "The Use of the Old Testament in the New Testament," in *New Testament Criticism and Interpretation*, eds. David Alan Black and David S. Dockery (Grand Rapids: Zondervan, 1991); Robert B. Sloan, "Use of the Old Testament in the New Testament," in *Reclaiming the Prophetic Mantle*, ed. G. L. Klein (Nashville: Broadman, 1992).

6. Cf. R. T. France, "The Formula-Quotations of Matthew 2 and the Problem of Communication," *New Testament Studies* 27 (1981): 223–51; Donald Juel, *Messianic Exegesis: Christological Interpretation of the Old Testament in Early Christianity* (Philadelphia: Fortress, 1988).

7. F. F. Bruce, *New Testament Development of Old Testament Themes* (Grand Rapids: Eerdmans, 1968), 20–21. When one accepts the Gospel presentations as authentic, there is a continuity which is expressed in Jesus preeminently in the history of salvation. Cf. Baker, *Two Testaments, One Bible*; Carson and Williamson, eds. *It is Written*.

8. Birger Gerhardsson, *Memory and Manuscript: Oral Tradition and Written Transmission in Rabbinic Judaism and Early Christianity*, trans. E. J. Sharpe (Lund: Gleerup, 1961), 327.

9. Robert M. Grant, ed., *The Apostolic Fathers: A New Translation and Commentary*, 6 vols. (New York: Thomas Nelson, 1964). See also Michael W. Holmes, ed., *The Apostolic Fathers* (Grand Rapids: Baker, 1989).

10. Grant, *Apostolic Fathers*, 1:v; see also J. Ramsey Michaels, "Apostolic Fathers," *International Standard Bible Encyclopedia*, 1:203–13.

11. Cf. Donald A. Hagner, *The Use of the Old and New Testaments in Clement of Rome*, Supplement to *Novum Testamentum*, no. 34 (Leiden: Brill, 1973). It must be noted, however, that Clement does not use any single known standardized LXX text; see Kliest, *Epistles of St. Clement of Rome*, 6.

12. Ibid.

13. Grant, *Apostolic Fathers*, 1:58–59.

14. Willis A. Shotwell, *The Biblical Exegesis of Justin Martyr* (London: SPCK, 1965), 2–5.

15. Justin Martyr, *Dialogue* 33, 53; Shotwell, *Biblical Exegesis in Justin Martyr*, 8,31–33.

16. Shotwell, *Biblical Exegesis of Justin Martyr*, 48–64, 88–93.

17. Ibid., 93.

18. Karlfried Froehlich, *Biblical Exegesis in the Early Church* (Philadelphia Fortress, 1984); cf. Justin Martyr, *Dialogue* 86–91; cf. also Cullen I. K. Story, *Nature of Truth in "The Gospel" and in the Writings of Justin Martyr: A Study of the Pattern of Orthodoxy in the Middle of the Second Century* (Leiden: Brill, 1970); Oskar Skarsaune, *Proof from Prophecy: A Study in Justin Martyr's Proof-Text Tradition* (Leiden: Brill, 1987).

19. J. N. D. Kelly, *Early Christian Doctrines*, 36; cf. Robert M. Grant, *Greek Apologists of the Second Century* (Philadelphia: Westminster, 1988).

20. Robert M. Grant, "From Tradition to Scripture and Back," in *Scripture and Tradition*, ed. Joseph F. Kelly (Notre Dame, Ind.: Fides, 1976), 20–21.

21. Irenaeus, *Against Heresies* 3.11.7

22. Irenaeus, *Against Heresies* 5.20.1; cf. P. Hefner, "Theological Methodology in St. Irenaeus," *Journal of Religion* 44 (1964): 294–309.

23. The terms rule of faith and rule of truth are used interchangeably for *regula fidei* (or *regula veritaitis*). While not specifically defined from the apostolic fathers through the third century, it was particularly prominent in Irenaeus, Tertullian, Clement of Alexandria, and Origen. Each of these theologians used the term as the creedal expansion of the baptismal formula to define the apostolic tradition of faith against Gnostics and other heretics.

24. Irenaeus, *Against Heresies* 1.10; 22; 2.25; 3.4.2.

25. Irenaeus could interpret the prophetic and apostolic texts in light of other texts taken from the whole of Scripture. Like Justin, he did not seem interested in the original literary or cultural context.

26. Tertullian, *On Prescription Against Heretics* 20.1

27. Tertullian, *On Prescription Against Heretics* 233; also Jean Danielou, *The Origins of Latin Christianity* (Philadelphia: Westminster, 1977), 139–60, 209–14, 261–328. Whereas Justin before Tertullian, and Origen after him, attempted to synthesize Christianity with philosophy, particularly with forms of Platonism, Tertullian's reactionary and separitistic approach is evident with his dealings with philosophy in general and with heretical

uses of Scripture. Just as heretics had no right to interpret Scripture, so Christianity had nothing to do with philosophy, or in his famous words, "What has Jerusalem to do with Athens?"

28. Froehlich, *Biblical Interpretation in the Early Church*, 15.

29. R. P. C. Hanson, *Allegory and Event: A Study of the Sources and Significance of Origen's Interpretation of Scripture* (Richmond: John Knox, 1959), 360.

30. Clement of Alexandria , *Miscellanies* 6.15.126.

31. Cf. Rowan A. Greer, "A Framework for Interpreting a Christian Bible," in *Early Biblical Interpretation* (Philadelphia: Westminster, 1986), 155–76; idem, "Applying the Framework," *Early Biblical Interpretation*, 177–99.

32. Origen, *Against Celsus* 1.18

33. Ibid., 4.71

34. Origen, *First Principles* 4.2.4–17; cf. Kelly, *Early Christian Doctrines*, 70–75; cf. Robert M. Grant, *The Letter and the Spirit* (New York: Macmillan, 1957). Origen based this upon his translation of Proverbs 22:20, "write them in a threefold way."

35. R. J. Daly, "The Hermeneutics of Origen: Existential Interpretation of the Third Century." in *The Word in the World* (Cambridge: Weston College Press, 1973), 135–44.

36. Origen, *Against Celsus* 4.13, 6.16.

37. Ibid., 6.4; 6.58.

38. See J. N. D. Kelly, *Early Christian Doctrines*, 4th rev. ed. (San Francisco: Harper and Row, 1978), 76–77.

39. Rowan A. Greer, *Theodore of Mopsuestia* (London: Faith, 1961), 94.

40. Wiles, "Theodore of Mopsuestia," 489–90, notes that because of this, he was given the title The Interpreter.

41. Ibid., 509–10.

42. Jack B. Rogers and Donald K. McKim, *The Authority and Interpretation of the Bible: An Historical Approach* (Grand Rapids: Eerdmans, 1979), 20.

43. Chrysostom, *Commentary on the Epistle to the Galatians* 4.24.

44. Chrysostom, *Homily on the Epistle to the Philippians* 10.

45. G. W. H. Lampe, "The Reasonableness of Typology," in *The Reasonableness of Typology* compiled by G. W. Lampe and K. J. Woolcombe (London: SCM, 1957), 29.

46. Jerome, *Letters* 57.5.

47. Rogerson, Rowland, and Lindars, *The Study and Use of the Bible*, 43–44.

48. Robert M. Grant with David Tracy, *A Short History of the Interpretation of the Bible*, rev. ed. (Philadelphia: Fortress, 1984), 69.

49. Cf. R. H. Barrow, *Introduction to St. Augustine's "The City of God"* (London: Faber and Faber, 1950).

50. Augustine, *The City of God* 10.25.

51. Ibid., 17.4.

52. Ibid., 15.8; 16.2.

53. Ibid., 15.23.

54. Ibid., 15.26.

55. Ibid., 16.38, For a thorough analysis of Augustine's exegesis in *The City of God*, see R. A. Markus, *Saeculum: History and Society in the Theology of St. Augustine* (Cambridge: Cambridge University Press, 1970).

56. A. Hilary Armstrong, *St. Augustine and Christian Platonism* (Villanova, Pa.: Villanova University Press, 1967), 1–2. Armstrong, 288–94, notes that "Augustine's limited knowledge of Greek forced him to read the Platonists and Neoplatonists through the Latin translations of Victorinus."

57. Augustine, *On Free Will* 2.4.6.

58. Bernard Ramm, *Protestant Biblical Interpretation: A Textbook of Hermeneutics*, 3d rev. ed. (Grand Rapids: Baker, 1970), 34–35; Belford D. Jackson, "Semantics and Hermeneutics in Saint Augustine's De doctrina Christiana" (Ph.D. diss., Yale University, 1967), 171–87.

59. Ibid., 34–35.

60. Augustine, *On Christian Doctrine* 2.1.1.

61. Ibid., 2.2.3.

62. Ibid., 3.15.

63. Ibid., 3.10.

64. See Beryl Smalley, *The Study of the Bible in the Middle Ages*, 2d ed. (Oxford: Blackwell, 1952), 22–23.

65. Augustine, *Confessions* 6.4.6; 5.14.24.

66. Augustine, *City of God* 13.22.

67. Cf. Robert E. McNally, *The Bible in the Early Middle Ages* (Westminster, Md.: Newman, 1959), 50–54.

68. Augustine, *Against the Epistle of Manichaeus Called Fundamental* 5.6.

69. See Beryl Smalley, *The Study of the Bible in the Middle Ages*, 26–36. Cf. Gillian R. Evans, *The Language and Logic of the Bible: The Earlier Middle Ages* (Cambridge: Cambridge University Press, 1984); G. W. H. Lampe, ed., *The Cambridge History of the Bible* 2: *The West from the Fathers to the Reformation* (Cambridge: Cambridge University Press, 1969).

70. See James Houston's introduction in *Bernard of Clairvaux, The Love of God and Spiritual Friendship*, ed. with an introduction by James Houston (Portland: Multnomah, 1983), 32–33. Also see John Rogerson, Christopher Rowland, and Barnabas Lindars, vol. 2 of *The History of Christian Theology*, ed. Paul Avis, 3 vols. (Grand Rapids: Eerdmans, 1988); Beryl Smalley, "The Bible in the Middle Ages," in *The Church's Use of the Bible Past and Present*, ed. D. E. Nineham (London: Macmillan, 1963), 60.

71. Cf. Thomas Aquinas, *On Interpretation*, trans. J. T. Oesterle (Milwaukee: Marquette University Press, 1962).

VII

REFORMATION AND
POST-REFORMATION
HERMENEUTICS

In this chapter we will survey the contribution to biblical interpretation since the time of the Reformation. Because there have
been so many significant persons and movements during the past
five hundred years, we cannot examine these with the same detail as
we did those in the early church. The purpose of these survey chapters is to establish a foundation on which we can offer a framework
for interpretation in the contemporary church.

THE SIXTEENTH CENTURY

Martin Luther (1483–1546), the great Reformer, started his
career as a biblical interpreter by employing the allegorical method
but later abandoned it.[1] Yet it was Desiderius Erasmus (1466–1536)
more so than Luther, who through the influence of John Colet
(1466–1519) rediscovered the priority of the literal sense. As the
chief founder of modern biblical criticism and hermeneutics, Erasmus must always hold a cherished position among interpreters of

the Bible. He exemplified the finest in Renaissance scholarship that emphasized the original sources.[2] The ultimate source to which he returned was the Greek New Testament. Erasmus possessed a truly historical understanding of ancient texts, but he also desired that the texts bring edification to the readers through the spiritual sense as well. His approach to biblical interpretation developed toward a more critical-historical and philological approach as his method matured, though he always, following his hero, Origen, emphasized the spiritual sense as well.[3]

ERASMUS

Erasmus recognized the need for a Greek Testament as early as 1507, and from 1511 onward he carefully studied and collated more Greek manuscripts of the New Testament than has been generally realized. He produced successive editions of the Greek New Testament in 1516, 1519, 1522, 1527, and 1535. In 1516 he published a revised Vulgate alongside his Greek text. His own fresh Latin translation appeared in 1519. From 1517 onward, he produced several editions of his own paraphrases of the New Testament Epistles and Gospels.[4]

As significant and innovative as Erasmus' works were, the pivotal figures in biblical studies during the Reformation period were Martin Luther and John Calvin (1506–1564). Calvin was the greatest exegete of the Reformation. He developed the grammatical-historical method of interpretation as revised by Erasmus, focusing the place of meaning in the historical interpretation and developing the spiritual message directly from the text.[5] In his commentary on Romans, he inscribed a dedication that read:

> Since it is almost the interpreter's only task to unfold the mind of the writer who has undertaken to expound, he misses his mark, or at least strays outside his limits, by the extent to which he leads his readers away from the meaning of his author. . . . It is presumptuous and almost blasphemous to turn the meaning of Scripture around without due care, as though it were some game that we were playing. And yet many scholars have done this at one time.[6]

While Erasmus and Luther broke tradition to establish a new Protestant hermeneutic, Calvin exemplified it with his touch of genius. Where Luther was bold, sweeping, and prophetic, Calvin was more scholarly and painstaking. Luther was a prophet, a preacher; Calvin a scholarly lecturer. Indeed in the eyes of some, he is regarded as the greatest interpreter in the history of the Christian church.[7]

LUTHER

With his use of a christological method of interpretation, Martin Luther broke the stronghold of allegorical interpretation. From his commitment to *sola scriptura*, Luther felt he must stress first of all that the historical sense is the true sense and the only sense that provides a framework for sound doctrine. In rejecting allegorical interpretation, Luther said, "When I was a monk, I allegorized everything. But after lecturing on the Epistle to the Romans, I came to have some knowledge of Christ. For therein I saw that Christ is not an allegory, and I learned to know what Christ actually was."[8]

Luther also insisted that the Bible itself is its own best interpreter. In this principle he followed the great Augustine. The source from which the methodology of hermeneutics is to be derived is that of Scripture itself. And the true principles of biblical interpretation are to be developed from the biblical sources.

Underlining these commitments was a complete trust in the Bible's truthfulness and authority. Luther believed that Scripture was to be understood above all human thinking—for it is the Word of God itself. Believing that the God of truth had spoken in Scripture, Luther believed that humans must stand under Scripture's authority.[9]

Luther carefully differentiated between the ministerial use of reason and the magisterial use of reason. This principle demanded that human intellect adjust itself to the teachings of Holy Scripture.[10] Reason can be used to understand truth, but it cannot be used to judge the truth value of Scripture. However, Luther's practice did not often match his theory. He did not accept Esther, James, and Jude as canonical. Even with these inconsistencies, Luther maintained that theology had to be brought in line with the Bible rather than the other way around.[11]

Luther wrote important commentaries on Romans and Galatians. He failed as mentioned above to find equal value in all the writings of Scripture, judging those that most clearly conveyed the biblical gospel to be superior. He observed:

> In short, St. John's Gospel and his first Epistle; St. Paul's Epistles, especially those to the Romans, Galatians and Ephesians; and St. Peter's first Epistle—these are the books which show you Christ and teach everything which is necessary and blessed for you to know, even if you never see or hear any other book or teaching. Therefore in comparison with them, St. James's Epistle is a right strawy epistle, for it has no evangelical quality about it.[12]

Luther's bold advance over the fourfold allegorical methodology of the Middle Ages paved the way for the Reformation. However, it was John Calvin who, in a sense, "out-Luthered" Luther to develop a wholistic model of biblical interpretation for the Reformation.

CALVIN

Calvin wrote commentaries on every book in the New Testament except Revelation and 2 and 3 John. His works evidenced and applied theological exegesis. Always insisting that Scripture interprets Scripture, Calvin rejected allegorical interpretation and emphasized the necessity of examining the historical and literary context while comparing Scriptures that treated common subjects.[13]

Calvin more consistently developed an inductive and literal approach to exegesis. His adherence to the principle of *sola scriptura* made him less free with his criticism of Scripture. Calvin attempted to synthesize James and Paul rather than reject one or the other. His sound method of harmonization still can serve the church in a healthy way.[14]

Though Calvin was undeniably committed to the absolute truthfulness and ultimate authority of Scripture, he was not driven to harmonize every tension or potential problem. If he had no solution; he simply let a problem stand, rather than give an artificial solution or question Scripture's authority. Above all, Calvin appealed to the witness of the Holy Spirit as a guide for understanding and interpreting Scripture.[15] He maintained that the testimony of the Holy Spirit is more important than all reason. It is the inward testimony of the Spirit that binds the Scriptures upon a person's heart and conscience. Calvin maintained the same Spirit who inspired the biblical writings must also work in the hearts and minds of interpreters to persuade them of the meaning and authority of the Bible. Calvin consistently appealed to the illumination of the Spirit above human judgment so as to affirm the full authority of the Bible. Thus Calvin, like Luther, believed the Scripture must ultimately be interpreted, applied, and experienced in order to be truly and redemptively understood.

THE SEVENTEENTH AND EIGHTEENTH CENTURIES

PROTESTANT SCHOLASTICISM

It is commonly believed that the followers of the Reformers shrank from the exegetical creativity and freedom employed by Luther and Calvin. They instead produced their expositions along newly-established theological boundaries, resulting in a Protestant scholasticism. Yet as F. F. Bruce has noted, there were several independent thinkers during this period, including Matthias Flacius Illyricus (1520–1575), Joachim Camerarius (1500–1574), John Lightfoot (1602–1675), Christian Schottgen (1687–1751), and Johann Jakob Wettstein (1693–1754). The Counter-Reformation also made its contribution to the revival of sound exegesis. At a time when the book of Revelation was too often used as an arsenal for weapons to be used in the Reformation cleavage by one group against the other, F. Ribera and L. Alcasar went back to the earlier Christian fathers to find a more satisfactory method of interpreting that book. On the Reformed side, the first person to abandon the identification of antichrist with the papacy was the Dutch Jurist Hugo Grotius (1583–1645).[16]

It is true, however, that the followers of Luther and Calvin tended to systematize their exegesis into an Aristotelian mold.[17] Primarily this approach was exemplified on the Lutheran side in Philip Melanchton (1497–1560) and the Calvinist side by Francis Turretin (1623–1687). This new form of scholasticism exercised an authoritative and dogmatic hermeneutic. The new scholasticism coupled with the rise of the Enlightenment, which rejected both authoritative and dogmatic approaches, issued in two responses: (1) a new-found pietism in Philipp Jakob Spener (1635–1705) and

August Herman Franke (1663–1727),[18] and (2) a historical-critical method that stressed the importance of the historical over against the theological interpretation of the Bible pioneered by Johann Semler (1725–1791) and Johann Michaelis (1717–1791).[19]

PIETISM AND RATIONALISM

Pietism began in Germany in the seventeenth century and later spread to Western Europe and America. It represented a reaction to the scholastic dogmatism that had developed. Pietism sought to renew the practice of Christianity as a way of life through group Bible study, prayer, and the practice of personal devotion. Pietists stressed the devotional and practical study of the Bible, though they did not reject careful grammatical exegesis. They always focused on practical applications of the Bible. The leading pietist in England was John Wesley (1703–1791), who also sought to recover the personal and spiritual significance of the Bible.[20]

Jonathan Edwards (1703–1758) represented the Pietist movement in America. Edwards was America's greatest theologian, and undertook two major exegetical projects seeking to advance a Reformed theological exegesis that was open to multiple levels of meaning in the biblical text. It was not bound to the literal sense, but assumed that every passage held the possibility of multiple interpretations. In the same passage he often found a literal meaning, a statement about Christ, the church, and last things (heaven/hell). Edwards' spiritual approach has greatly influenced American pulpits for the past two hundred years.[21]

In the seventeenth century Bernard Spinoza developed an approach to biblical studies that undercut the authority of Scripture. In his originally anonymous work entitled *Tractatus Theologio-Politicus* (1670), Spinoza argued for the priority of reason over Scripture.[22] He suggested that the Bible, like any other book, should be studied as a human document and argued for the importance of asking questions about the authorship, date, occasion, and purpose of particular biblical writings. It was this approach that opened the door for the work of Semler and Michaelis. This embryonic approach to historical criticism argued that purely historical questions should be asked without reference to doctrine. For the next 250 years biblical scholarship would continue to wrestle with the issues related to biblical criticism (which we will discuss in the latter part of this chapter).

One cannot fail to mention the valuable contribution to biblical studies from the pietist tradition that arose during this period from the works of Johann Albert Bengel (1687–1752). He was the first scholar to classify the New Testament manuscripts into families on the basis of similarities. His commentary, the well-known *Gnomon of the New Testament* (1742) served as a model for its combination of historical roots, explanation of figures of speech, and suggestions for devotional applications.[23]

Bengel's work moved against the tide of his day, which was characterized by philosophical and theological rationalism. Two leading thinkers, H. S. Reimarus (1694–1768) and G. E. Lessing (1729–1781), subsumed biblical revelation under the role of reason. F. D. E. Schleiermacher (1768–1834) combined aspects of pietism with rationalism and developed new hermeneutical concerns. Schleiermacher granted that the historical-critical approach helped disclose the intention of the biblical writers in the context of their day, but he also raised the question of what their message might mean to readers and hearers in a different age and culture. In so doing, he became not only the "Father of Theological Liberalism," but also the "Father of Modern Hermeneutics."[24]

THE NINETEENTH CENTURY

The nineteenth century was a revolutionary one in many aspects. Kenneth Scott Latourette labeled it "The Great Century" because it saw both an unprecedented expansion in missions efforts and an increased repudiation of Christianity as well.[25] Radical advances in history, philosophy, and science developed during this time led by the works of Frederic Hegel and Charles Darwin. In the midst of this revolutionary time, historical-critical interpretation began to impact all aspects of biblical studies. Scholars began to treat the Bible as they would any other literature rather than as God's Word to His people.[26]

HISTORICAL CRITICISM

A new approach to biblical studies had been introduced by Johann Semler, who approached the New Testament text only on a historical basis. Unsatisfied with the pietist tradition, Semler made a distinction between the "Word of God," which has abiding authority unto salvation, and the "Scriptures," which contain information important only for the time in which they were written.[27] Inspiration thus gave way to "objective history." A contemporary of Semler, Johann A. Ernesti, in his *Institutio Interpretis Novi Testamenti* (1761), applied to the New Testament the philological-historical method he had successfully used earlier in editing classical texts. Ernesti did not divorce historical study from biblical inspiration as did Semler, and continued to affirm the complete truthfulness of the Bible.[28] He introduced eleven rules of grammatical interpretation that are as useful today as they were at the time they were penned.[29]

These new beginnings pioneered what has become known as the historical-critical interpretation of Scripture. Historical criticism is used as a comprehensive term designating several techniques used to discover the historical situation, the sources behind the writings, the literary style and relationships, the date, the authorship, approach to composition, destination, and recipients. In contrast to textual criticism, historical criticism was often referred to as higher criticism, but this term is now virtually obsolete. Historical criticism opened the door for studying the Bible apart from confessional presuppositions. To the degree that it has provided methodologies for understanding the historical context, culture, and theological intentions of the writers, it has been a valuable tool. To the degree that it has questioned the divine authority of the biblical text, it has been an ongoing challenge for the church for the last 250 years. Whether or not one approaches the text with faith presuppositions, affirming the complete truthfulness and authority of the Bible, is determinative as to the value of historical criticism for the study of the Scriptures in the church.[30]

During this period, a fragmentation of approaches to biblical interpretation developed. On the one hand the rationalistic-historical critics promoted the divorce of theology and biblical studies whereas the pietists, on the other hand, continued to search the Scriptures for guidance in the life of believers on a daily basis and in the corporate life of the church. Since the eighteenth century, the church has continued to be divided into two basic camps:

those who approach the biblical text with presuppositions related to the divine authority of the Bible and those who approach the Bible as any other human book.[31]

In Old Testament studies, Julius Wellhausen focused attention on the written sources behind the Pentateuch. In his work on *Prolegomena to the History of Israel* (1878), Wellhausen argued that behind the Pentateuch stood four separate written sources that could be dated between 850 and 550 B.C. Wellhausen's work concluded that Moses could not have written the first five books of the Bible; that the law contained in the first five books originated after the writing of the historical books and not before them; and that the history of Israel was significantly different from that portrayed in the Old Testament narrative.[32]

On the New Testament side F. C. Baur, professor of theology at the University of Tübingen (1826–1860), argued that Paul's letters reflected a deep division in apostolic Christianity between Jerusalem, led by the apostle Peter, and the Gentile church, led by the apostle Paul. Baur and other members of the infamous Tübingen school reconstructed the history of the apostolic and sub-apostolic age by developing the thesis of the ongoing confrontation between Peter and Paul.[33] The solution for Baur came in his suggested synthesis that the New Testament writings were not first-century apostolic documents, but second-century documents that presented a developing Catholicism. This approach to critical reading of the New Testament came to dominate New Testament research and still strongly influences various schools of thought today. However, further research has shown that there is an obvious unity in the biblical text that was not allowed for by Baur and his followers.

The last one hundred years of study has demonstrated that the work projected by Wellhausen in the Old Testament and Baur in the New Testament cannot stand. British scholarship has particularly challenged the conclusions of their German counterparts. The Cambridge trio of J. B. Lightfoot (1828–89), B. F. Westcott (1825–1901), and J. A. Hort (1828–92) refuted the unwarranted conclusions regarding the supposed conflict between Pauline and Petrine Christianity in the apostolic era. Lightfoot also wrote exemplary commentaries on several New Testament epistles including Galatians, Philippians, and Colossians. The works of Lightfoot,

Westcott, and Hort modeled an exacting scholarship that brilliantly influenced both British and American evangelicals for generations to come.[34]

LIFE OF JESUS STUDIES

In contrast to the works of these important British scholars, German scholarship continued its quest to reconstruct the Gospels and the sources behind the Gospels in order to understand and interpret Jesus in purely historical and human categories. The phrase driving this approach achieved widespread usage from the title of Albert Schweitzer's (1875–1965) volume, *The Quest for the Historical Jesus* (1906). Schweitzer summarized over 250 authors who, from the end of the eighteenth century to the beginning of the twentieth century, investigated the life of Jesus.[35]

Most nineteenth and early twentieth century New Testament scholars felt the importance of interacting with this movement. Rudolf Bultmann (1884–1976) declared that the historical Jesus was inaccessible to the historian.[36] T. W. Manson, a significant British New Testament scholar, responded to this movement saying, "Indeed, it may be said of all theological schools of thought: by their lives of Jesus, ye shall know them."[37] Problems were created by "either/or" choices when the gospel picture is "both/and." We do not have to choose between the historical Jesus and divine Jesus or the human Jesus and the Christ. Jesus is historical and supernatural, He is the God-man. Portraits of Jesus in the synoptic Gospels and in the gospel of John are complementary, not contradictory. Jesus inaugurated the kingdom of God when He came to earth the first time, but the kingdom yet waits a consummation at His second coming.

The nineteenth and early twentieth century unearthed a complex and seemingly contradictory context of historical sayings and sources behind the Bible. These views severely undermine the historical reliability of the Bible and its authority as a source of divine revelation.[38] The entire scope of biblical interpretation was changed from interpreting the meaning of the text we have to trying to find the sources standing behind the Bible. Twentieth-century biblical studies continued to fragment with the further development of source criticism,[39] form criticism,[40] redaction criticism[41] and genre criticism.[42]

As we have seen, source criticism attempted to discover the sources behind the biblical text. Form criticism attempted to reconstruct the biblical "forms" of the early tradition by classifying principal forms such as legal, poetic, legend, or parable. The process included examining these forms to discover their content, how they were handed down, and what their successive life settings were until they assumed their present shape and position. Some scholars, particularly in the Gospels, have undertaken to recover the exact words of Jesus by removing the so-called additions attached to the sayings in the course of transmission. The threefold task of form criticism included: (1) the interpretation of the present Gospels through (2) the interpretation of the tradition lying behind them to (3) the reconstruction of the proclamation of Jesus.

The work of source and form criticism left us with a contradictory Bible where the parts did not relate to the whole. Redaction criticism moved beyond the findings of form criticism as the limits of form criticism became obvious. Redaction criticism developed out of a concern to see the relationship of authors to written sources. The approach has four basic concerns: (1) the original situation of the biblical event or saying, (2) the tradition and process of transmission, (3) the situation in Israel or the early church, and (4) the situation and purpose of the biblical writer/editor. Basic to understanding redaction criticism is the theological motivation of the biblical author/editor. Redaction criticism is thus concerned with the entire framework, not individual units of material. Pioneering studies that developed these approaches included H. Conzelmann's *The Theology of Luke* (1954); W. Marxen's *Mark the Evangelist* (1959); and G. Bornkamm, G. Barth, and H. J. Held's *Tradition and Interpretation in Matthew* (1960). Of these approaches, redaction criticism can be the most helpful for the evangelical scholar in understanding the theological framework of the biblical writer. However, when redaction criticism or other critical methodologies are employed apart from faith presuppositions, they can be deadly to the life of the church.[43]

SCHLEIERMACHER

The major two figures in biblical studies in the Modern Period have been F. D. E. Schleiermacher and Rudolf Bultmann. Schleiermacher shaped nineteenth-century studies and Bultmann shaped twentieth-century studies as no two other persons have done.[44] Schleiermacher (1768–1834) was a mystical pietist, a philosopher, and a theologian, who developed new hermeneutical approaches. Schleiermacher granted that the historical-critical approach helped disclose the intention of the biblical writers in the context of their day, but he questioned what their message meant to modern readers and hearers in a different age and culture. Schleiermacher argued that interpretation consisted of two categories: grammatical and psychological.[45] Prior to Schleiermacher, hermeneutics was understood as special hermeneutics and general hermeneutics. Special hermeneutics was concerned with how the Bible ought to be interpreted and general hermeneutics was used to interpret other kinds of literature. Schleiermacher, however, insisted that the understanding of linguistic symbols, whether biblical, legal, or literary texts, should be derived from a consideration of how understanding in general takes place; thus, a shift from special hermeneutics to general hermeneutics developed.

Schleiermacher saw that what was to be understood must, in some sense, be already known. Acknowledging that this appeared circular or even contradictory, he maintained that this very account of understanding remained true to the facts of everyday experience. This was emphasized in his comment that "every child arrives at the meaning of a word only through hermeneutics."[46] The child must relate the new word to what is already known; otherwise, the word remains meaningless. On the other side the child must assimilate "something alien, universal, which always signifies a resistance for the original vitality. To that extent it is an accomplishment of hermeneutic."[47]

Schleiermacher added that since understanding new subject matter depended on positive relations to the interpreters' own known horizons, lack of understanding was never completely removed. Therefore, understanding constituted a progressive process, not simply an act that can be definitively completed.[48] Schleiermacher held that a preunderstanding must take place before interpretation can happen. For Schleiermacher, understanding was related to the author's intention. In his section on grammatical interpretation, the early Schleiermacher, following Ernesti, articulated some of the most incisive statements found in all hermeneutical literature on the principles useful for grasping what an author wanted to communicate.

However, the grammatical meaning was not enough for Schleiermacher. He argued that the theme of an author's text was a product of an author's nature. The ultimate aim, therefore, was to get through to an author's unique individuality, a psychological interpretation.[49] Understanding required a knowledge of grammatical concerns, but also intuition through empathy with and imagination of the author's experience. The goal was for the author and the interpreter to share a life-relationship. Thus the interpreter is to seek an immediate knowledge of the author's individuality. Understanding, then, involved more than rethinking what an author thought; it included re-experiencing what was in the life of the author who generated the thought. Schleiermacher was thus able to contend that if this re-experiencing could take place, the interpreter could understand the author's work as well or even better than the author.[50]

THE TWENTIETH CENTURY

The Schleiermacher tradition was continued into the twentieth century through the works of Wilhelm Dilthey (1833–1911), Gottlob Frege (1848–1925), Edmund Husserl (1857–1939), Ludwig Wittgenstein (1889–1951), and Martin Heidegger (1889–1976). It is important to note the development that took place from an emphasis on epistemology in Schleiermacher to existential emphases with Heidegger. Heidegger was skeptical that it was possible to achieve determinant meaning in textual interpretation. While Schleiermacher opted for the possibility of an objective interpretation, Heidegger, followed by Rudolf Bultmann, moved away from this position, away from the possibility of determinant meaning and objectivity.[51]

BULTMANN

That Rudolf Bultmann was primarily responsible for Heidegger's hermeneutical insights entering the field of biblical studies is well known.[52] What was important for Bultmann was not the objectifying language of the New Testament, but the existential possibilities of the human being projected through it. One such possibility obviously rested in the New Testament concept of faith. The New Testament was written from the vantage point of faith and called for faith from its readers. Bultmann drew attention to the considerable diversity of theological interests in the primitive church and denied the coherence of an objective doctrinal norm. As he theologized in his *New Testament Theology*, "In the beginning faith is the term which distinguishes the Christian congregation from the Jews and the heathen, not orthodoxy (right doctrine). The latter, along with its correlate, heresy, arises out of the differences that develop within the Christian congregations."[53] By faith, New Testament doctrine, couched in the objectifying mode of language, which Bultmann called "myth," was to be interpreted in terms of the primordial possibilities of human-being. What Bultmann intended by his radical program of demythologizing was not the removal of myth but rather its existential interpretation. In fact, it may be more correct to call Bultmann's approach remythologization rather than demythologization.

Bultmann stood in the Schleiermacher tradition, even though his proposals were major modifications of it.[54] He wished not to reject his tradition, for he remained convinced that the chief interest in reading many texts, particularly philosophical and theological ones, was to have a personal encounter with authors. His objections lay in the tradition's one-sidedness in supposing that grasping the author's individual personality was the only goal in interpreting texts. The broader goal of interpretation, according to Bultmann, included gaining the possibilities of human-being as they exist in relation to the concrete historical world.[55] Understanding, then, may occur when the existential possibilities of the language of faith are appropriated by faith and result in a new self-understanding or understanding of existence.[56]

The presupposition that made understanding possible was that both the interpreter and author share the same historical world as humans. In this, human-being occurs as being in an environment and understanding discourse with objects as well as with other men and women.[57] Bultmann argued for prior understanding or presuppositions in reading the biblical text. Without such a prior understanding and the questions initiated by it, Bultmann maintained that the biblical texts are mute.[58] Thus, Bultmann thought biblical exegesis without prior understanding to be an impossibility. By deemphasizing the cognitive aspect of the biblical text and shifting the notion of interpretation to existential encounter, Bultmann redirected the focus of New Testament interpretation in particular and biblical studies in general in the twentieth century.

The Marburg scholar argued that exegesis without presuppositions is impossible. The interpreter must approach the text with specific questions or with a specific way of raising questions, bringing to the text a certain idea of the subject matter with which the text is concerned. Bultmann raised significant points awakening biblical scholarship from its Cartesian, dogmatic slumbers,[59] but his approach was not accepted by all contemporary theologians or interpreters.[60]

Both Karl Barth (1886–1968)[61] and Wolfhart Pannenberg (1928–),[62] in addition to many American and British evangelical scholars, responded to Bultmann. They claimed that with Bultmann the biblical content is narrowed down from the outset. Anything other than the possibilities of human existence cannot become relevant for existential interpretation. Both of these theological giants maintained that it is rather doubtful that the text, which is to be interpreted on the basis of a Bultmannian model, could still say what it has to say on its own: the New Testament texts, for example, are concerned, at least explicitly, with many things other than the possibility of understanding human existence, although everything with which they are concerned will also be an element of the understanding of the existence of the New Testament author.

In Old Testament studies, German Old Testament scholar Hermann Gunkel, developed critical methodologies similar to those of Bultmann.[63] Biblical studies began to focus on the specific cultural life and original settings of the biblical material. Obviously there is value in the use of these methodologies for serious Bible students.

However, not all scholars, especially those in Britain and North America reached the same conclusions as Bultmann and Gunkel.[64]

EVANGELICAL SCHOLARSHIP

British scholars like C. H. Dodd, T. W. Manson, Vincent Taylor, F. F. Bruce, and I. Howard Marshall have ably defended the substantial historical reliability of the Gospel accounts.[65] In North America, a consistent echo continues the Calvinist tradition's grammatical-historical exegesis, built upon what was established at Princeton Seminary in the nineteenth century on the works of Charles Hodge (1797–1878), who published masterful volumes on the Pauline epistle from 1835–59, J. A. Alexander, A. A. Hodge, and B. B. Warfield.[66] This North American evangelicalism contributed to the advancement of the theological exposition of the Bible, defending its complete veracity and full authority. The work of Hodge and Warfield still stands as a monumental defense of the complete authority of Holy Scripture. Moses Stuart, the great Andover scholar, concentrated in Old Testament studies but also wrote important New Testament commentaries that interacted with critical European scholarship. Stuart did not reject the critical methodologies but reinterpreted them for use within a faith-oriented community. Basil Manly, John Broadus, and A. T. Robertson followed the Stuart tradition by affirming the inerrancy of Scripture while advancing the cause of scholarship in a most significant way.[67] Since World War II, the existential interpretation of Scripture has been at the forefront of scholarship. However, more fruitful approaches such as salvation history hermeneutics, developed by Oscar Cullmann, and the canonical hermeneutics of Brevard Childs have offered new and helpful approaches for bringing together the biblical canon, its message, and the ministry of the church. In the next chapter, we will return to the issue of interpretation as we seek to develop a working model for the contemporary church.

ENDNOTES

1. See Jaroslav Pelikan, *Luther the Expositor* (St. Louis: Concorida, 1959); David S. Dockery, "The Christological Hermeneutics of Martin Luther," *GTJ* 4 (1983): 198–203; Raymond Barry Shelton, "Martin

Luther's Concept of Biblical Interpretation in Historical Perspective" (Ph.D. dissertation, Fuller Theological Seminary, 1974).

2. A. Rabil, *Erasmus and the New Testament: The Mind of a Christian Humanist* (San Antonio: Trinity University Press, 1972), 43–45; cf. J. H. Bentley, *Humanist and Holy Writ* (Princeton: Princeton University Press, 1983), 115–26.

3. Cf. J. W. Aldridge, *The Hermeneutics of Erasmus* (Richmond: John Knox, 1966); also J. B. Payne, *Erasmus: His Theology of the Sacraments* (New York: Bratcher, 1970), 54–70.

4. Traditionally negative evaluations have been given to Erasmus' work, e.g., A. T. Robertson, *An Introduction to the Textual Criticism of the New Testament* (New York: Doubleday, 1925), 19–20; Bruce M. Metzger, *The Text of the New Testament* (Oxford: Oxford University Press, 1968), 97–103. Recently more balanced and positive renderings have been offered by Bentley, *Humanist and Holy Writ*, 114–24; and Henk Jan De Jonge, "The Character of Erasmus' Translation of the New Testament as Reflected in His Translation of Hebrews 9," *Journal of Medieval and Renaissance Studies* 14 (1984): 81–87; idem, "*Novum Testamentum A Nobis Versum:* The Essence of Erasmus' Edition of the New Testament," *Journal of Theological Studies* 35 (1984): 394–413.

5. Hans-Joachim Kraus, "Calvin's Exegetical Principles," *Interpretation* 31 (1977): 8–18; cf. Timothy George, *Theology of the Reformers* (Nashville: Broadman, 1988).

6. John Calvin, *The Epistles of Paul the Apostle to the Romans and to the Thessalonians*, eds. D. W. Torrance and T. F. Torrance (Grand Rapids: Eerdmans, 1961), 1.4.

7. Even a rival like J. Arminius said Calvin's interpretation was incomparable, saying, "He stands above others, above most, indeed, above all." Cited by C. Bangs, *Arminius: A Study in the Dutch Reformation* (Nashville: Abingdon, 1971), 287–88.

8. Martin Luther, *Luther's Works*, ed. J. Pelikan (St. Louis: Concordia, 1955), 42:173.

9. See Martin Luther, *Bondage of the Will* (Edinburgh: T & T Clark, 1957), 67.

10. A. S. Wood, *Luther's Principles of Biblical Interpretation* (London: Tyndale, 1960), 14–15.

11. *Luther's Works*, 16:363–93.

12. *Luther's Works*, 35:361–62.

13. See P. A. Verhoef, "Luther and Calvin's Exegetical Library," *Concordia Theological Journal* 3 (1968): 5–20; also B. A. Gerrish, *The Old Protestantism and the New: Essays on the Reformation Heritage* (Chicago: University of Chicago, 1982), 51–68.

14. Dan McCartney and Charles Clayton, *Let the Reader Understand: A Guide to Interpreting and Applying the Bible* (Wheaton: BridgePoint, 1994), 97.

15. See R. C. Gamble, "*Brevitas et Facilitas*: Toward an Understanding of Calvin's Hermeneutic," *Westminster Theological Journal* 47 (1985): 1–17.

16. F. F. Bruce, "History of New Testament Study," *New Testament Interpretation*, ed. I. H. Marshall (Grand Rapids: Eerdmans, 1975), 34–37.

17. See J. P. Donnelly, "Calvinist Thomism," *Victor* 7 (1976): 41–51; also J. K. S. Reid, *The Authority of Scripture: A Study of Reformation and Post-Reformation Understanding of the Bible* (London: Methuen, 1962).

18. Spener, in *Pia Desideria* (1675) offered six proposals for reform that became a short summary of pietism. Chief among these proposals was the appeal for a more extensive use of the Word of God among us. The Bible must be the chief means for reform. See J. O. Duke, "Pietism versus Establishment: The Halle Phase," *Classical Quarterly* 73 (1979): 3–20.

19. Edgar Krentz, *The Historical-Critical Method* (Philadelphia: Fortress, 1975), 16–23.

20. See William W. Klein, Craig L. Blomberg, and Robert L. Hubbard, Jr., *Introduction to Biblical Interpretation* (Dallas: Word, 1993), 42–43.

21. Stephen J. Stein, "The Quest for the Spiritual Sense: The Biblical Hermeneutics of Jonathan Edwards," *Harvard Theological Review* 70 (1977): 99–113.

22. See Robert M. Grant with David Tracy, *A Short History of the Interpretation of the Bible*, rev. ed., (Phildelphia: Fortress, 1984), 105–08.

23. Johann Albert Bengel, *Gnomon of the New Testament*, ed. Andrew R. Faucet (Edinburgh: T & T Clark, 1857–58); cf. W. C. Kaiser, Jr., *Toward an Exegetical Theology* (Grand Rapids: Baker, 1981), 60–63.

24. See F. D. E. Schleiermacher, *Hermeneutics: The Handwritten Manuscripts*, ed. H. Kimmerle, trans. James Duke and H. J. Forstman (Missoula, Mont.: Scholars, 1977).

25. Kenneth Scott Latourette, *A History of Christianity* (New York: Harper, 1953), 495–98.

26. See W. Neil, "The Criticism and Theological Use of the Bible 1700–1950," *Cambridge History of the Bible* 3, 255–65.

27. W. G. Kümmel, *The New Testament: The History of the Investigation of its Problems*, trans. S. M. Gilmour and H. C. Kee (Nashville: Abingdon, 1972); cf. Stephen Neill and N. T. Wright, *The Interpretation of the New Testament 1861–1986*, 2nd. ed., (New York: Oxford, 1988), 65.

28. See F. Lau, *Neue Deeustsche Biographie* (Berlin: Dunker and Humbolt, 1959), 4:605.

29. Cited and discussed by W. C. Kaiser, Jr., "Legitimate Hermeneutics," *Inerrancy*, ed. N. Geisler (Grand Rapids: Zondervan, 1979), 117–47.

30. See David Alan Black and David S. Dockery, eds., *New Testament Criticism and Interpretation* (Grand Rapids: Zondervan, 1991).

31. See L. Paige Patterson, in *Beyond the Impasse?* eds. Robison B. James and David S. Dockery (Nashville: Broadman, 1992).

32. See Julius Wellhausen, *Prolegomena to the History of Israel* (Edinburgh: Adam and Charles Black, 1885).

33. See Kümmel, *New Testament*, 98–104.

34. See Bruce, "History of New Testament Study," 46.

35. See D. E. Nineham, "Schweizer Revisited," *Explorations in Theology*, 1 (London: SCM, 1977), 112–33.

36. See Rudolf Bultmann, *The History of the Synoptic Tradition* (New York: Harper, 1968).

37. T. W. Manson, "The Failure of Liberalism to Interpret the Bible as the Word of God," *The Interpretation of the Bible*, ed. C. W. Dugmore (London: SPCK, 1944), 92, though the Cambridge trio of Lightfoot, Hort, and Westcott neglected this area in their research.

38. For an excellent defense of the Bible's historical trustworthiness, see Craig L. Blomberg, *The Historical Reliability of the Gospels* (Downers Grove, Ill.: InterVarsity, 1987).

39. See Scot McKnight, "Source Criticism," *New Testament Criticism and Interpretation*, 137–72.

40. See Darrell L. Bock, "Form Criticism," *New Testament Criticism and Interpretation*, 175–96.

41. Grant Osborne, "Redaction Criticism," *New Testament Criticism and Interpretation*, 199–224.

42. Craig L. Blomberg, "The Diversity of Literary Genres in the New Testament," *New Testament Criticism and Interpretation*, 507–32.

43. See D. A. Carson, "Redaction Criticism," *Scripture and Truth*, 126.

44. See McCartney and Clayton, *Let the Reader Understand*, 98–110; also cf. Mark A. Noll, *Between Faith and Criticism* (San Francisco: Harper and Row, 1986).

45. See Schleiermacher, *Hermeneutics*, 66–68.

46. Ibid., 40.

47. Hans-Georg Gadamer, "The Problem of Language in Schleiermacher's Hermeneutic," *Journal for Theology and the Church* 7 (1970): 70.

48. Schleiermacher, *Hermeneutics*, 141.

49. See Anthony C. Thiselton, *Two Horizons: New Testament Hermeneutics and Philosophical Description* (Grand Rapids: Eerdmans, 1980), 103–06.

50. See R. E. Palmer, *Hermeneutics* (Evanston, Ill.: Northwestern University Press, 1969), 84–97.

51. See Martin Heidegger, *Being and Time*, trans. J. Macquarrie (Oxford: Blackwell, 1962); idem, *On the Way to Language*, trans. P. D. Hertz (New

York: Harper and Row, 1971); the best discussion of *Heidegger* is found in Thiselton, *Two Horizons*, 143–204, 327–56; see also Michael Gelvin, *A Commentary on Heidegger's "Being and Time"* (New York: Harper and Row, 1970).

52. Thiselton, *Two Horizons*, 205–51; also cf. Donald G. Bloesch, *Holy Scripture* (Downers Grove, Ill.: InterVarsity, 1994), 223–53.

53. Rudolf Bultmann, *Theology of the New Testament*, trans. Kendrik Grobel, 2 vols. (New York: Scribners, 1955), 135.

54. Thiselton, *Two Horizons*, 233–44.

55. Rudolf Bultmann, "The Problem of Hermeneutics," *Essays Philosophical and Theological*, trans. and ed. James Greig (London: SCM, 1955), 238–43.

56. See Paul Ricoeur, *Essays on Biblical Interpretation*, ed. L. S. Mudge (Philadelphia: Fortress, 1980), 49–70.

57. Bultmann, "The Problem of Hermeneutics," 253.

58. As Bultmann so brilliantly articulated in his classic article, "Is Exegesis Without Presuppositions Possible?" *Existence and Faith*, ed. Shubert M. Ogden (London: Hodder and Stoughton, 1961), 789–96.

59. See Helmut Thielicke, *Prolegomena*, vol. 1 of *The Evangelical Faith*, trans. G. W. Bromiley, 3 vols. (Grand Rapids: Eerdmans, 1974), 38–218.

60. E.g. R. C. Roberts, *Rudolf Bultmann's Theology: A Critical Appraisal* (Grand Rapids: Eerdmans, 1976); also P. E. Hughes, *Scripture and Myth: An Examination of Rudolf Bultmanns's Plea for Demythologization* (London: Tyndale, 1956).

61. See Karl Barth, *Rudolf Bultmann: Ein Versuch ihn zu Verstehen, Theologischen Studien und Kritiken* 34 (Zurich: Evangelischer Verlag, 1952).

62. Wolfhart Pannenberg, "Hermeneutics and Universal History," *History and Hermeneutics*, ed. R. W. Funk (Tübingen: Mohr, 1967), 132.

63. See H. F. Hahn and H. D. Hummel, *The Old Testament in Modern Research* (Philadelphia: Fortress, 1970), 289–91; also Paul House, ed., *Form Criticism* (Winona Lake, Ind.: Eisenbrauns, 1992).

64. See the discussion in Klein, Blomberg, and Hubbard, *Biblical Interpretation*, 44–46.

65. Ibid., 47.

66. Especially through N. B. Stonehouse and J. G. Machen, cf. M. Silva, "Old Princeton, Westminster, and Inerrancy," *Inerrancy and Hermeneutic*, ed. H. Conn (Grand Rapids: Baker, 1988), 67–80.

67. See Noll, *Between Faith and Criticism*.

VIII

THE USE AND INTERPRETATION OF CHRISTIAN SCRIPTURE

The church has used the Bible in a variety of ways. Because of the multifaceted character of the Bible, its use and interpretation have taken a variety of forms. We will briefly examine some of these uses, some basic approaches to interpretation, and some principles for applying the Bible in our modern context. The goal of this chapter is to enable us to set forth a model for reading and hearing God's Word in our contemporary culture.[1]

BIBLICAL INTERPRETATION: THE EARLY CHURCH PATTERN

The writers of the New Testament adopted a christological understanding of the Old Testament. This pattern was based on the way that Jesus Christ Himself read the Old Testament text. Following the current rabbinic practices, the apostles employed various approaches to the Old Testament. Moral injunctions were generally interpreted literally. Other Old Testament passages took on an obvious christological reference, primarily through the use of typological interpretations. Yet no single image or pattern, no one motif or theme adequately expresses the apostles' interpretation of the Old Testament. The New Testament emphasizes that numerous themes, images, and motifs of revelation and response are fulfilled in Jesus Christ. The note of Philip's jubilant words "We have found him" (John 1:45) was echoed by the New Testament writers as the way to interpret the Old Testament events, pictures, and ideas. It was not so much one fulfillment idea, but a harmony of notes presented in a variety of ways by different methods of interpretation.

Jesus became the direct and primary source for the church's understanding of the Old Testament. The apostles, probably subconsciously rather than intentionally, practiced the procedures of interpretation followed by later Judaism. Jewish context, however, in which the New Testament was born, was not the primary aspect or the formation of Christian interpretation. At the heart of their interpretation a christocentric perspective can be found. What was needed was a perspective that could transform Torah into the Messianic Torah. Through the pattern that Jesus had set and through His exalted Lordship expressed through the Holy Spirit, Jesus served as the ongoing source of the early church's approach to the Scriptures.

From the earliest days of Christian history, individual Christians and the church have used the Bible in various ways. This rich heritage influences today's Christians in the ways they use the Bible for individual and corporate purposes. Some of the ways the Bible is used today include the Bible as: (1) a source for information and understanding of life; (2) a guide for worship; (3) a wellspring to formulate Christian liturgy; (4) a primary source for the formulation of theology; (5) a text for preaching or teaching; (6) a guide for pastoral care; (7) the sustenance for spiritual formation in the Christian life; and (8) literature for aesthetic enjoyment. A look at some of the primary uses of Scripture will help us understand the inestimable value of the Word of God and help us see its particular importance for all aspects of life.[2]

THE BIBLE AND PRIVATE STUDY

Because copies of the Bible were so expensive to produce in the time of the early church, most copies were owned by communities, not individuals. Because common people could not possess their own Scriptures, they depended on public readings. Not until after the eighth century A.D. was a smaller and more affordable copy of the Bible made available to a large number of people. From this time on, it was popular for wealthy individuals to purchase copies of the Bible and to provide them for others. However, many individuals were illiterate and thus prohibited from private reading. With the invention of the printing press and the development of the doctrine of the priesthood of believers in the Reformation, the private reading of Scripture increased. The practice of private study had been encouraged since Jerome (A.D. 341–420) and Augustine (A.D. 354–430), but the emphasis on the believer's reading and interpreting Scripture is one of the mainstays of post-Reformation Protestantism. The strong renewal movement has stressed the supreme importance of the devotional use of the Bible. Certainly that has been the case with the movement known as Pietism in its best form, which called for a clear Spirit, enabled reading, and application of Holy Scripture.

THE BIBLE AND THEOLOGY

In the early church, theological construction was vitally related to, if not inseparable from, biblical interpretation. The basis of all true biblical theology in the history of the church is a sound exegetical understanding of Scripture. Most, if not all, theological deviations are caused by the neglect of biblical truth or by faulty interpretation of the biblical text. Theology at its best is developed from the sequence of biblical exegesis to biblical theology to systematic theology. It is important as we will note in studying the biblical material to interpret it against the historical and cultural background of the time. We must guard against either modernizing or de-culturizing the Bible. The Bible must be allowed to say first what it was saying to the readers and hearers of that time rather than what we think it should have said, or what we think it is saying to us.

151

The theologian should recognize that the whole Bible provides the context for interpretation and theologizing. The Old and the New Testaments should be approached with the expectation that a unity between the two exists.

The Bible is a starting point for understanding and articulating a theology for the church. To be truly biblical, however, does not ordinarily mean to repeat the words of Scripture precisely as they were written. Indeed, at times that would be unbiblical. Theology that is biblically grounded involves interpreting, analyzing, synthesizing, and contextualizing the biblical text to our contemporary world. Theology involves seeing what Jesus, the prophets, and the apostles would say today to our situation. The Bible is the supreme source of our understanding, but that does not mean theology excludes all other sources. But these other sources remain secondary to Holy Scripture. A theological interpretation of the Bible is mandatory for faithful preaching.[3]

THE BIBLE AS LITERATURE

Although the Bible was never intended to be read solely as literature, it has undeniable literary qualities and has undoubtedly greatly influenced other literature, particularly in the English-speaking world. From a literary point of view, the Bible contains drama, poetry, narrative, and prose. The intimacy of the New Testament letters has especially exerted broad appeal. The Bible is worthy of literary study. This usage has increased greatly in the past decades. Yet the literary study of the Bible is not the reason that the Bible is the best-selling and the most frequently read book in the world. It is because the Bible is God's Word to men and women of all ages, addressing the most important spiritual needs in their lives and revealing truth about God to His world.

THE BIBLE AND WORSHIP

We do not know for certain what procedure the earliest churches adopted to include Bible reading as a regular feature of worship. But it is certain that the first and primary use of the Bible was in the church's worship. It is imperative to remember that biblical interpretation was grounded in the church's use and understanding of the sacred text, not in the theoretical analysis of scholars. Following the pattern established in the Jewish synagogue, the exposition of the sacred word was of utmost importance in the church's worship. This pattern started with Jesus' exposition of Isaiah 61 at the beginning of His ministry, which He interpreted in light of His own Messianic mission (see Luke 4:16–22), and was continually practiced in the early church's worship (see Acts 13:14–44; 14:1; 17:1; 19:8).

In 1 Timothy 4:13 young Timothy was exhorted to devote attention to the public reading of Scripture. Private study was encouraged in 2 Timothy 2:15, but private study was not available to all. The matter of the public reading of Scripture was therefore given a high priority. It was the apostles' conviction that Scripture was given by the inspiration of God and was able to make the hearer wise unto salvation, which is in Jesus Christ (2 Tim. 3:15–17). Thus the place of the reading in exposition of Scripture held in public worship was always central. The model Christian service, like the worship in the synagogue, was a Word-of-God service. The reference in 1 Timothy is the first historical allusion to the use of the Scriptures in the church's worship.

The New Testament letters were read in the public meeting of the churches (see Col. 4:16; Rev. 1:3). Apparently, the apostles expected their letters to be accepted as authoritative in their own lifetime (see 2 Thess. 2:15; 2 Pet. 3:15–16). The letters were gradually accepted, circulated, and read aloud in public gatherings. In this way they became the objects of study and meditation.

The reading of Scripture was accompanied by its exposition. Almost all of the church's interpretation of Scripture and corresponding theologizing developed from the sermon. The real meaning of preaching was set forth by the apostle Paul in 1 Corinthians 1:17–23. He claimed that he came to preach the gospel, which he identified as the message of the cross, Christ crucified. This preaching was to demonstrate the Spirit's power so that faith would demonstrate God's power (see 1 Cor. 2:1–6). The apostle's theology of preaching was built on the elements of the *kerygma*: the incarnation, death, burial, resurrection, and exaltation of Christ. In this sense, preaching in the context of the worshiping community reenacted the event of Christ, the event that provided shape and meaning not only to worship, but also to the lives of the worshipers. The church's preaching interpreted the Old Testament Scripture in terms of Christ's coming, as evidenced in the church's attitude toward the Old Testament. The church regarded the Law and the Prophets, as well as the events and worship of Israel, as part of the Christian tradition, because it believed that they testified of Jesus Christ. For example, in 1 Corinthians 15:3–4 Paul insisted that everything concerning Christ took place "in accordance with the Scriptures." Soon a typological interpretation of the Old Testament became a standard way of expounding the Scriptures in the church's worship. Thus, through the early church's preaching the initial typological exegesis was practiced. The preaching of the early church was not a dispassionate recital of historical facts, a sort of nondescript presentation of certain truths, interesting enough but morally neutral. No, the facts were meant to become factors in the lives of the worshipers; hence the constant offer of repentance, pardon, and a place in the new age inaugurated by the coming of God's Son.

The church was given the gifts of pastors and teachers so that the community of faith could be built up through reading, preaching, and teaching Holy Scripture to the measure of the stature of Christ in His fullness (see Eph. 4:11–16; Col. 1:28). The early church heavily emphasized that Christians are to be instructed in the Scriptures (see Heb. 5:11–14) and that Christian leaders are to remain faithful to the tasks of interpreting and expounding the Bible (see Col. 4:16–17; 1 Pet. 4:10–11). Thus, as in the synagogue, the church's worship was a Word-of-God worship, grounded in the Holy Scripture. This set the pattern for the church's use of Scripture throughout the ages.[4] Let us now turn our attention to the primary hermeneutical practices adopted in recent times.

BIBLICAL INTERPRETATION IN THE TWENTIETH CENTURY

The prominent approach to biblical studies in both Protestant and Roman Catholic schools of interpretation until the middle of this century was an author-oriented approach in line with Schleiermacher tradition. This view has been called the "literal-grammatical," "historical-contextual," or "historical-critical" method of interpretation. Advocates of this approach, such as Krister Stendahl and John L. McKenzie, writing in the *Journal of Biblical Literature* (1958), defined interpretation as determining the meaning intended by the human author and understood by the original readers. Followers of this approach considered the meaning of biblical texts to be stable and univocal. They considered meaning to be located in the historical situation. Stendahl defined the task of interpretation as furnishing the original, reconstructing the transaction of the author to the original audience by way of the text.

In an early edition of *A Short History of the Interpretation of the Bible* (1963), Robert M. Grant affirmed a very similar position.[5] He did this even while recognizing the shifts toward existential hermeneutics under the widespread influence of Martin Heidegger and Rudolf Bultmann. Grant maintained: "It would appear the primary task of the modern interpreter is historical, in the sense that what he is endeavoring to discover is what the texts and contexts he is interpreting meant to their authors in their relationships with their readers."[6]

In 1967, a University of Virginia literary scholar, E. D. Hirsch, Jr., published a major work titled *Validity in Interpretation* that advocated an author-oriented, normative hermeneutic. He followed this work in 1976 with *The Aims of Interpretation*.[7] Working within the Schleiermacher tradition of general hermeneutics, Hirsch called for a grammatical and historical interpretation that attempts to grasp the meaning an author intended to convey in what was written. His influence in biblical interpretation is praised by many scholars of diverse traditions.

Hirsch distanced himself from the Schleiermacher tradition, however, by maintaining that it was not the task of the interpreter to have access to the mental process by which an author produced a work. He affirmed that the author's verbal meanings can be grasped because the interpretation of texts is concerned with shareable meanings. Hirsch contended that authors choose language conventions that will bring to readers' minds the things they are attempting to communicate, so the readers can also know what the authors wanted to share with their audience by words. Language is efficient in transmitting these meanings because it consists of conventions, of elements that the society using that language has agreed should stand for all its various aspects of common experience. Thus, "an author's verbal meaning is limited by linguistic possibilities, but is determined by his actualizing and specifying some of these possibilities."[8] The meaning of words is thus limited by a context that has been determined by the author. Interpreters cannot, then, understand what writers meant except by what they have actually written. With reference to biblical studies, G. B. Caird has summarized:

> We have no access to the mind of Jeremiah or Paul except through their recorded words. Afortiori, we have no access to the word of God in the Bible except through the words and the minds of those who claimed to speak in his name. We may disbelieve them, that is our right; but if we try, without evidence, to penetrate to a meaning more ultimate than the one the writers intended, that is our meaning, not theirs or God's.[9]

To summarize E. D. Hirsch's position concerning an author-oriented interpretation, we can note that he claimed the task of the interpreter is to understand what an author meant at the time of the writing. This is possible because the text's meaning is controlled by language conventions that exist between the speaker and hearer or author and reader. Hirsch acknowledged that interpretation takes the form of process, a process that takes the form of a guess, and there are no rules for making good guesses.

There are, however, methods for validating guesses, as Hirsch himself has elucidated: "The act of understanding is at first a genial (or a mistaken) guess and there are no methods for making guesses, no rules for generating insights; the methodological activity of interpretation commences when we begin to test and criticize our guesses."[10]

Paul Ricoeur, agreeing with Hirsch, has likewise observed:

> As concerns procedures of validation by which we test our guesses, I agree with Hirsch that they are closer to a logic of probability than a logic of empirical verification. To show that an interpretation is more probable in light of what is known is something other than showing that a conclusion is true. In this sense, validation is not verification. Validation is an argumentative discipline comparable to the judicial procedures of legal interpretation. It is a logic of uncertainty and of qualitative probability. . . . A text is a quasi-individual, the val-

idation of an interpretation to it may be said, with complete legitimacy, to give a scientific knowledge of the text.[11]

The most important contribution Hirsch's theory has made to biblical studies is the distinction between "meaning" and "significance." Meaning is what the writer meant when addressing the original readers. Hirsch emphasized that there is one primary normative meaning—that which the author intended. However, he suggested the more important or meaningful a text is the greater the possibility of deeper, fuller meanings. The significance of the text includes all the various ways a text can be read and applied beyond the author's intention.

I would like to suggest that exegesis focuses on the primary normative meaning of the biblical text. Exposition entails bringing out the fuller meaning or significance of the biblical text in line with the way the early church read Scripture, through the vehicles of typological and allegorical interpretation, plus the developments of *sensus plenior* (the fuller meaning of the text) and the analogy of faith employed since the second century.

The goal, then, of interpretation is not to psychologize an author, but to determine the author's purpose as revealed in the linguistical structure of the text. In other words, the goal of interpretation concerns itself with what the author achieved. Ricoeur has stressed that, generally when one reads a text, the author is not present to be questioned about any ambiguous meaning in the text. This is certainly the case with the human authors of the biblical text, though the Holy Spirit who inspired the text can illuminate it for us today.

Paul Ricoeur, like E. D. Hirsch, maintains a text's meaning is intelligible across the historical and cultural distance. Because of the nature of writing, the text opens a possible world to the interpreter (the text world); the interpreter may enter into that world and appropriate the possibilities it offers. When that occurs, the meaning of the text is actualized in the interpreter's understanding. What is understood or appropriated, then, is the text itself, the result of the author's writing. Thus, the goal of biblical interpretation is to understand meaning from the standpoint of what the author actually wrote or to focus on the text as the result of the author's writing.[12] Now, let us look at ways in which we can both interpret and apply the biblical text in the life of the contemporary church.

TOWARD INTERPRETATION OF THE HOLY SCRIPTURE

Hermeneutical models and presuppositions outlined in the first portion of this chapter have prepared us to talk about a method of biblical interpretation. Before identifying steps involved in the process of New Testament interpretation, I would like to highlight the issues that need to be addressed. Each biblical document and each part of a biblical document must be studied in its context. This includes not only its historical context, but its immediate literary context, as well. This means that to interpret a text, we must have an understanding of the biblical languages, the types of literature that are being employed, the historical background, the geographical conditions, and the life-setting of both the author and readers or hearers of this text. The meaning of a piece of writing is seldom clearly self-evident. This is especially true for an ancient document like the Bible, which was written for people who lived in a very different cultural and historical setting. This means in order to get at the issues we have just identified we must ask at least five questions of the text under consideration:

1. Who was the writer and to whom was he writing?

2. What was the cultural-historical setting of the writer?

3. What was the meaning of the words used at the time of the writing?

4. What was the purpose for the author's writing and why was he saying it the way he said it?

5. What does this mean for believers in the contemporary church?

We must also recognize that before we come to a text we must identify our own presuppositions. All understanding requires a framework or context within which to interpret. The more knowledge the reader has about a text the more likely it is that it can be understood properly. If the Bible is God's revelation to His people, then the essential qualification for a full understanding of the Bible is to know the revealing God. To know God we must have a relationship with Him. The Bible describes this relationship by using the term faith. Only those who believe and trust in God can rightly understand what God has spoken in His Word. It is impossible to understand the biblical text if one denies that there is a God or that the Bible is not from God.

A second commitment that is necessary is the willingness to submit to the text and to obey what it says. Hermeneutics cannot be limited to the grammatical-historical techniques that help the interpreter understand the original meaning of the text. For those who accept the Bible as a sacred text, the church's book, the record of God's unique self-revelation, its interpretation cannot be conducted on the grammatical-historical level alone. That level is fundamental, but there is a theological level that cannot be ignored. The grammatical-historical level of interpretation may bring out the historical meaning in the Bible, but the theological exegesis presupposes that there is an overall unity for the entire Bible in light of which the diversity can be appreciated in its proper perspective.[13]

Thus, to understand the Bible theologically and to obey its teaching, we need to rely upon the illuminating work of the Holy Spirit. It is through the ministry of the Holy Spirit that God provides the resource for such obedient understanding of His truth. The illuminating work of the Holy Spirit does not dispense with hard work and solid principles of hermeneutics. It does mean that the Spirit brings the text alive so that it can be properly understood and applied to our lives individually, as well as to the life of the church. This latter aspect must not be ignored when we preach the Bible in our contemporary setting. As interpreters of the biblical text, we must be constantly aware of the temptation of individualism. We need to recognize our participation in the body of Christ and do our work as interpreters for the good of others in the community of faith. The church is the instrument that the Spirit uses to provide accountability for our interpretation and to guard against wrongheaded and individualistic approaches to the text. It provides a check against self-serving conclusions that may be limited by our own circumstances. We also recognize that the church of Jesus Christ is a worldwide fellowship that crosses cultural boundaries.

This means that our interpretation must make sense to others in Christ's worldwide body, as well as to those in our local setting.

A MODEL FOR CONTEMPORARY
BIBLICAL INTERPRETATION

We must begin our work as interpreters recognizing that we build upon the work of those who have gone before us. We must interpret Scripture in our confessional setting recognizing that it is, indeed, the inspired and inerrant word of God.[14] We can learn from the different models that have been identified in the previous section, recognizing that there are strengths in each of these models. We must affirm the real possibility that the entire biblical text in its canonical context contains a theological meaning that is not unlike what traditionally has been called *sensus plenior*. This term indicates a fuller meaning in the Scripture than what was possibly intended or known by the original human author. The more significant the text, the more this is the case. Because of the canonical shape and divine nature of the biblical text, a passage may have a surplus of meaning or a full depth of meaning, which by its very nature can never be exhausted. It is with this humility that we approach the text, recognizing that the meaning of a text may actually exceed the conscious intention of the original authors or the understanding of the original readers.

How can these fuller meanings be determined? What parameters exist to limit fanciful excesses? The parameters are located in the text itself and in the biblical canon. The fuller meanings must be consistent with the canonical message. Some guidelines will prove helpful as we seek to develop a contemporary model. These include the following:

1. Approach the text with right presuppositions which we have previously identified as biblical faith, accepting the Bible as fully truthful and authoritative.

2. Recognize that the historical and literal meaning of the Bible is the primary meaning, but not the limit of meaning.

3. Acknowledge the possibility of deeper meanings in the prophetic-apostolic witness.

4. Affirm the human authorship of the text, as well as its divine origin.

5. See the biblical text, rather than the author's mind, as the place where meaning is concentrated.

6. Understand that a text rests in it canonical context, thus Scripture serves as the best commentary on Scripture.

7. Expect the enabling help in illumination from the Holy Spirit to assist in interpretation.

8. Expect the Bible to speak to the reader's contemporary concerns.

9. Interpret the Bible in light of the centrality of Jesus Christ and for the good of the church.

Thus we read the Bible both christologically and ecclesiologically.[15]

It is true that all reading is perspectival; that is, the reader participates in understanding the text, but the reader is not the determiner of meaning. We would suggest that there are indicators in the text itself, contextual markers that are not there by accident, but to guide us toward an objective meaning. An objective meaning is thus mediated by the biblical text itself. Textual indicators limit the possibilities so that the number of meanings available to the reader is not infinite. While stressing the historical meaning of the text, we cannot neglect the concerns of the contemporary reader. The concept of the text's significance, in this way, is as important as its meaning, thought not equated with it.[16]

Focusing meaning in the biblical text, rather than in the author or reader, acknowledges that a text's verbal meaning can be construed only on the basis of its own linguistic possibilities. These are not given from some other realm, but must be learned or guessed at; this is a process which is entirely intrinsic to a particular social and linguistic system. Paul Ricoeur has claimed that what was to be appropriated for understanding to be completed is nothing other than the power of disclosing the "text-world" that is the reference of a text. The gulf between reader and author has been bridged by the text itself. A text is, indeed, historical in its origin, but is also present in its power to communicate its sense and to open a world to its reader by its reference. It is in this sense that Ricoeur can suggest that the letters to the Romans, Galatians, Corinthians, and Ephesians, as well as other books, are addressed to contemporary readers as much as to original readers. If that is the case, what are some steps that will help the interpreter achieve an understanding of the biblical text? Here we would like to identify seven helpful steps that will move us from the then to the now in the process of interpreting the Bible for its use in the church.

STEP 1. INTRODUCTION

The interpretive process begins with prayer. God's direction and enablement must be sought at each step. Then we bring our questions to the text at hand. Three questions help us deal with introduction issues. First and foremost we must ask, "What presuppositions do we bring to the biblical text?" We have already identified these as faith, obedience, the expectation of the illuminating work of the Spirit, a commitment to the truthful text, and a recognition of our place within the community of faith. Our basic assumption is that the Scriptures are fully inspired and constitute a truly truthful, divine-human book. We must also seek to determine, "What is the historical situation behind the author?" And "What is the cultural context out of which the author wrote?"

STEP 2. OBSERVATION

As we observe the text being considered, we ask: "What are the limits of the text?" We must look for keys or structural signals, such as conjunctions, particles, etc., that serve as markers in the text. While the basic unit for consideration is the paragraph, we must pay attention to sentences and word meanings, as well. Much that is identified as interpretation is little more than word studies. Seeing the text's structure in paragraph units will enable us to see the major idea being communicated by the author.

STEP 3. TRANSLATION

Here we ask, "What is the text?" Through textual criticism and comparison of various translations, we establish the text from which we will work. It is likely that most interpreters will work from one basic, favorite translation and do minimal comparison with other translations. We would encourage the comparison of translations before accepting one translation. Here the use of the original language is extremely helpful, if not mandatory.

STEP 4. BASIC EXEGESIS

Before moving to our primary step, we need to ask, "What kind (genre) of text are we interpreting?" Is it poetry, narrative, prophetic, parabolic, gospel, epistolary, or apocalyptic? Then we can begin to do basic work with Bible dictionaries, concordances, and grammars. Diagraming a sentence flow at this point can be extremely helpful for seeing the major emphases of the text. Gordon Fee's step-by-step instructions for analyzing the text with the use of sentence flow charts will be most helpful in this process.[17] For certain genres, discovering the plot or macrostructure of the text will be necessary at this point.

STEP 5. INTERPRETATION

This is the most important step in seeking the textual meaning from an author-oriented perspective. We bring the question: "What did the text mean in its historical setting to the initial readers?" Here the question moves from what to why. We move beyond asking "What does the text say?" to "Why was it said in this way?" Now, we must examine commentaries, trace the history of interpretation of our passage, and move toward seeing the meaning of the text in its literary and canonical context.

STEP 6. THEOLOGY

Three important questions will help us seek the theological significance of the passage. First, "What does the text mean to contemporary readers?" Second, "What cultural factors need to be contexualized or retranslated?"[18] Third, "What is the theological significance of the passage?"

STEP 7. PROCLAMATION AND SIGNIFICANCE
FOR THE CHURCH

Finally, we must raise two questions, "How can the historical meaning and the contemporary significance be communicated to our contemporary world?" and, "How will the text be heard and understood today?"[19] The final step of the process also includes finding and proclaiming the relevance and normative application for modern readers and hearers. It is to the issue of application that we now turn our attention.

CONCLUSION: THE RELEVANCE AND APPLICATION OF THE BIBLE

We have affirmed that the Bible is God's authoritative Word to men and women. Guidelines for interpretation enable us to hear and respond to God's Word in our various cultural settings. Yet we need to ask, "How do we apply these guidelines to such contemporary issues as decision-making and ethical practices?"

INTERPRETATION AND AUTHORITY

We must recognize that God's truth is revealed not through our human capacities but through the Holy Spirit's illumination (see 1 Cor. 2:6–16). Jesus claimed: "If you hold to my teaching, you are really my disciples. Then you will know the truth, and the truth will set you free" (John 8:31–32).

To live in accordance with the truth of Scripture and obey its authority, it is necessary to handle the Word of God accurately (see 2 Tim. 2:15). Care must be taken to interpret the Scriptures faithfully. We can suggest the following practical guidelines.

1. We must be careful not to interpret the Scriptures by our experiences or cultural norms, though, of course, we cannot deny our experiential or cultural presuppositions. Instead, we need to interpret our experience and culture by the Bible. If we allow the Scriptures to be interpreted by our experience, our experience will become the higher authority.[20]

2. We must be cautious, not dogmatic, in our interpretations where the Scriptures are not conclusive. Often we are guilty of saying more than the Bible says in such areas as dress, appearance, or cultural practices (see Rom. 14; 1 Cor. 8:10–13). Where the Bible speaks, we should speak; where it is silent, we must take care that our response is consistent with the general teachings in Scripture.

3. We must avoid rationalizing the Bible so as to undercut its authority. Although Scripture is time- and culture-related, we

Introduction	Observation	Translation	Basic Exegesis	Interpretation	Theology	Proclamation
Step 1	Step 2	Step 3	Step 4	Step 5	Step 6	Step 7
Ask:	Ask:	Ask:	Ask:	Ask:	Ask:	Ask:
What presuppositions do I have when I approach this text?	What are the limits of the text?	What is the text?	What kind (genre) of text is this?	What does the text mean in its context?	What does the text mean to the contemporary reader?	How can the hist. meaning and contemp. significance be communicated?
What is the historical situation?	Basic translation	Establish the text	Advanced observation	Why was it said this way? canonical meaning?	What cultural factors need to be contextualized?	How will the text be heard and understood today?
What is the cultural context?	Observe structure		Lexical Exegesis	see commentaries	What is the theological significance?	
	paragraph		What does the text say?	survey history of interpretation		
			macrostructure			
	sentence					
	words		plot			

must be cautious before dismissing a scriptural teaching as time- or culture-bound. Anytime we allow current philosophical or scientific theories or cultural movements to become the standard by which Scripture is understood, we may fall into the trap of usurping Scripture's authority.[21]

4. At the same time, we must recognize that we are separated from the prophets and apostles by time and culture. Meanings of words and practices change from generation to generation. We should carefully seek to determine whether a passage is figurative rather than literal. Recent examples from our own culture may prove helpful. Not long ago if something was said to be hot, it meant something had a high or warm temperature. Now to say that something is hot means it is considered "in" or good. The same could be said for the word cool. Present generations use terms cool or hot to describe something that is good and they often describe good as "bad." So the use of words and their meanings change from generation to generation.

5. The use of the term *lion* in 1 Peter 5:8 can refer to Satan, and it can refer to Christ in Revelation 5:5. Paul exhorted the Philippian church to be aware of the "dogs" (Phil. 3:2). He does not mean a pack of angry animals but a group of false teachers. These examples point Bible students to the need to take the word usage and cultural practices into account when interpreting Scripture. In our attempt to find the spiritual truths in a passage, we must not read a spiritual meaning into a passage where no spiritual meaning can be substantiated by the immediate context or by a broader canonical understanding. Fuller meanings must always be extensions of the primary historical meaning and consistent with the Bible's canonical or overall message. A good general principle is to attempt to interpret the Bible in light of its primary historical meaning. The meaning is found by diligently examining the context of a passage, the customs of the time, and the meanings of words and phrases. Only when we understand Scripture's meaning can we rightly live under its authority.

6. We need to remember that the purpose of biblical interpretation is to bring about Christlikeness in our lives so we will be

equipped for service in Christ's church (see 2 Tim. 3:17). Biblical authority means putting God's Word into practice (see Ps. 119:59–60). We must not limit biblical interpretation to one particular method or technique, but we must employ every legitimate means to understand the Bible's message. The benefit of interpretation is hearing and obeying the Word of God—receiving what the Lord Himself says and prayerfully putting it into practice. Biblical authority begins with a willing acceptance of truth. A right response to scriptural authority is characterized by trust, obedience, praise, and thanksgiving.[22]

SCRIPTURAL AUTHORITY AND CONTEMPORARY CHALLENGES

Challenges to biblical authority often arise when we apply biblical teachings to our twentieth-century context. The questions we bring to the Bible shift from "What did the Scriptures mean to those to whom it was first given?" to "What do the Scriptures mean to us?" Biblical context and our context are sometimes embedded in different cultures and world views. I. Howard Marshall asks, "How is meaning found when what is common sense in one culture is not common sense in another?" Paul's command to obey one's master in all things (Col. 3:22–23) is addressed to a culture of involuntary slavery. Our economic system and understanding of the extended household differs greatly from that world.[23]

Today, workers or employees are often partners in their work with employers. Does this kind of relationship call for loyalty or obedience? If we say that for today the biblical command means that we would give appropriate respect and loyalty to employers rather than unconditional obedience, are we diluting the exhortation of the passage or expressing the essential meaning in terms appropriate for contemporary working conditions? Cultural differences challenge us to hear God's Word clearly.

A missionary has related an account of telling the Joseph story (see Gen. 37–50) to a group of Europeans and to a group of Third World people. The Europeans heard the story of Joseph as a man who remained faithful to God no matter what happened to him. The Third World group, on the other hand, pointed to Joseph as a man who, no matter how far he traveled, never forgot his family. Different cultural backgrounds prompted each response.[24] Can we say that one is more consistent with the authority of the biblical story? Is the other one incorrect? Is it possible that both are legitimate understandings—or at least legitimate applications? How can an ancient text speak to us authoritatively so that our cultural, temporal, and social meanings do not become dominant over the historical meaning of the Bible?[25] Certainly, D. A. Carson is right when he says, "No human being living in time and speaking any language can ever be entirely culture-free about anything."[26]

In line with our divine-human (christological) understanding of Scripture, Harvie Conn has suggested six helpful clues on this subject. From the divine perspective he offers three important guidelines:

1. The beginning point is a commitment to Scripture's total truthfulness. The only proper control for our judgments remains the primary historical meaning of the biblical text.

2. The cultural patterns of the biblical time period do not simply provide God with sermon illustrations. That culture becomes the providentially controlled matrix from which His revelation comes to us (for example, see Exod. 3:12; Luke 22:19–20). That context is the place from which the history of God's unfolding special revelation has been manifested. From that cultural particularity come the universals that link the faith of the biblical characters to ours.

3. The Holy Spirit, who brought the first horizon of the text into being (see 2 Pet. 1:20–21), must open our hearts and illumine our minds to open the biblical text for our world. The Spirit does not become some mechanical or magical answering service. Nor does the Spirit become an intermediary between God and us; He is God who addresses us.

Conn also provides three helpful insights from the human perspective:

1. A distancing must take place before we can hear the ancient biblical text for our day. This might sound like just the opposite thing we want to accomplish. But many biblical stories (such as the parables of the prodigal son in Luke 15 or the

repentant publican in Luke 18) need to be distanced from our setting so the parables' "punch lines" can be heard.

2. Our presuppositions and world view must be reshaped by the Bible. Our values and perspectives must become more and more what God wants them to be. Our vantage point must be shaped by creation, the fall, redemption, and consummation. In this sense, our cultural and temporal distinctions can become a help, not a hindrance, to understanding and responding to the biblical message.

3. Holy Scripture is presented in cultural forms that are different from ours. These cultural forms often need to be restated and translated for our day to address contemporary challenges.[27]

We can maintain our confession of biblical authority, recognizing the divine-human aspects of the nature of Scripture and the interpretation of Scripture. The Bible's truth is untainted by either the culture from which it comes to us or the culture to which it goes. The message of Scripture uses various cultures while simultaneously and authoritatively standing in judgment over them.

AUTHORITY AND APPLICATION

We have seen that the Bible is authoritative since it is God's Word to men and women. Guidelines for interpretation enable us to hear and respond to God's Word in our cultural settings. Yet we need to ask, "How do we apply these guidelines to such contemporary issues as decision-making and ethical practices?" We can recognize that some biblical teachings are specific and universal commands that speak directly to people in all cultures. Some general teachings have universal application. Some biblical principles have implicit authority.[28] Finally, some matters can be addressed only by finding biblical guidelines that can be applied to that issue or question. The following examples will help us understand these guidelines:

1. Passages such as prohibitions against stealing (see Exod. 20:15; Eph. 4:28) are direct teachings that apply to all people in all times.

2. General teachings on love or justice or some broader theme can be applied to various situations in different settings. Peo-

ple in employee-employer relationships, family relationships, or broader societal situations must seek to apply principles of justice and/or love in these settings.

3. Teachings about drunkenness (see Eph. 5:18) must be obeyed. Applications about abstinence from alcoholic beverages are implied rather than being direct teachings of Holy Scripture. Thus, the level of authority is different from the previous examples.

4. Some contemporary issues are not addressed specifically in Scripture. Where should we work? Whom should we marry? What church should we join? We must approach each of these matters by trying to apply biblical principles. The answer to these issues must be dealt with differently by each of us under the Holy Spirit's guidance.[29]

Understanding that various levels of authority are present in the Bible helps us understand that a commitment to scriptural authority is not out-of-date.[30] The general teachings of Holy Scripture reveal God's will in a variety of ways. The direct, implied, and applied principles of Scripture can cross the temporal, social, linguistic, and cultural barriers. Thus, we can affirm the adequacy, sufficiency, and authority of the Bible for modern men and women. The Bible can and does speak, at various levels, to challenges and issues we face in our modern world.

ENDNOTES

*The major portion of this article is based on my chapter "The Use and Interpretation of Scripture" in *Foundations for Biblical Interpretation*, ed. David S. Dockery, et al., (Nashville: Broadman and Holman, 1994).

1. See R. T. France, *Jesus and the Old Testament: His Application of Old Testament Passages to Himself and His Message* (London: Tyndale, 1971); also my fuller discussion of this matter in David S. Dockery, *Biblical Interpretation Then and Now* (Grand Rapids: Baker, 1992).

2. William W. Klein, Craig L. Blomberg, and Robert L. Hubbard, Jr., *Introduction to Biblical Interpretation* (Dallas: Word, 1993), 377–99.

3. See the chapter by Robert Sloan, "Canonical Theology of the New Testament," in *Foundations for Biblical Interpretation*, eds. David S. Dockery, K. A. Mathews, and Robert B. Sloan (Nashville: Broadman and Holman, 1994), 565–94.

4. See Leland Ryken, *How to Read the Bible as Literature* (Grand Rapids: Zondervan, 1984); also see Ralph P. Martin, *Worship in the Early Church* (Grand Rapids: Eerdmans, 1964), 68–76.

5. See Robert M. Grant, *A Short History of the Interpretation of the Bible* (New York: Macmillan, 1963).

6. Ibid., 186.

7. See E. D. Hirsch, Jr., *Validity in Interpretation* (New Haven: Yale University Press, 1967); idem, *The Aims of Interpretation* (Chicago: University of Chicago Press, 1976).

8. Idem, *Aims*, 47.

9. G. B. Caird, *The Language and Imagery of the Bible* (Philadelphia: Westminster, 1980), 61.

10. Hirsch, *Validity*, 19–20.

11. Paul Ricoeur, *Hermenuetics and the Human Sciences*, ed. and trans. J. B. Thompson (Cambridge: Cambridge University Press, 1986), 212.

12. I have discussed these matters in *Biblical Interpretation Then and Now* (Grand Rapids: Baker, 1992), 161–83.

13. F. F. Bruce, "Interpretation of the Bible," *Evangelical Dictionary of Theology*, ed. W. Elwell (Grand Rapids: Baker, 1984), 565–68.

14. See David S. Dockery, *The Doctrine of the Bible* (Nashville: Convention, 1991), 65–92.

15. Ibid., 120–22; see also Dan McCartney and Charles Clayton, *Let the Reader Understand* (Wheaton: Victor/BridgePoint, 1994), 51–58; Richard B. Hayes, *Echos of Scripture in the Letter of Paul* (New Haven: Yale, 1989), 162.

16. See David M. Scholer, "Issues in Biblical Interpretation," *Evangelical Quarterly* 88 (1988): 5–22; cf. Grant Osborne, *The Hermeneutical Spiral* (Downers Grove, Ill.: InterVarsity, 1992).

17. See Gordon D. Fee, *New Testament Exegesis* (Philadelphia: Westminster, 1983), 60–77.

18. See the helpful principles articulated in David Hesselgrave, *Communicating Christ Cross-Culturally* (Grand Rapids: Zondervan, 1978).

19. See John R. W. Stott, *Between Two Worlds: The Art of Preaching in the Twentieth Century* (Grand Rapids: Eerdmans, 1982); also the different approaches identified and discussed in Michael Duduit, ed., *A Handbook for Contemporary Preaching* (Nashville: Broadman, 1992).

20. See R. P. Richard, "Application Theory in Relation to the New Testament," *Bibliotheca Sacra* 143 (1986): 210–12.

21. See Jack Kuhatschek, *Taking the Guesswork Out of Applying the Bible* (Downers Grove, Ill.: InterVarsity, 1990).

22. See Oletta Wald, *The Joy of Discovery* (Minneapolis: Bible Banner, 1956).

23. I. Howard Marshall, *Biblical Inspiration* (Grand Rapids: Eerdmans, 1982), 105.

24. See Harvie M. Conn, "Normativity, Relevance, and Relativism," *Inerrancy and Hermeneutic*, ed. Harvie M. Conn (Grand Rapids: Baker, 1988), 186–89.

25. See Gordon D. Fee and Douglas Stuart, *How to Read the Bible for All It's Worth* (Grand Rapids: Zondervan, 1982), 58–60.

26. D. A. Carson, ed., *Biblical Interpretation and the Church: The Problem of Contextualization* (Nashville: Nelson, 1984), 19.

27. Conn, "Normativity, Relevance, and Relativism," 197–209.

28. E. E. Johnson, *Expository Hermeneutics: An Introduction* (Grand Rapids: Zondervan, 1990), 229.

29. I am dependent on insights gained from Ebbie C. Smith's biblical ethics class at Southwestern Seminary.

30. W. W. Klein, C. L. Blomberg, and R. L. Hubbard, Jr., *Introduction to Biblical Interpretation* (Dallas: Word, 1993), 406–20.

CONCLUSION

This volume has addressed the major issues surrounding the crisis of biblical authority that we face today. It would be naive to think that the only issue creating division among Christians—and even among evangelical Christians—is the issue of Scripture. Many of our misunderstandings and divisions are created by regional and cultural differences. Others are fostered because we have diverse understandings of the church, of education, of pastoral leadership, of church-state issues, and a variety of other matters. Yet, we cannot move forward in our discussions in these areas without a common commitment to the truthfulness and authority of Holy Scripture that remains the foundational concern of this book.

Evangelicals must continue to affirm that the Bible is totally true and trustworthy because this foundational commitment serves other primary and fundamental affirmations of the Christian faith. A commitment to a completely truthful and fully authoritative Bible is the first step toward healing the deadly sickness in today's theological and ethical trends that threaten the very heart of the Christian faith and message. When approaching the Bible, we recognize its authoritative and normative character which can enable us to discover truth and its implications for the answers to life's ultimate questions. We also can find guidance for godly living in our world. We want primarily to stress the truthful and trustworthy character of God's faithful revelation to humanity and believe it is impossible to move forward together in ministry, missionary, and evangelistic efforts apart from such a common affirmation. We need people who will proclaim the truthfulness and authority of God's word while seeking to live under its authority.

We need not only to affirm the Bible's inspiration, truthfulness, and normative nature, but we need to evidence our concern for these matters by careful theological reflection, faithful proclamation, repentance, and prayer. A confession that the Bible is fully inspired and totally truthful is necessary because it is the foundation that establishes the complete extent of Scripture's authority. The contemporary church must choose to articulate a view of the Bible that is faithful to historic evangelical and orthodox positions that have characteristically confessed that the Bible is the written Word of God, is truthful, infallible, and is the only sufficient, certain, and authoritative rule of all saving knowledge, faith, and obedience. We can thus relate to one another in love and humility, bringing about true fellowship and community, resulting not only in orthodoxy but orthopraxy before a watching world. In conclusion, we can commit ourselves wholeheartedly to the following brief confession of the Bible's complete reliability and place our total trust and confidence in it. It is my hope that this brief confessional statement can serve as a foundation for a new consensus in a broad evangelical world.

1. We believe all knowledge of God comes by way of revelation, which is God's manifestation of Himself to humankind in such a way that men and women can know and fellowship with Him.

2. We believe God has revealed Himself to all peoples at all times in all places through nature, history, and in human consciences and experiences. He has revealed Himself specifically to specific people in specific places through redemptive acts

and prophetic and apostolic words. Ultimately, He has revealed Himself in Jesus Christ, the Living Word of God. We believe this special revelation of God is made available to us today through Holy Scripture, an inspired Word from God. We believe that while God's general revelation is to be interpreted in light of His special revelation; they are not in conflict with one another, but are complimentary and harmonious.

3. We believe these acts of special revelation have been interpreted by God's prophets and apostles and under the providential hand of God have been gathered together and recognized by the church to form the canon of Sacred Scripture, consisting of thirty-nine books in the Old Testament and twenty-seven books in the New Testament. We believe that God's revelation is personal and that God reveals Himself personally and redemptively, but His revelation is also propositional in that it reveals truths about God and His creation. This special revelation is progressive, which means in the witness of biblical history there is a developing disclosure of God, His will, and His truth in the Old and New Testaments. The development is not contradictory in any fashion, but is supplementary to what has been previously revealed.

4. We believe Scripture is inspired and is entirely and completely the Word of God as well as the words of human authors. It is inadequate to affirm that the Bible is only a human witness to divine revelation because the Bible is also God's witness to Himself. Through the superintending influence of God's Spirit on the writers of Holy Scripture, the accounts and interpretations of God's revelation have been recorded as God intended so that the Bible is actually the written Word of God.

5. We believe inspiration was the work of God in which God, by His Spirit through human writers and editors, gave us His Word. The origin of Scripture is divine; and as such, the Holy Scriptures are the authoritative Word of God and are the supreme written norm by which God binds the conscience. While the process of divine inspiration remains largely a mystery, we believe that the work of inspiration can best be

described as concursive and plenary. God, in His work of inspiration, utilized the distinctive personalities and literary styles of the human writers whom He had chosen and prepared.

6. We believe that the Spirit's work of inspiration results in a Bible that is God's Word written to all people for all times. We also believe that when all the facts are known, this written Word of God properly interpreted in light of which culture and communication means had developed by the time of its composition will be shown to be completely true (and therefore not false) and truthful in all that it affirms, to the degree of precision intended by the author, in all matters related to God and His creation.

7. We believe in the Spirit's work of illumination that enables believers to interpret the biblical text in its original context in such a way as to understand the biblical authors' meanings, as well as its canonical significance for our contemporary world. Ultimately, the Bible is to be interpreted in light of the centrality of Jesus Christ, who affirms the complete veracity of the Bible and lived His life in fulfillment of Holy Scripture.

8. We believe the Bible is the ultimate standard of authority for God's people. We further believe the Bible is our only and all-sufficient rule of faith and practice. The Holy Spirit, who inspires Holy Scripture, leads believers today to recognize the authority of Scripture and to respond to and obey its message.

This confessional statement is not intended as a final word, but as a place to develop a common consensus grounded in Holy Scripture. It is not intended to address every issue or provide all the answers, but it does address the significant issues of biblical authority that we need to heartily confess for us to move ahead together, united in our common faith and witness to Jesus Christ before a changing and fragmented world. The twenty-first century will be filled with new challenges that we cannot yet comprehend. One thing, however, is for sure. The message of the Bible, written two thousand years earlier, remains the foundation on which we can together move forward in mission and ministry.

APPENDIX

THE INSPIRATION AND AUTHORITY OF SCRIPTURE IN THE SOUTHERN BAPTIST CONVENTION (1845–1994)

The Southern Baptist Convention (SBC) is a large, powerful, Protestant denomination that has found itself wrenched by controversy over the nature and interpretation of Scripture for almost twenty years.[1] The Southern Baptist Convention has not been alone in this controversy, however, for there are similar debates taking place in Christianity-at-large. Yet the intensity of the debate within the Southern Baptist Convention outdistances the issues in other Christian bodies.

During their first 150 years, Southern Baptists have changed in several obvious ways. What was once a small, Southern, predominantly white denomination has become large, multi-regional, and multi-ethnic. Southern Baptists now worship and serve in dozens of languages throughout the United States. What was originally and primarily a group with white, male-dominated leadership has begun to make room in some places for others to serve in leadership roles.[2]

This particular section of our book is not an attempt to wrestle fully with matters of Southern Baptist identity and heritage, but to examine the history of the inspiration and authority of the Bible, particularly as the debate has heightened over the past forty years. The forty-year period represents that time since the death of W. T. Conner (d. 1952), the convention's last "shaping theologian" and generally the time period since the rise of programmatic emphases in the convention's "glory days" (such as the "Million More in '54" campaign). Before looking at Southern Baptist history and attempting to place Southern Baptists on the contemporary theological map, trying to see how they are related to mainstream Protestants, Evangelicals, and Fundamentalists, we will take a brief look at Baptist foundations and confessions that have informed Southern Baptist theology.[3]

Traditionally Baptists have been cautious about the use of doctrinal confessions.[4] Yet Baptists have published numerous confessions of faith since the early years of the seventeenth century. It is our purpose to examine the statements regarding Holy Scripture in representative Baptist confessions from the seventeenth century to the present.[5]

BAPTIST CONFESSIONS AND BIBLICAL INSPIRATION

Thomas Helwys' confession (1611) in Article 23 sets forth the following view on Scripture:

> That the scriptures off the Old and New Testament are written for our instruction, 2 Tim. 3:16 and that we ought to search them for they testifie off CHRIST, Io.5:39. and therefore to bee used with all reverence, as conteyning the Holie Word off God, which onlie is our direction in all things whatsoever.

The Standard Confession (1660–63) in Article 23 sets forth the characteristic General Baptist understanding of Scripture:

That the Holy Scripture is the rule whereby Saints both in matters of Faith, and conversation are to be regulated, they being able to make men wise unto salvation, through Faith in Christ Jesus, profitable for Doctrine, for reproof, for instruction in righteousness, that the man of God may be perfect, thoroughly furnished unto all good works, 2 Tim. 3.15,16,17. John 20.31. Isa. 8.20.

The First London Confession (1644), a Calvinistic confession that predates the Westminster Confession, in Articles 7 and 8, states:

The Rule of this Knowledge, Faith, and Obedience, concerning the worship and service of God, and all other Christian duties, is not man's inventions, opinions, devices, lawes, constitutions, or traditions unwritten whatsoever, but onely the word of God contained in the Canonicall Scriptures.

In this written Word God hath plainly revealed whatsoever He hath thought needfull for us to know, beleeve, and acknowledge, touching the Nature and Office of Christ, in whom all the promises are yea and Amen to the praise of God.

The Second London Confession (1677, 1689), basically following the wording and emphases of the Westminster Confession, contains ten articles on the Scriptures. In comparison to earlier Baptist confessions, there is a significant shift whereby the articles of Scriptures are located in the first section of the document. In addition to articles on the canon (21), a denial of the authority in the apocrypha (3), statements on illumination (6), the original languages (8), and the perspicuity of Scripture in regards to salvation (7), it affirms:

1. The Holy Scripture is the only sufficient, certain, and infallible rule of all saving Knowledge, Faith, and Obedience.

4. The Authority of the Holy Scriptures for which it ought to be believed dependeth not upon the testimony of any man, or Church; but wholly upon God (who is truth itself) the author thereof; therefore it is to be received, because it is the Word of God.

5. We may be moved and induced by the testimony of the Church of God, to an high and reverent esteem of the Holy Scriptures . . . and it doth abundantly evidence itself to be the Word of God; yet, not withstanding, our full persuasion, and assurance of the infallible

truth, and divine authority thereof, is from the inward work of the Holy Spirit, bearing witness by and with the Word in our Hearts.

9. The infallible rule of interpretation of Scripture is the Scripture itself: And therefore when there is a question about the true and full sense of any Scripture (which is not manifold but one) it must be searched by other places that speak more clearly.

10. The supream judge by which all controversies of Religion are to be determined, and are Decrees of Counsels, opinions of ancient Writers, Doctrines of men, and private Spirits, are to be examined, and in whose sentence we are to rest, can be no other but the Holy Scripture delivered by the Spirit, into which Scripture so delivered, our faith is finally resolved.

The Philadelphia Confession (1742), which so greatly influenced Baptists in America, followed the Second London Confession. At no place was the Philadelphia statement more influential than in Charleston, where the theological formation and development of Richard Furman, J. P. Boyce, and Basil Manly, among others, took place.

The Orthodox Creed (1678), a General Baptist statement, contains a lengthy statement on sacred Scripture, which is positioned at the conclusion of the confession. Article 37 concludes by confessing the Scriptures "are given by the inspiration of God, to be the Rule of faith and life."

In 1833 the New Hampshire Confession, an altogether new document for Baptists in America, articulates a high view of Scripture with language that has been officially adopted by many other Baptist bodies. Article 1 declares:

We believe that the Holy Bible was written by men divinely inspired, and is a perfect treasure of heavenly instruction; that it has God for its author, salvation for its end, and truth, without any mixture of error, for its matter; that it reveals the principles by which God will judge us; and therefore is, and shall remain to the end of the world, the true centre of Christian union, and the supreme standard by which all human conduct, creeds, and opinions should be tried.

Since 1845 the Southern Baptist Convention has approved only three documents that have served as confessions or statements of faith. These include the Abstract of Principles (1858), the Baptist

Faith and Message (1925), and the revised Baptist Faith and Message (1963).

The Abstract of Principles maintains that the "Scriptures are given by inspiration of God, and are the only sufficient, certain and authoritative rule of all saving knowledge, faith and obedience." The two Baptist Faith and Message statements were born in the midst of controversy. The 1925 document responded to the evolution controversy and the 1963 statement developed in light of the convention's rejection of Ralph Elliott's Genesis commentary.

Basically both adopted the wording of the New Hampshire Confession with minor changes. The 1925 statement, edited by E. Y. Mullins, inserted the adjective "religious" to modify the word "opinions." The 1963 confession's description of inspired Scripture added the phrase, "and is the record of God's revelation of Himself to men." A hermeneutical guide was also provided, stating: "The criterion by which the Bible is to be interpreted is Jesus Christ."

Readily apparent is the confidence that Baptists have and have had in the Bible, its inspiration and authority. Yet the affirmations indicate developmental and contextual differences. The nuances and distinctions are worthy of notation, but all the statements evidence a commitment to the Bible's truthfulness, reliability, and infallibility.[6]

Theological development is to be expected, though some would claim that any development of orthodox doctrine is corruption, deviation into heterodoxy, or heresy. But since any survey of historical theology, even one as brief and selective as the one in this section, recognizes some change; the challenge is to explain the development.

Recognizing that there exists a smorgasbord of options in Baptist life today on the matter of biblical inspiration we must somehow differentiate orthodox doctrinal development from unorthodox development, doctrinal corruption, or apostasy. We must make positive contributions to the theological task which, whether carried on in the areas of academy, society, or church, must produce true statements about God and His relationship to this creation. Baptists are generally united in their commitment to a common belief of the priority of Scripture over tradition. Yet this has worked itself out in at least four identifiable ways in the current context.

VARIETIES IN SOUTHERN BAPTIST LIFE

Among Southern Baptists, there are at least four different groups represented in the discussion over the nature of Scripture, its interpretation, and its relation to tradition: (1) fundamentalists, (2) conservatives or evangelicals, (3) moderates, and (4) liberals. The understanding of these four groups is decisive for interpreting the current context within which the Southern Baptist Convention operates. The following section analyzes the doctrine of Scripture in each of these groups, noting other theological or social commitments that inform the beliefs, traditions, and agendas of the various groups.[7]

FUNDAMENTALISTS

Fundamentalism in the Southern Baptist Convention is closely related to the unique phenomenon in American Christianity in the areas of theological conviction and social agenda. Southern Baptist fundamentalists, however, are not generally as militant or separatistic as other bodies of American fundamentalism. In the Southern Baptist Convention, fundamentalists include different groupings and theological structures. Among these differences, there are two major groupings: (1) a mystical-pietistic body that emphasizes evangelism and missions, and (2) a more scholastic theological group that often stresses the importance of either Calvinistic or dispensational theology. Recognizing these significant differences, they should still be treated as one group because in theory their doctrine of Scripture is virtually identical.

The fundamentalists' doctrine of Scripture emphasizes the Godward side of inspiration, sometimes seemingly ignoring the human writers. The prophetic model, "Thus says the Lord," becomes the paradigm through which all of Scripture is seen. Revelation is understood entirely or almost entirely in propositional terms and the concept of inspiration borders on dictation. The dictation theory places the emphasis on God's actual dictation of His Word to the human writers. It is sometimes uncritically affirmed that the Bible is the writing solely of the living God, with little attention given to the human authors. Each sentence is dictated by God's Holy Spirit. This de-emphasizes the human nature of Scripture.

Fundamentalists affirm a full and absolute inerrancy of Scripture that stresses not only the truthfulness of Scripture, but its precise accuracy as well. For this to be maintained, a philosophical framework is often superimposed on the text, whereby literary features and genre differences are diminished in importance as the entire Bible is read as a set of propositional statements, each expressing divine affirmation. Likewise, in their approach to biblical interpretation, historical-critical methods are strongly rejected. The problem passages, such as apparent discrepancies or conflicting accounts, are often explained as errors in the transmission of manuscripts or are eliminated through a harmonization approach to the biblical text. There is a stress on the overall unity of Scripture and a virtual ignoring of the variety and development within the Bible.

CONSERVATIVES OR EVANGELICALS

For nearly fifty years, there has existed a growing movement in conservative Protestantism in Europe and America known as Evangelicalism that is distinct from fundamentalism. Among Southern Baptists, there are many who identify with this movement and affirm its basic theological convictions, while functioning in a Baptist context.

Concerning the doctrine of Scripture, Evangelicals affirm that revelation is both personal and propositional. While emphasizing propositional revelation, Evangelicals are careful to maintain that Scripture's literary diversity is more than a historic accident or decorative device; it is a vehicle for imaginative thought and creative expression about things difficult to grasp. Commands, promises, parables, analogies, metaphors, symbols, and poetry cannot be forced into propositional form without loss. The recognition of literary diversity brings a healthy realization of the human aspect in Scripture, thus balancing the divine-human authorship of the Bible. Evangelicals maintain that the Bible attests to its own inspiration that can be characterized as plenary (meaning all of Scripture is inspired) and concursive (meaning inspiration includes both human and divine aspects). While Evangelicals affirm verbal inspiration, they remain cognizant of contemporary linguistic theory that suggests that meaning is at the sentence level and beyond.

Based upon plenary inspiration of Scripture, an Evangelical view infers the inerrancy of Scripture that stresses that what the Bible affirms is completely true. Evangelicals attempt to be sensitive to the diversity and development in Holy Scripture, recognizing different literary genres while seeking to determine the original meaning of Scripture. Harmonization is accepted as a legitimate means of handling diversity in the biblical text, but not at the expense of running roughshod over the context and forcing the Bible to say what it does not say. Because the Bible is a divine-human book, the interpretative tools of literary and historical criticism are employed with care and faith-oriented presuppositions.

MODERATES

Moderates in the Southern Baptist Convention include representatives from different theological strands entailing neoevangelicalism, neo-orthodoxy, and neoliberalism, as well as the newer aesthetic and narrative theologies. This group would generally identify with the larger "mainline" movement in Protestantism.

Moderates in the Southern Baptist Convention prefer to think of themselves as loyalists to the denomination's history, though the diversity of understanding of Baptist tradition and the rise of the Cooperative Baptist Fellowship calls this self-understanding into question. Some moderates would accept the term "evangelical," some with and some without a theological commitment to biblical inerrancy. Such would be true of laypeople, pastors, and theologians, while others stand in the tradition of Karl Barth and Emil Brunner—including laypeople, pastors, and theologians.

Moderates generally see Scripture as a witness to God's revelation and prefer the term infallibility instead of inerrancy. When moderates employ the term inerrancy in reference to Scripture, it is generally limited to religious or doctrinal matters (following the tradition of the 1925 Baptist Faith and Message statement). They understand inspiration in a dynamic fashion by which the Holy Spirit directs the writers-redactors to the concepts they should have and then allows them great freedom to express these ideas in their own styles, through their own personalities, and with their own choice of words, in a way consistent with and characteristic of their own situation and contexts. Some have creatively expanded the view, looking beyond the human author's role to see the place of the community in the composition of Scripture.

For moderates, Scripture is characteristically understood in light of the central message of salvation. There is an emphasis on Scripture's infallibility and its ability to accomplish its purposes because it will not deceive humanity about matters of salvation. Most moderates would identify with the posture of Dutch theologian G. C. Berkouwer, who states, "The purpose of the God-breathed Scripture is not at all to provide a scientific gnosis in order to convey and increase human knowledge and wisdom, but to witness of the salvation of God unto faith." Scripture is thus understood as a functional and living instrument serving God for the proclamation of the salvation message to its readers and hearers.

LIBERALS

This group is most difficult to describe. While there is much talk about "liberalism" in the SBC, there is little that identifies with the classical liberalism of the nineteenth-century, though there are a variety of representatives of the more radical theologies of the twentieth-century: existentialism, process thought, liberation movements, and feminist theologies.

Characterizing a view of Scripture among these diverse theologies is nearly impossible. A common agreement would be the de-emphasis of the divine nature of Scripture and elevation of the human dynamic. Most of these movements would find the Bible in its current form to be of little value and would seek to retranslate it almost entirely for contemporary issues in modern contexts. They would understand inspiration to involve the Spirit's working within the human writers to raise their religious insight and express themselves with eloquent language. These theologies generally posit that inspiration lifts the authors beyond their normal abilities to express themselves creatively. People reflecting these diverse theologies read the Bible from a subjective, reader-oriented approach and typically disallow objective readings of Scripture. Inspiration, authority, and interpretation are bound together in inseparable ways that make traditional discussions about inspiration seemingly meaningless.

While all four groups, and many other subsections among these are present in Southern Baptist life, it is our observation that the Southern Baptist Convention is composed primarily of conservative evangelicals and moderates. Generally, Southern Baptist fundamentalists are not as separatistic as the rest of American fundamentalism, nor are Southern Baptist liberals as radical as most of American liberalism. Yet each of these groups claims to represent the primary tradition of Southern Baptist thinking over the last 150 years. While there has been variety and development within Southern Baptist life there has also been much continuity.

Since 1845, there have doubtless been hundreds of professors and pastors who have influenced the shape of Southern Baptist theology through their lectures, writings, and sermons. Yet for the purposes of this volume, we will focus primarily on major theologians, denominational leaders, and writing pastors, though the influence of popular evangelists, pastors, and teachers has been more formative for shaping Southern Baptists thinking than most of us realize. Let us examine the current variety in Southern Baptist life in light of our 150-year tradition.

BIBLICAL INSPIRATION, INTERPRETATION, AND AUTHORITY: 1845–1952

The first one hundred years were largely shaped by three major theologians: James P. Boyce (1827–88),[8] E. Y. Mullins (1860–1922),[9] W. T. Conner (1877–1952).[10] From the early years of Boyce to the death of Conner, Southern Baptists witnessed the diminishing influence of Calvinism, the decline of postmillennialism, the rise of revivalism, and an advancement in the understanding of Baptist origins and identity. Also there was during this time the basic introduction into SBC life of such matters as historical criticism, theistic evolution, and experiential apologetics. We could say that Southern Baptist theology moved from a hermeneutic of divine sovereignty with John L. Dagg, J. P. Boyce, and Basil Manly to one of personal revelation and experience with Mullins, and to a lesser degree with Conner. From these changes a growing consensus emerged around the moderate Calvinistic theologies of Mullins and Conner, with additional programmatic, pragmatic, and revivalistic emphases. Shaped by these shifts and concerns, Southern Baptists navigated their way through the first century of their existence.

JOHN L. DAGG[11]

Prior to the establishment of the Southern Baptist Theological Seminary in 1859, Mercer University was a well-known Baptist school with an established Department of Theology. J. L. Dagg (1794–1884) served as president and professor of theology at Mercer from 1844–54. During his lifetime, Dagg was the most prominent theologian among Southern Baptists. Among his many works was included an article on the "Origin and Authority of the Bible," which was penned in 1853 and was also included in *A Manual of Theology* (1858).

Dagg both led the way for Southern Baptists, and mirrored them in almost all areas of theology, including the doctrine of Scripture. His theological contributions were largely isolated from European thinkers of his day, who discussed the nature of revelation in great detail. Dagg did not enter that dialogue. He was quite content with his understanding that the Bible was to be understood as divine revelation.

In his *Manual of Theology*, he explained: "We shall here assume that the Bible is a revelation from God."[12] For Dagg, revelation is information about the Christian religion. He continued saying: "To us in these last days God speaks in his written word, the Bible, which is the perfect source of religious knowledge and the infallible standard of religious truth."[13]

Inspiration was understood to be the means by which the matter of revelation was conveyed to human minds and also the means by which this revelation was put in permanent form as a written document. Revelation and inspiration are so closely related that as they meet in the Bible they become interchangeable. Dagg's wording "the origin of the Bible" points simultaneously to the revelation and inspiration of the Bible. He affirmed that inspiration was to be understood as both plenary and verbal. He emphasized the divine control of the human authors, though he refuted the charge of mechanical dictation.

Dagg maintained that inspiration brought about the close relationship between human language and divine revelation that created the Bible and that can be received as inspired revelation and read as the very Word of God. Dagg believed inspiration guaranteed that God's people had received a revelation from God that could be characterized as infallible and authoritative. He believed that infallibility meant that the Bible was absolutely truthful in all of its statements. He believed this to be entirely consistent with human authorship and claimed that the Bible was divine truth without error. Though he acknowledged difficulties in the biblical text, which he referred to as alleged imperfections, he believed these difficulties had "very little weight when compared with the amount of evidence on which the belief of plenary inspiration rests."[14] J. L. Dagg's affirmations regarding the complete inspiration of Scripture as the process by which God conveyed His revelation to the world paved the way for reaffirmations of the Bible's ultimate authority and further advances by the founders of the Southern Baptist Theological Seminary.

JAMES P. BOYCE AND BASIL MANLY, JR.

James P. Boyce (1827–88) and Basil Manly, Jr. (1825–92) formed half of the original faculty of the Southern Baptist Theological Seminary when it opened in 1859. Boyce previously taught at Furman University and Manly was principal of the Female Institute of Richmond, Virginia. Both were equally adept at administrative work, as well as teaching theology. While each made important contributions in several areas, Boyce's major work was his *Abstract of Systematic Theology* (1887) and Manly's primary effort was his *The Bible Doctrine of Inspiration* (1888). Both volumes were the results of their class lectures. The issue of inspiration was not dealt with in detail in Boyce's theology class, because that subject was dealt with in Manly's course on "Biblical Introduction." It is not beyond reason to conclude that Manly's work on Scripture is reflective of Boyce's position on this subject.[15]

Manly's landmark volume was published as a response to the resignation of Old Testament professor, C. H. Toy. Though Manly was an original member of the faculty, he had departed in 1871 to become president of Georgetown College. The fact that he returned following the Toy controversy again confirms Boyce's confidence in Manly's position on the subject of biblical inspiration.

The key to understanding the thought of Boyce and Manly is to recognize their common opposition and response to the work of Toy. Both Boyce and Manly disagreed with Toy's doctrine of Scripture and its practical implications.

Both men built their understanding of Scripture on the work of their Princeton mentors, as well as Alvah Hovey and J. L. Dagg, all of whom affirmed the inspiration and inerrancy of Holy Scripture. J. P. Boyce affirmed the Bible as "infallible."[16] Infallibility for Boyce meant "without error," and there is nothing in his writings that would imply that he distinguished between infallibility and inerrancy.

The most important and informative work on the inspiration and authority of Scripture among Baptists in the nineteenth century was certainly Basil Manly's *The Bible Doctrine of Inspiration* (1888). Manly argued that an uninspired Bible would furnish no infallible standard of thought, no authoritative rule for obedience, and no ground for confidence and everlasting hope.[17] It is important to note the inseparable relationship between inspiration, infallibility, and authority in Manly's work (which diminishes any importance in the change of wording between the term "infallible" in the Second London Confession and the word "authoritative" in the Abstract of Principles). Manly was careful to distinguish inspiration from revelation, which he defined as "that direct divine influence that secures the accurate transference of truth into human language by a speaker or writer, so as to be communicated to another."[18]

While affirming plenary inspiration, Manly carefully refuted any theory of mechanical dictation, because it ignored genuine human authorship. He maintained that every aspect of Scripture is characterized as infallible truth and divine authority. Manly believed that infallibility was the corollary of inspiration. Manly, like Boyce, took seriously the human authorship of the Bible, as well as its divine origin, and balanced this tension more effectively than Dagg while contending for the complete truthfulness of Holy Scripture. Perhaps with less scholarly erudition, but with equally persuasive power, B. H. Carroll sounded similar concerns in the Southwest.

B. H. CARROLL (1843–1914)[19]

B. H. Carroll was the founder and first president of Southwestern Baptist Theological Seminary (1908–14). Unlike Boyce and Manly, who were educated at Princeton, Carroll lacked formal training in theology. However, Carroll was the superior intellect and by self-education taught himself theology. Carroll regularly taught the entirety of the English Bible in four-year cycles while he was on the faculty at Baylor and at Southwestern Seminary. His work, entitled *An Interpretation of the English Bible*, represents the publication of these lectures.[20] Over a decade after Carroll's final lectures on the inspiration and authority of Scripture, J. B. Cranfill edited the professor's lectures, which continue to serve as a primary source for understanding early Southern Baptist views of Scripture.

The Bible was the focus of Carroll's career. His widespread reputation as a champion of Baptist orthodoxy was closely associated with his doctrine of Scripture. He understood the Bible to be the written revelation of God. The affirmation undergirded Carroll's entire theology and exegesis of Scripture. While noting a close relationship between revelation and inspiration, Carroll nevertheless went to great lengths to differentiate between revelation, inspiration, and illumination.

Carroll wrongly built his understanding of inspiration on the Latin term *inspiro* rather than the Greek word *theopneustos*, causing him to think of inspiration as God breathing on or breathing into the Scriptures rather than breathing out the Scriptures. Nevertheless, Carroll emphasized that inspiration insured a perfect standard of instruction, conviction, and a profitable work for correction and instruction in righteousness.[21]

Carroll believed that inspiration did not apply to the writers, but the writings of Scripture. He carefully set his argument for biblical inspiration within a Baptist context, building on the affirmation of Scripture in Article One of the New Hampshire Confession of Faith. Carroll built his case for inspiration by piling up the Bible's testimony about itself. He defended the inspiration of every word in Scripture almost excessively, for in doing so he even defended the Hebrew vowel points. While this excess was wrong-headed, his bottom-line conclusion that the very words of the Bible were chosen by God is consistent with the work of J. L. Dagg, Basil Manly, and J. P. Boyce. Carroll rejected all forms of partial or limited inspiration, saying that, "When you hear the silly talk that the Bible contains the Word of God and is not the Word of God, you hear a fool's talk."[22]

Because Carroll emphasized the product of inspiration, he was silent on the method of inspiration. He focused on the result of inspiration, which he believed to be an infallible Bible. In addition to the description "infallible," Carroll also used the terms inerrant, true, trustworthy, irrevocable, and irrefragable to describe Scripture. He applied this inerrant quality only to the original writings of the sixty-six books of the Protestant Bible.

While Dagg, Boyce, and Manly clearly stand as giants among Southern Baptists, it is impossible to measure how vast and enormous has been the influence of B. H. Carroll on the life and thought of Southern Baptists. Carroll, perhaps more than any other Baptist leader, has served as a model and resource for hundreds of Southern Baptist pastors. Much of the motivation for change in the Southern Baptist Convention over the past two decades reflects Carroll's beliefs that churches, schools, and evangelistic/mission agendas rise or fall according to one's understanding of biblical inspiration. Before moving to the significant contributions of E. Y. Mullins and W. T. Conner, it is important to note some of the many other expressions regarding the nature of Scripture in Southern Baptist life near the turn of the century, or from the time of C. H. Toy's resignation at Southern Seminary to the rise of the evolution controversy. The issue of biblical inspiration and authority was as important in the closing years of the nineteenth century as it has been in the later years of the twentieth.

DENOMINATIONAL LEADERSHIP (1879–1920)

In 1867 Thomas F. Curtis, a professor at several eastern universities, who served as director of the SBC Home Mission Board from 1851–1853, challenged the early consensus regarding the inspiration and infallibility of Holy Scripture. His work on *The Human Element in the Inspiration of the Sacred Scriptures* [23] emphasized the freedom of the human authors in a similar fashion to the work of C. H. Toy. Toy, one of the most brilliant Old Testament scholars of his time, can be credited with introducing Southern Baptists to European biblical studies and the world of critical scholarship. In 1869 he wrote "The Claims of Biblical Interpretation on Baptists," a work representative of the other young faculty members at Southern Seminary. However, a decade (1879) later, Toy was forced to resign his position at the Seminary due to significant shifts from his earlier positions. In a series of six articles published in the *Religious Herald* in 1880, he raised questions regarding the plenary inspiration of the Scripture in light of the challenge of modern science and German criticism. George Washington Simpson analyzed the issues raised by C. H. Toy in two articles in 1880 also published in the *Religious Herald*. His articles, entitled "German and English Theories of Inspiration" enabled the paper's readers to understand the issues raised by Toy.

In a mighty chorus, Baptist leaders all over the Convention, seemingly in response to the issues raised by Toy, sounded a nearly unanimous affirmation of the full inerrancy and authority of Scripture. In addition to the work mentioned above by Basil Manly, Jr., numerous works addressed the burning issue of the day. J. B. Jeter, editor of the *Religious Herald*, answered Toy with three articles on the "Inspiration of the Bible" and an edited volume on Baptist Doctrines in 1880. C. Tyree, also in 1880, in the *Religious Herald* with more apologetic strength, defended the "Verbal Inspiration of the Scriptures."

Two leading Landmark Baptists, James M. Pendleton and his work on *Christian Doctrine* (1878) and J. R. Graves in *The Work of Christ in the Covenant of Redemption* (1883) foreshadowed the inerrancy affirmations of B. H. Carroll. Indicating the apparent unanimous opposition to Toy's position on inspiration were the works on the subject by three of Southern Baptists' greatest biblical scholars, John A. Broadus, A. T. Robertson, and John R. Sampey. Broadus, who authored the outstanding volume on *Matthew* in *The American Commentary* series, wrote "Three Questions as to the Bible" (1883) in which he gave a positive answer of "completely" to the question "To what extent ought we to regard the sacred writings of the Old and New Testament as inspired?" In 1887 he basically agreed with the works of Boyce and Manly in his work "The Paramount and Permanent Authority of the Bible," though Broadus was more independent and creative in his articulation.[24]

A. T. Robertson and John R. Sampey both advocated the inerrancy of Scripture during the early years of their careers in the 1890s, so indicating in annual sessions of the Baptist Congress for the Discussion of Current Questions. Robertson authored "The Relative Authority of Scripture and Reason" (1892) and Sampey defended the complete truthfulness of the biblical text in his address on "The Interpretation of the Old Testament." Robertson produced the most important Greek grammar of the twentieth century in addition to a six-volume commentary on the New Testament focusing on the meaning and portraits presented in the Greek New Testament.[25]

The discussion regarding the infallibility of Scripture dominated theological discussions in the Southern Baptist Convention during the last two decades of the nineteenth Century. The discussion reached its zenith with articles in the *Word and Way* (1896) and a compendium of essays in *Baptists Why and Why Not*, edited by J. M. Frost in 1900.[26] R. L. Davidson brilliantly discussed the nature of Scripture in six articles in the *Word and Way* entitled "The Inerrant Word of God." A. C. Rafferty's work echoed Davidson's conclusions in three similar articles entitled "The Bible: What is It?"; "The Inspiration of the Bible"; and "The Bible: A Living Book."

The opening chapter by J. M. Frost, T. T. Eaton, and F. H. Kerfoot in *Baptists Why and Why Not* expressed the consensus Baptist position on the Bible. Frost explained in the introduction that the foundation of all the articles in the book was the presupposition that the Bible is inerrant. Perhaps a quotation from Frost, the founding editor and first secretary of the Baptist Sunday School Board, is indicative of this theological consensus: "We accept the Scriptures as an all-sufficient and infallible rule of faith and practice, and insist upon the absolute inerrancy and sole authority of the Word of God."[27]

This encyclopedic listing, while not analytical, nevertheless puts to rest the repeated charges that the doctrine of biblical inerrancy is a recent innovation in Southern Baptist theology. Nothing could be further from the truth. The last two decades of the nineteenth century and the first two decades of the twentieth century are filled with writings representing an affirmation of the complete infallibility and authority of Scripture.

In addition to what we have previously noted, we can observe the contributions of Edgar Estes Folk, editor of the *Baptist and Reflector*, who urged his son to maintain "loyalty to God's Word in God's Book" in the Sunday School Board publication *Letters to My Son* (1909).[28] His work followed E. C. Dargan, who argued from tradition, the Bible's internal witness, and its character that the Bible is God's authoritative revelation in *Doctrines of the Faith* (1905).[29]

J. Van Ness, executive-secretary of the Baptist Sunday School Board, spelled out what is meant by advocating the Bible as "our authoritative rule" in *The Baptist Spirit* (1914). He maintained that the Bible is: (1) sufficient; (2) certain in its teachings; (3) to be believed and accepted in all things as it stands; (4) the final authority for us. He concluded that Baptists need to be a Bible-knowing people and a Bible-teaching people, who must have a Bible-loving ministry.[30]

J. R. Sampey followed up on his previous work in "Jesus and the Old Testament" in the 1921 Conference on Baptist Fundamentals. Based on his interpretation of 2 Timothy 3:16 and 17, Sampey articulated his belief in the sufficiency and veracity of the Old Testament. He gladly affirmed that God's revelation is progressive and culminates in Christ, and that it is entirely inspired and infallible.

There is no hint in any of these writers that they differentiated between inerrancy and infallibility. On to this united front that unhesitatingly maintained that the Bible is fully inspired, inerrant, and authoritative came the dynamic and creative work of E. Y. Mullins and W. T. Conner, Southern Baptists' two most formative and shaping theologians.

E. Y. MULLINS

E. Y. Mullins (1860–1928) served as the fourth president and professor of theology at the Southern Baptist Theological Seminary from 1899 to 1928. Mullins represents a paradigmatic shift in Southern Baptist theology. Nowhere is this better illustrated than his volume on systematic theology entitled *The Christian Religion in Its Doctrinal Expression* (1917).[31] Not only was his book used as the major textbook at Southern and Southwestern Seminary for decades, but Mullins also powerfully influenced W. T. Conner, who served as professor of theology at Southwestern Seminary for thirty-nine years. Mullins' emphasis on the role of experience and his work on the relationship between science and Scripture paved the way for a new generation of Baptists to raise new questions about the nature and interpretation of Scripture.

Mullins remained very much in the mainstream of conservative Baptist thought during his decades of leadership, while nevertheless engaging wide intellectual interests and contemporary theological formulations. This conservatism became increasingly apparent during his latter years, and is especially evident in his handling of the "Fundamentalist-Modernist" debates in the early twentieth century. The release of his final major publication, *Christianity at the Crossroads* (1924),[32] testifies to this shift of emphasis in Mullins' work. E. Y. Mullins moved in a different direction from Boyce, Manly, Robertson, and the early Sampey (Sampey in his later years seemed to be more willing to embrace the findings of historical criticism and less sure about traditional views of inspiration—at least according to an interpretation offered by W. O. Carver in his oral history of Southern Seminary commissioned by Duke K. McCall).[33] This means that Mullins' ministry, though representing diversity within unity, nevertheless continued the united consensus regarding Scripture that existed in the Southern Baptist Convention during its first seventy-five years.

Mullins' shift may have been more a shift of methodology and context than of content. He was hesitant to equate the Bible with revelation, at least as it had been stated by Manly and Carroll before him. For Mullins, the primary characteristic of the Bible was its authority, not its inspiration or inerrancy. A major shift for Mullins was his insistence that the authority of the Bible was limited to the religious life of the Christian believer, seemingly overemphasizing the characteristic affirmation regarding the Bible's authority in "faith and practice."

Mullins followed A. H. Strong in his affirmation of a dynamic model of inspiration rather than a plenary verbal one, though he quickly commended the plenary view's intent to "preserve and maintain the authority of Scripture as the very Word of God." Mullins argues that the difference between the two approaches was more one of method than of content relating to the Bible. Even though Mullins shifted his methodological understanding of Scripture, he nevertheless emphasized the truthfulness of the Bible. His description of the dynamic theory of inspiration included the affirmation "that men were enabled to declare truth unmixed with error." He rejected any charge of contradictions in the Bible, claiming that Holy Scripture cannot dispute what it is not intended to affirm. The most important shift in the thinking of E. Y. Mullins was his emphasis on experience, which represents both the best of pietism and the experiential emphasis of F. D. E. Schleiermacher. Mullins defended the Bible on the basis of Christian experience both as to what was recorded in Scripture and also what was confirmed by other believers throughout the centuries.[34]

E. Y. Mullins pioneered new ways to theologize in Southern Baptist life, though in essence he seems to restate, in different ways, traditional Southern Baptist tenets. He contended that the Bible is a fully reliable and authoritative guide. Nowhere is his traditional emphases better seen than in his 1923 address to the Southern Baptist Convention on "The Dangers and Duties of this Present Hour," where he concluded that the Bible is "God's revelation of himself and is the sufficient and authoritative guide" for all life.[35]

W. T. CONNER

W. T. Conner (1877–1952) carried out the role at Southwestern Seminary which had been played by E. Y. Mullins at Southern Seminary. Conner began his career at Southwestern Seminary in 1910 as professor of theoretical theology. During his career he taught almost everything in the curriculum, but his interest rested primarily in New Testament and systematic theology. Conner's contribution to the matter of biblical interpretation and authority is found in his discussions of the broader subject of revelation contained in his writings on *Revelation and God* (1936)[36] and *Christian Doctrine* (1937).[37] Conner's theology represented a conflation of his mentors: Calvin Goodspeed, B. H. Carroll, A. H. Strong, and E. Y. Mullins. During his tenure, the influence of Carroll waned and that of Mullins increased; though both shaped his personal theological synthesis.

Conner wrote very little on the issue of inspiration. He seemed to have followed Mullins' lead on many of the matters related to the Bible, though unlike Mullins, he did not technically affirm a particular view of the inspiration of the Bible. At this point, he followed Carroll's silence. The bottom line for Conner was the authoritative character of Scripture as expressed in his 1918 article in a Southwestern Seminary publication on "The Nature and Authority of the Bible." He maintained that: "The only way to realize true freedom is by submission to rightful authority. The Bible then is the medium through which God's authority is made known." Conner unhesitatingly affirmed the fact of the Bible's inspiration and was careful to allow for human agency. In his writing on *Christian Doctrine* he rightly answered that the Bible is both a divine book, as well as a human book. Conner's work did not discuss either inerrancy or infallibility. Though Conner could be considered a "functional inerrantist," he was less comfortable with the idea of inerrancy than even E. Y. Mullins had been. Yet W. T. Conner did not in any way want to affirm an inspiration only in a partial or limited sense. He did acknowledge that biblical authority is reserved for the spiritual dimensions of life. Conner was ultimately concerned with the function of Scripture in leading men and women toward freedom in Christ.

Conner was open-minded on the relationship of science and the Bible. Yet he adamantly rejected evolution, maintaining that it leaves out God and maintains that without God's creative power or guidance the universe came uncaused out of nothing, and has kept on evolving until it produced humanity. One of the first Southern Baptist leaders to endorse evolution was W. L. Poteat, professor and president at Wake Forest College. Poteat wrote widely on this topic and his words received a strongly negative review from Conner in *The Southwestern Evangel* in May, 1925.

While Conner relegated discussions regarding theories of inspiration to theological obscurity, he unhesitatingly confessed the Bible as the product of God's revelation, with redemption its central interest and Jesus Christ as its center and key to its unity. Though Conner would not affirm the term inerrancy,[38] he retreated from discussing any errors in the Bible, while emphasizing the Bible's divine origin and absolute authority in all matters spiritual.[39]

DENOMINATIONAL LEADERSHIP (1920–1952)

We can conclude this section on the first century of Southern Baptist thought on this subject by highlighting other important contributions to this subject. In a major work published by the Baptist Sunday School Board in 1922 entitled *Fundamentals of the Faith*, William B. Nowlin critiqued historical-critical approaches to the Bible and supported the Scriptures' own self-testimony to its complete inspiration.[40] New Testament scholar, H. E. Dana, defended the historical reliability of the Bible in a 1923 work called the *Authenticity of the Holy Scriptures*.[41]

J. J. Reeve, a professor at Southwestern Seminary, who had previously embraced historical-critical methods and conclusions, contributed an article called "My Experience with Higher Criticism" for *The Fundamentals*, edited by R. A. Torrey and A. C. Dixon (1917).[42] Here he affirmed the absolute truthfulness of Scripture while critiquing the dangers of historical criticism.

The inerrancy of Scripture was popularized by the pulpit oratory of R. G. Lee, who in 1930 penned, *The Word of God: Not Broken and Not Bound*.[43] O. C. S. Wallace in *What Baptists Believe* (1934) discussed the need of the Scriptures, the process of writing, and the purpose of the Scriptures.[44] In his conclusion he reaffirmed the 1925 Baptist Faith and Message terminology that the Bible is a "perfect treasure of heavenly instruction." The same year, the Sunday School Board also published J. B. Weatherspoon's *The Book We Teach*, in which he maintained the Bible as a book of revelation and sure guidance, that is not only a book of Christian faith, but of Christian mission and education.[45]

In 1936 J. B. Tidwell, professor at Baylor University, authored *Thinking Straight About the Bible or Is the Bible the Word of God*.[46] In many ways, Tidwell's work reflects the consensus viewpoint about the nature of Scripture for the first one hundred years of the SBC's existence, though he has more in common with B. H. Carroll and Basil Manly than W. T. Conner or E. Y. Mullins. Tidwell identified direct and indirect claims regarding the Bible's inspiration and absolute truthfulness. He then offered fourteen evidences for the complete veracity and divine origin of the Bible.

Yet, it must be noted that the syncretistic position of W. O. Carver, the first Southern Seminary faculty who did not study with J. P. Boyce, the latter positions of J. R. Sampey, and other Southern Baptist scholars, coupled with the openness not only to the new methodology of historical criticism, but in some cases to the conclusions of historical criticism as well, paved the way for shifts in the doctrine of biblical inspiration and authority in the post-World War II era. That being the case, nevertheless, we have seen that a strong consensus existed, represented by scholars, pastors, and denominational leaders. This diverse group affirmed with deep convictions the common heritage regarding the divine origin, the complete truthfulness, and the full authority of the Bible. The historic Southern Baptist position during the first century of its existence was primarily the commonly held conviction that the Bible is the inspired, written, reliable, and authoritative Word of God.

BIBLICAL INSPIRATION, INTERPRETATION, AND AUTHORITY (1952–1994)

Two historic changes were initiated in the 1950s in Southern Baptist life. The first, and most important for our discussion, was the open practice of historical-critical studies in the curriculums of Baptist seminaries and colleges. The other more wide-ranging shift was the movement to a program-oriented approach to ministry. This shift brought about a generation of leaders committed to programmatic expansion. Nothing typifies this organizational and programmatic growth more than the "Million More in '54" campaign, which resulted in almost 750,000 new Sunday School members in Southern Baptist churches.

With this and other similar successful programs, a movement away from theological commitments to pragmatic ones consciously or unconsciously began to take place. I do not for one minute think it was a malicious attempt to undermine the orthodox theological consensus developed during the convention's first century. The pragmatic outlook was what was central for growing a successful denomination in the post-World War II era. Orthodoxy was understood in terms of "doing the right program" rather than articulating the right belief system. What resulted was not so much a heterodox people but an "a-theological" generation.

When controversies over the nature of Scripture entered the public arena in 1961, 1969, and 1979, the theological understanding necessary to examine and evaluate such issues was lacking.[47] Even men and women who never questioned the reliability of the biblical message nor ever doubted the miraculous claims of the Bible were confused by terms like "inerrant" and "infallibility," which we have seen were widely employed in previous generations. The programmatic and pragmatic emphases of the 1950s help us understand how the paradigm shifted in the SBC from the early 1950s to the late 1970s.[48]

Yet, even during the 1950s there were ongoing examples that were in basic continuity with the doctrinal affirmations of previous generations. Works such as those by W. R. White, "The Authoritative Criterion" in *Baptist Distinctives* (1950);[49] J. B. Lawrence, "The Word and Words of God" and "The Bible, Our Creed" in *Southern Baptist Home Missions* (1952, 1957);[50] J. Clyde Turner, "That Wonderful Book" in *Things We Believe* (1956) indicate the ongoing commitments to the trustworthiness and authority of Scripture at this time.[51] Yet, things were changing all around.

RECENT THEOLOGICAL DEVELOPMENT (1952–1979)

Theology in the post-Conner/Mullins era introduced an innovative and exciting time in a denomination coming of age. During this period southern society began to take on a new shape. After World War II the New South started to emerge from its previous isolation. The agricultural economy and culture of the Old South gave way to urban and suburban structures. Populations grew and became more pluralistic, employment trends destabilized, and racial tension soared. Old South values were being visibly disturbed.

Southern Baptists struggled to deal with these challenges, as well as urbanization, growing denominational bureaucracies, territorial expansion, and new emphases in theology, which some identified as "liberal." New tensions were created. New questions were raised in this context. How were people to combine intellectual rigor with personal religious experience?[52] The mid-twentieth century in SBC academic life wrestled with this question, particularly focused on the rise of biblical criticism. The practitioners of this new art sought somehow to combine a belief in biblical inspiration with biblical criticism, as publicly evidenced in the debates surrounding the publication of *The Message of Genesis* (1961), by Ralph Elliott, as well as the first volume of *The Broadman Bible Commentary* (1969).[53] Both of these works openly challenged the historical reliability of the Bible.

Many of the public issues dealt with historical matters of the Old Testament, but the influence of form criticism was beginning to be seen on the New Testament side as well. Many of these struggles in particular dealt not only with the use of historical criticism, but with the place of Darwinism in the theological arena. Interestingly, E. Y. Mullins, almost a half century earlier, had opened the door, following James Orr and A. H. Strong, in acknowledging some form of theistic evolution. This issue became a major concern for two theological leaders in this period. Both Dale Moody (1915–1991) and Eric Rust (1910–1991) pioneered new explorations in the area of the relationship between theology and science. Together with others, such as Frank Stagg (1911–), a new theological paradigm was being forged. This paradigm had little use for traditional Calvinistic or popular dispensational systems of thought. Nowhere was the "arminianizing" of the SBC better exemplified than in the writings of Moody and Stagg. Moody's concerns focused on issues of predestination and perserverance,[54] ultimately rejecting both; while Stagg endeavored to redefine the meaning of the cross in terms other than vicarious or substitutionary atonement.[55]

Frank Stagg, in the eyes of many, was the leading and most influential Southern Baptist theologian during this period, having placed his stamp on two theological institutions: New Orleans Seminary (1945–64) and Southern Baptist Seminary (1964–77). Stagg's commentaries and books, including his major work on *New Testament Theology*,[56] all reject the Calvinistic understanding of God's purposes in salvation. Stagg's understanding of the cross of Jesus Christ represents what could be called an exemplary theory of the atonement. For Stagg, the cross represents the revelation of the divine self-denial that was always at the very heart of God and thus demands that humans find their authentic existence as God's creatures. In addition to his treatment of the cross, Stagg reinterpreted the concept of atonement, election, and predestination so as to stand diametrically opposed to Calvinism. The only thing God has predetermined, maintained Stagg, is that "whoever is in Christ will be saved."[57]

Though Moody and Stagg greatly influenced the academic theology of the Convention, two popular theological movements held sway in numerous pulpits across the Convention: the "deeper life movement" and "dispensationalism." These two movements merged to bring about unique approaches to the Christian life, eschatology, social ministries, and denominational affiliation. The legendary pastor of the First Baptist Church of Dallas, Texas, W. A.

Criswell (1909–) personified this popular grass roots theology.[58] As was to be proven during the decade of the eighties, this group's strength may not have been necessarily its vigorous theological reflection, but its numerical predominance.

The SBC thus entered the second half of the twentieth century divided between the progressivism that characterized the moderate leadership in denominational agencies and seminaries and the popular traditionalism in the pulpits. As most major denominational leadership posts were claimed by the progressive or moderate wing of the Convention, the traditionalist or conservatives became defensive and separatistic, focusing on their local churches instead of on the denomination.

The conservatives tended to retreat to a position in opposition to a changing American culture. They saw the American culture of the sixties heading toward an age of insanity. Living in a time of presidential assassinations, racial unrest, civil rights' protests, rock-and-roll celebrations, "love-ins," "sit-ins," and Vietnam war protests, the traditionalists lambasted these crazy trends and found their own emphasis on a completely truthful Bible to be extremely useful for bringing sense out of this chaos. Nowhere was this better illustrated than in the classic volume by W. A. Criswell published while he was president of the Convention and entitled *Why I Preach that the Bible is Literally True* (1969).[59] For it was the optimism among conservatives that the "truth" eventually would be victorious, after the craziness of that present age had passed, that spurred them onward. The way to protect the truth in the meantime was through a form of separatism, consistent with either their "deeper life" and/or "dispensational" theology, though they remained somewhat active in the denomination and generally faithful to denomination programs.[60]

The moderates, however, marched into the sixties and seventies seeking to avoid the negative reaction of the traditionalists and hoping to gain respect in the larger cultural context. Further changes in American culture in a post-Watergate and post-Vietnam era created an anti-authoritarian mood among progressives. Thus another shift away from earlier SBC theology can be seen in a movement away from authority. For as W. T. Conner maintained, "If God is not a God of authority, he is not God at all. If God does not reveal himself, religion is impossible. Therefore, if God reveals himself to man, it must be in an authoritative way."[61] The new generation of progressive leadership was open to dialogue and interaction with other traditions, while evidencing a renewed concern for social responsibility; contemporary, existential, or reader-oriented hermeneutics; and the ecumenical nature of the church, while basically rejecting all forms of fundamentalism and seeking to embrace mainstream protestantism, accompanied by the theme that "Baptist means freedom."[62]

During the decade of the seventies the progressive leadership of the denomination moved in directions that forged larger gaps between the moderates and the conservatives. However, two popular heroes, who were greatly admired by both groups, helped both groups to maintain some common ground with each other both within the Convention itself, as well as in the larger sphere of American Christianity. One of these was Herschel Hobbs; the other was Billy Graham. Herschel H. Hobbs (1907–)[63] has often been called "Mr. Southern Baptist." He preached for eighteen years on the "Baptist Hours," was president of the Southern Baptist Convention from 1961–1963, and chaired the 1963 Committee of the Baptist Faith and Message. Hobbs held to a high view of biblical inspiration, while embracing the classical Arminian interpretation of the doctrine of God, so as to affirm complete divine knowledge of every free human choice, yet in such a way that the choices are not predetermined. In addition to his Arminian tendencies, Hobbs moved away from being a pre-millennialist without a program toward a thoroughgoing amillennialism. The Arminian and amillennialist position were welcomed by those espousing the progressive perspective.

On the other hand, Billy Graham (1918–),[64] the most well known international evangelist of our time and a member of the First Baptist Church of Dallas, Texas, proclaimed his simple gospel message to thousands. This message was undergirded by the evangelist's commitment to a completely truthful Bible and augmented by a "deeper life" approach to the Christian life and an apocalyptic dispensational eschatology, both of which were widely accepted and repeated in thousands of churches throughout the SBC. The nation as a whole during this time of unsettling transition was looking for stability and authority. Many were ready to hear the Word of God announced with authority as demonstrated with Graham's now famous words, "the Bible says." Into this vacuum the traditionalists moved, appealing to a fully truthful and authoritative Bible and contending that this was the message needed to address these turbulent times. While the denomination seemingly appeared strong, healthy, and poised for "Bold Mission" endeavors, the conservatives charged that the moderate leadership had moved too far from the popular "orthodox" theology of the grass roots, people, and the heritage of Baptist giants of previous generations. Based on these concerns the SBC entered the decade of the eighties a very diverse movement with a multifaceted history, faced with its own version of the "modernist-fundamentalist" controversy. Now we turn to these most recent developments.

RECENT THEOLOGICAL DEVELOPMENT (1979–1994)

During the summer of 1979 in Houston, Texas, the Southern Baptist Convention took a major, and at that time unexpected theological turn. With the election of Adrian Rogers, pastor of the Bellevue Baptist Church in Memphis, Tennessee, as Convention president, the conservatives began a move out of their separatist mentality, accompanied by a clarion call for a commitment to the inerrancy of Holy Scripture. Where did this movement come from and why did this development take place?

The traditionalists' concern regarding the full truthfulness and trustworthiness of Scripture and their corresponding distrust of the progressives can be traced back to the controversies surrounding the works on Genesis by Ralph Elliott (1961) and the *Broadman Bible Commentary* (1969), and the widely circulated article by William Hull entitled "Shall We Call the Bible Infallible?"[65] The traditionalist's approach to Scripture had been articulated by W. A. Criswell in his *Why I Preach that the Bible is Literally True* (1969), but the gauntlet had been laid down by Harold Lindsell's *Battle for the Bible* (1976).[66]

Certainly as noted earlier, J. M. Frost, Basil Manly, B. H. Carroll and numerous others had maintained the truthfulness of Scripture, even readily employing the term "inerrancy" to describe the nature of Scripture. Both Mullins and Conner employed the language of the Baptist Faith and Message (1925), that Scripture is "truth, without any mixture of error," yet they did so without confessing a verbal or plenary view of biblical inspiration.

But with the rise of historical criticism, new approaches to biblical interpretation and new ways of describing the Bible's nature were articulated.[67] Many progressives were no longer comfortable describing the Bible in the tradition of B. H. Carroll or Basil Manly. As a matter of fact, the doctrine of inerrancy was virtually absent in academic circles from the mid-twenties to the eighties, usually being relegated to obscurantist thought and falsely equated with a mechanical dictation view of understanding. But now conservatives were calling for a return to Manly's position, though now in a more sophisticated dress enabled by two decades of discussion regarding Scripture in the broader evangelical world, culminating in the Chicago Statements on Biblical Inerrancy (1978) and Biblical Interpretation (1982).[68]

The Baptist Sunday School Board attempted to address the issue of biblical inerrancy by choosing the doctrine of Scripture as the Convention's doctrine study for 1983. Russell Dilday, president of Southwestern Baptist Seminary, was invited to write the doctrine book, *The Doctrine of Biblical Authority*, which was published in 1982.[68] Dilday carefully affirmed the inspiration and authority of the Bible, while pointing out the weaknesses of the inerrancy position. This, however, fueled the fires even further, supporting perceptions that leaders in the seminaries and those writing for Baptist Sunday School Board publications were not supportive of biblical inerrancy.

During the seventies and eighties a number of significant works were penned either challenging or upholding the inerrancy of Scripture. The most important work by conservatives during this time was *Baptists and the Bible* by Russ Bush and Tom Nettles, which attempted to show that biblical inerrancy had been a representative, if not dominant, view in the Baptist tradition.[69] The book met with mixed reviews and was countered by a series of essays edited by Rob James, entitled *The Unfettered Word*, which attempted to show that both the biblical position and historical interpretation in Baptist life differed from the Bush-Nettles proposal.[70]

The annual presentations at meetings of the National Association of Baptist Professors of Religion tried to show that Baptists had affirmed biblical inspiration, but had not advocated inerrancy. But as we have seen, this could only be done by selective readings of Mullins, Conner, and Carver as normative for all that went on before and after their time. Some tried to differentiate between infallibility and inerrancy, accepting the former and rejecting the latter. A carefully worded article representing this position was written in the *Review and Expositor* in 1986 by Roy L. Honeycutt, entitled "Biblical Authority: A Treasured Baptist Heritage."[71] Here he rejected inerrancy, suggesting that it was not a position consistent with Baptist tradition, while claiming that the Bible was authoritative and binding in all matters of faith and practice. This reading of Baptist theology followed the proposal of Jack Rogers and Donald McKim in *The Authority and Interpretation of the Bible*.[72] Major theologies during this period by Morris Ashcraft,[73] Dale Moody,[74] and James Leo Garrett[75] tended to follow this distinction with varying degrees, with Moody and Garrett closely following the models of their predecessors Mullins and Conner.

Though some of the articles that dealt with this issue were reactionary in their polemic against the progressives in the denomination, two contributions are especially noteworthy. William E. Bell wrote nine articles in *Southern Baptist Advocate* describing the meaning of inspiration and inerrancy and Daniel Vestal published a sermon called "The Word of God" (May, 1981), in which he concluded "Because God is truth and speaks truth, the Bible must be truthful. That is why I do not believe there are any errors in the Bible."

For the next decade, more heat than light was generated by both sides; though steadily the inerrancy position gained a hearing. Many thought inerrancy to be only a political position, but conservatives building on works of peripherally related or former Southern Baptists like Clark Pinnock's *A New Reformation* and *Biblical Revelation*[76] and Carl F. H. Henry's six-volume set, *God, Revelation, and Authority*[77] pressed on to re-establish the doctrinal consensus of previous generations.

Through the public appearances and effective strategy of Paige Patterson, Paul Pressler, and Adrian Rogers, undergirded by Patterson's theological insights and rhetorical skills, the traditionalists were able to elect presidents who helped appoint trustees with an inerrancy agenda for SBC agencies throughout the decade. The six seminary presidents, after taking an adversarial role opposing the conservative resurgence in the first half of the eighties, surprisingly issued the Glorieta Statement in 1986, which affirmed that the Bible did not err in any area of reality. Building on this affirmation, substantive changes began to take place in faculty appointments and denominational publications. A comparison of the 1992 doctrine study book with the book published a decade earlier by Russell Dilday (and mentioned above) is indicative of these changes. This work, entitled *The Doctrine of the Bible*, while interactive with modern thought, nevertheless reaffirmed the inerrancy of Scripture, echoing the consensus viewpoint reflective of earlier Baptist theologians.[78]

This most recent study affirms that revelation is both personal and propositional. While emphasizing propositional revelation, it notes that conservatives are careful to maintain that Scripture's literary diversity is more than a historic accident or decorative device; it is vehicle for imaginative thought and creative expression about things difficult to grasp. Commands, promises, parables, analogy, metaphor, symbol, and poetry cannot be forced into propositional form without loss. This recognition of literary diversity brings a healthy realization of the human aspect in Scripture, thus balancing the divine-human authorship of the Bible.

The 1992 doctrine book maintains that the Bible attests to its own inspiration, which can be characterized as plenary and concursive. While affirming verbal inspiration, there is an awareness of contemporary linguistic theory that suggests that meaning is at the sentence level and beyond.

Based on a plenary view on inspiration of Scripture, this view maintains the inerrancy of Scripture and stresses that what the Bible affirms is completely true. Such a position attempts to be sensitive to the diversity and development in the Bible, recognizing different literary genres while seeking to determine the original meaning of Scripture. Harmonization is accepted as a legitimate means of handling the diversity in the biblical text, but not at the expense of running roughshod over the context and forcing the Bible to say what it does not say. Because the Bible is a divine-human book, the interpretive tools of literary and historical criticism can be employed with care and faith-oriented presuppositions.

Such a view of Scripture, which now characterizes the new leadership in the SBC, places most Southern Baptists squarely in the evangelical world.[79] Some have called Southern Baptists "establishment evangelicals" or, perhaps better, "denominational evangelicals."[80] Others have issued a call for "Baptist evangelicals" or "evangelical Baptists." This certainly distances the SBC in the mid-nineties from the famous 1976 statement by then CLC executive, Foy Valentine: "Southern Baptists are not evangelicals. That's a Yankee word."[81]

CONCLUSION/FUTURE AGENDAS

Our brief survey has focused on developments in the doctrine of Scripture from 1845 to the present. A paradigm shift has taken place regarding the doctrine of Scripture, a shift demonstrating considerable continuity with the views of Boyce, Manly, and Carroll maintained in the early years of the SBC, though reflecting distance and discontinuity from the progressive positions adopted and advocated in the sixties–seventies. While there are several nuanced approaches to Scripture in the SBC, which we have discussed in several other places, generally it can be observed that the majority of Southern Baptists believe the Bible is God's truthful, written word. Likewise, they believe it can and should be trusted in all matters. What does this say about our theological identity? The past fifteen years of controversy have been fueled by political and personal differences, but the focal point of the differences has been the affirmation or denial of the doctrine of biblical inerrancy. The SBC of the nineties has clearly decided that inerrancy cannot be ignored, de-emphasized, or eliminated from the discussion. It is the focus of the developing new theological center in the SBC. It has now been heartily affirmed, but it must continue to be carefully clarified since the issue remains an emotional one, often misunderstood and misrepresented by progressives, moderates, and even many traditionalists as well.

I close with one final comment. Recently Archbishop George Carey ended his first official visit to the United States with a call for theologians to balance exploration and risk-taking with worship and ministry. Carey said "The unhealthy gap that frequently develops between academic theologians and churches can be avoided if theologians remember they are never superior to the revelation they explore." His observations basically summarize the concerns expressed by SBC conservatives about the nature of theological education over the past fifteen years. The theological explorer is not free to think anything, go anywhere, and be anything he or she likes, George Carey said. "Doxology undergirds theology and points the direction in which we must all travel" (Religious News Service).

Dr. Carey's point is well taken. The seminaries must not lose touch with the churches. Southern Baptists must work hard to bring the seminaries and churches together again as co-laborers for the cause of Christ.

Together Southern Baptists can help churches enable and educate leaders and enhance worship in order to bring about theological renewal in the SBC so that the church of Jesus Christ can grow as it lives in obedience to the command of our Lord, who has commissioned us to evangelize, disciplize, baptize, and teach. The same Lord who two thousand years ago commissioned us still calls us and gifts us to teach and equip His people for service and move them to maturity and unity.

As Southern Baptists build upon this new consensus and re-established foundation of the inspiration and authority of Scripture, with recognition of who we are consistent with our Southern Baptist heritage, let us move beyond articulations of the nature of Scripture and with heads, hearts, and hands seek to obey the divinely inspired, completed truthful, and fully authoritative written Word of God.[82]

ENDNOTES

1. See Robinson B. James and David S. Dockery, eds. *Beyond the Impasse? Scripture, Interpretation, and Theology in Baptist Life* (Nashville: Broadman, 1992); Nancy T. Ammerman, *Baptist Battles* (New Brunswick, N.J.: Rutgers, 1990); Bill J. Leonard, *God's Last and Only Hope* (Grand Rapids: Eerdmans, 1990); and the six volumes published under the title *Truth and Crises* by James C. Hefley (Hannibal, Mo.: Hannibal Books, 1986–1991).

2. An important indicator was seen at the 1994 Southern Baptist Convention in Orlando, Fla., where an African-American and Asian-American were elected vice-presidents. Interesting analyses of some changes can be found in Paul A. Basden, ed., *Has Our Theology Changed? Southern Baptist Thought Since 1845* (Nashville: Broadman and Holman, 1994).

3. A look at individuals who have shaped this theology can be found in Timothy George and David S. Dockery, eds., *Baptist Theologians* (Nash-

ville: Broadman, 1990); also see W. Wiley Richards, *Winds of Doctrine: The Origin and Development of Southern Baptist Theology* (Lanham, Md.: University Press of America, 1991).

4. See Herschel Hobbs, "Southern Baptists and Confessionalism: A Comparison of the Origins and Contents of the 1925 and 1963 Confessions," *Review and Expositor* 76 (1979); fuller treatments on this subject can be found in Thomas J. Nettles, "Creedalism, Confessionalism, and the Baptist Faith and Message," *The Unfettered Word*, ed. Robison B. James (Waco: Word, 1987), 138–54; William R. Estep, "Baptists and Authority: The Bible, Confessions, and Conscience in the Development of Baptist Identity," *Review and Expositor* 76 (1979): 35–42; Leonard, *God's Last and Only Hope*, 65–100; James Leo Garrett, Jr., "Biblical Authority According to Baptist Confessions of Faith," *Review and Expositor* 76 (1979): 43–54; idem, "Sources of Authority in Baptist Thought," *Baptist History and Heritage* 13 (1978): 47–49.

5. Citations from the confessions are found in William L. Lumpkin, *Baptist Confessions of Faith* (Philadelphia: Judson, 1959).

6. See Dwight Moody, "Doctrines of Inspiration in the Southern Baptist Theological Tradition," (Ph.D. dissertation, Southern Baptist Theological Seminary, 1982); also cf. David S. Dockery, "Biblical Inspiration and Authority in the SBC," (Page Lectures, Southeastern Baptist Theological Seminary, 1993); and Timothy George's assessment of these matters in *Baptist Theologians* (Nashville: Broadman, 1990).

7. See the discussion in David S. Dockery, ed., *Southern Baptists and American Evangelicals: The Conversation Continues* (Nashville: Broadman and Holman, 1993).

8. See the fuller treatment by Timothy George, "James P. Boyce," *Baptist Theologians*.

9. See Fisher Humpheys, "E. Y. Mullins," *Baptist Theologians*; also Thomas J. Nettles, "E. Y. Mullins," *Evangelical Theologians*, ed. W. A. Elwell (Grand Rapids: Baker, 1993).

10. See James Leo Garrett, Jr., "W. T. Conner," *Baptist Theologians*.

11. See Mark Dever, "John L. Dagg," *Baptist Theologians*.

12. J. L. Dagg, *A Manual of Theology* (Charleston, S.C.: Southern Baptist Publications Society, 1858), 21.

13. Ibid.

14. J. L. Dagg, *The Evidences of Christianity* (Macon, Ga.: J. W. Burke, 1869), 225.

15. I am indebted to Dwight Moody for his insights on this matter; see "Doctrines of Inspiration," 10–15. I have followed Moody closely in his analysis of Dagg, Boyce, Manly, Carroll, Mullins, and Conner.

16. J. P. Boyce, *Abstract of Systematic Theology* (Philadelphia: American Baptist Publication Society, 1887), 137.

17. Basil Manly, Jr., *The Bible Doctrine of Inspiration* (New York: A. C. Armstrong and Sons, 1888), 15.

18. Ibid., 37.

19. See James Spivey, "B. H. Carroll," *Baptist Theologians*.

20. See B. H. Carroll, *An Interpretation of the English Bible* (New York: Revell, 1913).

21. B. H. Carroll, *Inspiration of the Bible* (New York: Revell, 1930), 42.

22. Ibid., 20.

23. Thomas F. Curtis, *The Human Element in the Inspiration of the Sacred Scriptures* (New York: Appleton, 1867).

24. Though Broadus was careful to articulate a doctrine of inspiration as indicated by his statement in his *Commentary on the Gospel of Matthew* (Philadelphia: American Baptist Publication Society, 1886), 58. He comments, "we should be cautious in theorizing as to verbal inspiration." This warning does not detract from Broadus's commitment to the full reliability of the Bible contrary to what E. V. McKnight suggests in "A. T. Robertson: The Evangelical Middle," *The Unfettered Word*, 96.

25. See A. T. Robertson, *Word Pictures in the New Testament*, 6 vols. (Nashville: Broadman, 1934).

26. J. M. Frost, ed., *Baptists: Why and Why Not* (Nashville: Baptist Sunday School Board, 1900).

27. Ibid., 12.

28. E. E. Folk, *Letters to My Son* (Nashville: Baptist Sunday School Board, 1909).

29. E. C. Dargan, *Doctrines of the Faith* (Nashville: Baptist Sunday School Board, 1905).

30. J. Van Ness, *The Baptist Spirit* (Nashville: Baptist Sunday School Board, 1914).

31. E. Y. Mullins, *The Christian Religion in Its Doctrinal Expression* (Philadelphia: Judson, 1917).

32. E. Y. Mullins, *Christianity at the Crossroads* (Nashville: Baptist Sunday School Board, 1924).

33. This material is located in the James P. Boyce Library at Southern Baptist Theological Seminary, Louisville, Kentucky.

34. I am appreciative of the analysis of E. Y. Mullins in the 1982 dissertation by Dwight Moody.

35. Cited by R. Albert Mohler, Jr. in *Beyond the Impasse?*

36. W. T. Conner, *Revelation and God* (Nashville: Broadman, 1936).

37. W. T. Conner, *Christian Doctrine* (Nashville: Broadman, 1937).

38. See his review of *Fundamentals of Christianity*, by F. C. Patton in *The Southwestern Evangel* 10 (May 1926): 45.

39. I am largely dependent for the understanding of Conner's works on James Leo Garrett, Jr., "Theology of Walter Thomas Conner" (Th.D. dissertation, Southwestern Baptist Theological Seminary, 1954). Also, see L. Russ Bush and Tom J. Nettles, *Baptists and the Bible* (Chicago: Moody, 1980) and Dwight A. Moody, "The Bible," *Has Our Theology Changed?*, 7–40.

40. W. B. Nowlin, *Fundamentals of the Faith* (Nashville: Baptist Sunday School Board, 1922).

41. H. E. Dana, *Authenticity of the Holy Scriptures* (Nashville: Baptist Sunday School Board, 1923).

42. J. J. Reeve, "My Experience with Higher Criticism," *The Fundamentals*, eds. by R. A. Torrey and A. C. Dixon (1917; Grand Rapids: Baker, 1980).

43. R. G. Lee, *The Word of God: Not Broken and Not Bound* (Orlando: Christ for the World, 1930).

44. O. C. S. Wallace, *What Baptists Believe* (Nashville: Baptist Sunday School Board, 1934).

45. J. B. Weatherspoon, *The Book We Teach* (Nashville: Baptist Sunday School Board, 1934).

46. J. B. Tidwell, *Thinking Straight About the Bible or Is the Bible the Word of God* (Nashville: Broadman Press, 1936).

47. The 1961 controversy was over Ralph Elliott's *Message of Genesis* (Nashville: Broadman, 1961). The 1969 controversy focused on volume one of *The Broadman Bible Commentary* (Nashville: Broadman, 1969). The 1979 Southern Baptist Convention initiated the conservative resurgence in the SBC and has been referred to as the "inerrancy controversy." See the response in Ralph H. Elliott, *The "Genesis Controversy" and Continuity in Southern Baptist Chaos* (Macon, Ga.: Mercer, 1993).

48. This is not to find fault with the programmatic emphases in themselves, for they helped to create the strong church programs that gave identity to Southern Baptists as a people and provided a framework for effective outreach.

49. W. R. White, "The Authoritative Criterion," *Baptist Distinctives* (Nashville: Convention, 1950).

50. J. B. Lawrence, "The Word and Words of God," *Southern Baptist Home Missions* (Nashville: Convention, 1952); idem, "The Bible, Our Creed," *Southern Baptist Home Missions* (Nashville: Convention, 1957).

51. J. Clyde Turner, "That Wonderful Book," *Things We Believe* (Nashville: Convention Press, 1956).

52. I have profited from the social analysis in James Spivey, "The Millennium," *Has Our Theology Changed*, 230–62.

53. The controversy surrounding *The Broadman Bible Commentary*, edited by Clifton J. Allen, should not detract from the recognition that Southern Baptists had now produced a major work of biblical scholarship that provided exegetical help for many pastors, students, and Bible teachers. The contributions of Roy Lee Honeycutt, Frank Stagg, William Hull, Jack MacGorman, Marvin Tate, and Ray Summers were of especially high quality, though their critical conclusions at times detracted from their overall positive contributions.

54. See Dan Stiver, "Dale Moody," *Baptist Theologians*.

55. See the penetrating analysis of Stagg's theology in Robert Sloan, "Frank Stagg," *Baptist Theologians*.

56. See Frank Stagg, *New Testament Theology* (Nashville: Broadman, 1962).

57. Ibid., 88; see the discussion in Paul A. Basden, "Predestination," *Has Our Theology Changed?* 62–65.

58. See L. Russ Bush, "W. A. Criswell," *Baptist Theologians*.

59. W. A. Criswell, *Why I Preach that the Bible is Literally True* (Nashville: Broadman, 1969).

60. See Helen Lee Turner, "Fundamentalism in the Southern Baptist Convention: The Crystallization of a Millennialist Vision," (Ph.D. dissertation, University of Virginia, 1990).

61. See Conner, *Revelation and God,*

62. See Walter B. Shurden, *The Struggle for the Soul of the SBC* (Macon, Ga.: Mercer, 1992).

63. See Herschel Hobbs, *My Faith and Message* (Nashville: Broadman, 1993).

64. See J. D. Woodbridge, "William (Billy) Graham" in *Dictionary of Baptists in America*, ed. Bill Leonard (Downers Grove: InterVarsity, 1994), 135–37.

65. See William Hull, "Shall We Call the Bible Infallible?" *The Baptist Program* (1970).

66. See Harold Lindsell, *The Battle for the Bible* (Grand Rapids: Zondervan, 1976).

67. The use of historical criticism in and of itself can be very positive. However, some methodological approaches initially carried with them anti-supernatural biases that resulted in denying the veracity of Holy Scripture. Such was the case with the *Message of Genesis*. Positive employment of critical approaches can be found in David A. Black and David S. Dockery, *New Testament Criticism and Interpretation* (Grand Rapids: Zondervan, 1991).

68. Both statements were produced and signed by over one hundred evangelical scholars. The product of the 1978 conference can be found in

the volume edited by Norman Geisler, *Inerrancy* (Grand Rapids: Zondervan, 1979). The second conference resulted in the work edited by Earl Radmacher and Robert Preuss, *Hermeneutics, Inerrancy, and the Bible* (Grand Rapids: Zondervan, 1984). Southern Baptists who signed the "Inerrancy" (1978) statement included: L. Russ Bush, Larry Walker, and L. Paige Patterson. Southern Baptists who signed the "Interpretation" (1982) statement included: Bush, Walker, and David S. Dockery.

69. Russell Dilday, *The Doctrine of Biblical Authority* (Nashville: Convention, 1982).

70. L. Russ Bush and Tom J. Nettles, *Baptists and the Bible* (Chicago: Moody, 1980).

71. See James, *Unfettered Word*.

72. See Roy L. Honeycutt, "Biblical Authority: A Treasured Baptist Heritage," *Review and Expositor* 83 (1986): 605–22.

73. See Jack Rogers and Donald K. McKim, *The Authority and Interpretation of the Bible* (San Francisco: Harper and Row, 1981). The volume by Russell Dilday also was dependent on the Rogers-McKim thesis.

74. Morris Ashcraft, *Christian Faith and Beliefs* (Nashville: Broadman, 1984).

75. Dale Moody, *The Word of Truth* (Grand Rapids: Eerdmans, 1981). Moody tended to equate inerrancy with a mechanical dictation view of inspiration and thus rejected the term inerrancy. He did, however, later give his affirmation to the 1978 Chicago Statement and its careful nuances.

76. See James Leo Garrett, Jr., *Systematic Theology: Biblical, Historical, and Evangelical* (Grand Rapids: Eerdmans, 1990). Garrett follows Conner in not affirming a particular model of inspiration. He has, however, in this volume offered as full and significant treatment on the doctrine of Scripture yet offered by a Southern Baptist systematic theologian. His conclusions are a sound, balanced, and evangelical synthesis of the works of W. T. Conner, A. H. Strong, and Millard J. Erickson. He confesses the trustworthiness of the Bible (p. 161) and maintains its full divine inspiration. He says, "The greatest single need with respect to the doctrine of inspiration is for balance between divine agency and human involvement" (p. 110), a conclusion we emphasized in the chapter on "Inspiration" in this volume. Helpful analysis of the work of Garrett and Moody can be found in Dwight A. Moody, "The Bible," *Has Our Theology Changed?*

77. See Clark Pinnock, *A New Reformation* (Tigerville, S.C.: Jewel, 1968); idem, *Biblical Revelation* (Chicago: Moody, 1971).

78. See Carl F. H. Henry, *God, Revelation, and Authority*, 6 vols., (Waco: Word, 1976–83).

79. See David S. Dockery, *The Doctrine of the Bible* (Nashville: Convention, 1991). This work follows the conservative or evangelical position outlined earlier in this section.

80. Perhaps the most important indicator of this new paradigm is the publication of the *New American Commentary*, eds. David S. Dockery and E. Ray Clendenen (Nashville: Broadman, 1991–). Sixteen of a projected forty volumes have been published, and have been greeted by warm reviews and honors, demonstrating both the quality of scholarship and depth of commitment. Each writer agreed to write in accord with the Chicago Statement on Inerrancy (see editorial preface to each volume). The volumes by John B. Polhill (Acts), Robert Stein (Luke), and Duane A. Garrett (Proverbs, Ecclessiastes, Song of Songs) have been nominated for Gold Medallion Awards.

81. See the discussions in Dockery, ed., *Southern Baptists and American Evangelicals*.

82. See Foy Valentine, quoted in Kenneth L. Woodward, et al. "The Evangelicals," *Newsweek* 25 (1976): 76.

83. I am deeply appreciative of and dependent on Dwight A. Moody, Charles Chaney, and Timothy George for many of the observations and insights in this section.

BIBLIOGRAPHY

Abraham, William J. *The Divine Inspiration of Holy Scripture.* Oxford: University Press, 1981.

Ackroyd, Peter R., and C. F. Evans, eds. *The Cambridge History of the Bible: From Beginning to Jerome.* Vol. 1. Cambridge: Cambridge University Press, 1970.

Aland, Kurt. *The Problem of the New Testament Canon.* London: Mowbray & Co., 1962.

Aldridge, J. W. *The Hermeneutics of Erasmus.* Richmond: John Knox, 1966.

Allen, Clifton J., ed. *The Broadman Bible Commentary.* Nashville: Broadman, 1969.

Ammerman, Nancy T. *Baptist Battles.* New Brunswick, N.J.: Rutgers, 1990.

Aquinas, Thomas. *On Interpretation.* Trans. J. T. Oesterle. Milwaukee: Marquette University, 1962.

Armstrong, A. Hilary. *St. Augustine and Christian Platonism.* Villanova, Pa.: University Press, 1967.

Ashcraft, Morris. *Christian Faith and Beliefs*. Nashville: Broadman, 1984.

Athanasius. *De Incarnatione*. Ed. F. L. Cross. London: Macmillan, 1939.

Attwater, Donald. *St. John Chrysostom: Pastor and Preacher*. London: Harvil, 1959.

Augustine. *Against the Manichaens and Against the Donatists*. Trans. Richard Stothert, A. H. Newman, and J. R. King. vol. 4 of Nicene and Post-Nicene Fathers. Grand Rapids: Eerdmans, reprint 1983.

————. *City of God, and Christian Doctrine*. Trans. M. Dods and J. F. Shaw. Vol. 2 of Nicene and Post-Nicene Fathers. Grand Rapids: Eerdmans, reprint 1988.

Bailey, Raymond, ed. *Hermeneutics and Preaching*. Nashville: Broadman, 1992.

Baillie, John. *The Idea of Revelation in Recent Thought*. New York: Columbia, 1956.

Baker, D. L. *Two Testaments: One Bible*. 1976. Grand Rapids: Baker, 1993.

Bangs, C. *Arminius: A Study in the Dutch Reformation*. Nashville: Abingdon, 1971.

Barker, Kenneth L., ed. *The NIV: The Making of a Contemporary Translation*. Grand Rapids: Zondervan, 1986.

Barr, James. *Beyond Fundamentalism*. Philadelphia: Westminster, 1984.

————. *The Bible in the Modern World*. London: SCM, 1973.

————. *Fundamentalism*. London: SCM, 1977.

Barrow, R. H. *Introduction to St. Augustine's "The City of God."* London: Faber and Faber, 1950.

Barth, Karl. *Church Dogmatics*. Trans. and ed. G. W. Bromiley and T. F. Torrance. Edinburgh: T & T Clark, 1956 – .

———— and Rudolf Bultmann. *Ein Versuch ihn zu Verstchen*. Zurich: Evangelischer Verlag, 1952.

Basden, Paul A., ed. *Has Our Theology Changed? Southern Baptist Thought Since 1845*. Nashville: Broadman and Holman, 1994.

Beare, F. W. "Canon of the New Testament." *Interpreter's Dictionary of the Bible*. Nashville: Abingdon, 1962, 334–58.

Beckwith, Roger T. *The Old Testament Canon of the New Testament Church and Its Background in Early Judaism*. Grand Rapids: Eerdmans, 1985.

Beekman, John and John Callow. *Translating the Word of God*. Grand Rapids: Zondervan, 1974.

Bengel, J. Albert. *Gnomon of the New Testament.* Ed. Andrew R. Faucett. Edinburgh: T & T Clark, 1857–58.

Bentley, J. H. *Humanist and Holy Writ.* Princeton: University Press, 1983.

Berkouwer, G. C. *Holy Scripture.* Trans. Jack B. Rogers. Grand Rapids: Eerdmans, 1975.

Black, David A. and David S. Dockery. *New Testament Criticism and Interpretation.* Grand Rapids: Zondervan, 1991.

Black, Matthew. "The Christological Use of the Old Testament in the New." *New Testament Studies* 18 (1971): 1–14.

Bloesch, Donald G. *The Crisis of Piety.* Grand Rapids: Eerdmans, 1976.

_____.*Essentials of Evangelical Theology.* 2 vols. San Francisco: Harper & Row, 1978–79.

_____. *Holy Scripture: Revelation, Inspiration, and Interpretation.* Downers Grove, Ill.: InterVarsity, 1994.

Blomberg, Craig L. *Matthew.* In *New American Commentary.* Nashville: Broadman, 1992.

_____. *The Historical Reliability of the Gospel.* Downers Grove, Ill.: InterVarsity, 1987.

Bock, Darrell L. "Evangelicals and the Use of the Old Testament in the New." *Bibliotheca Sacra* 142 (1985): 209–23, 306–19.

Boice, James M., ed. *The Foundation of Biblical Authority.* Grand Rapids: Zondervan, 1978.

Boone, Kathleen C. *Because the Bible Tells Them So.* Albany, N.Y.: State University of New York Press, 1989.

Boyce, James P. *Abstract of Systematic Theology.* Philadelphia: American Baptist Publications Society, 1887.

Bray, Gerald L. *Creeds, Councils, and Christ.* Downers Grove: InterVarsity, 1984.

Broadus, John A. *Commentary on the Gospel of Matthew.* Philadelphia: American Baptist Publication Society, 1886.

Bromiley, Geoffrey W. "Authority." *International Standard Bible Encyclopedia.* 4 vols. Ed. Geoffrey W. Bromiley. Grand Rapids: Eerdmans, 1979, 1:346–71.

Brown, Colin. *Karl Barth and the Christian Message.* London: InterVarsity, 1967.

Bruce, F. F. *The Books and the Parchments.* London: Pickering & Inglis, 1963.

_____. *The Canon of Scripture.* Downers Grove: InterVarsity, 1988.

_____. *The English Bible.* New York: Oxford, 1970.

_____. *New Testament Development of Old Testament Themes.* Grand Rapids: Eerdmans, 1968.

_____. *The New Testament Documents: Are They Reliable?* Downers Grove: InterVarsity, 1960.

Brunner, Emil. *Revelation and Reason.* Trans. Olive Wyon. Philadelphia: Westminster, 1946.

_____. *The History of the Synoptic Tradition.* New York: Harper and Row, 1968.

Bultmann, Rudolf. "Is Exegesis Without Presuppositions Possible?" *Existence and Faith.* Ed. Shubert M. Ogden. London: Hodder and Stoughton, 1961.

_____. "The Problem of Hermeneutics." *Essays Philosophical and Theological.* Trans. James Greig. London: SCM, 1955.

_____. *Theology of the New Testament.* Trans. Kendrick Grobel. 2 vols. New York: Scribners, 1955.

Burtchaell, James Tunstead. *Catholic Theories of Biblical Inspiration Since 1810: A Review and Critique.* London: Cambridge, 1969.

Bush, L. Russ and Tom J. Nettles. *Baptists and the Bible.* Chicago: Moody, 1980.

Caird, G. B. *The Language and Imagery of the Bible.* Philadelphia: Westminster, 1980.

Calvin, John. *New Testament Commentaries.* Eds. D. W. Torrance and T. F. Torrance. Grand Rapids: Eerdmans, reprint 1961.

Campenhausen, H. F. von. *The Formation of the Christian Bible.* Philadelphia: Fortress, 1972.

_____. *The Case for Orthodox Theology.* Philadelphia: Fortress, 1959.

Carnell, E. J. *Christian Commitment: An Apologetic.* Grand Rapids: Eerdmans, 1957.

Carroll, B. H. *An Interpretation of the English Bible.* New York: Revell, 1913.

_____. *Inspiration of the Bible.* New York: Revell, 1930.

Carson, D. A., ed. *Biblical Interpretation and the Church: The Problem of Contextualization.* Nashville: Thomas Nelson, 1984.

_____. *The King James Version Debate.* Grand Rapids: Baker, 1979.

Carson, D. A. and H. G. M. Williamson, eds. *It is Written: Scripture Citing Scripture.* Cambridge: University Press, 1988.

Carson D. A. and John D. Woodbridge, eds. *Hermeneutics, Authority, and Canon.* Grand Rapids: Zondervan, 1986.

_____. eds. *Scripture and Truth*. Grand Rapids: Zondervan, 1984.

Chrysostom, John. *Homilies on Acts and Romans*. Trans. J. Walker, Vol. 2 of Nicene and Post-Nicene Fathers. Grand Rapids: Eerdmans, reprint 1979.

Clark, Gordon H. *God's Hammer: The Bible and Its Critics*. Jefferson, Mo.: Trinity Foundation, 1982.

Comfort, Philip W. *Early Manuscripts and the Modern Translations of the New Testament*. Wheaton: Tyndale, 1990.

Conn, Harvie M., ed. *Inerrancy and Hermeneutics*. Grand Rapids: Baker, 1988.

Conner, W. T. *Christian Doctrine*. Nashville: Broadman, 1937.

_____. *Revelation and God*. Nashville: Broadman, 1936.

Conzelmann, Hans. *The Pastoral Epistles*. Trans. Philip Buttolph and A. Yarbro. Philadelphia: Fortress, 1962.

Countryman, William *Biblical Authority or Biblical Tyranny*. Philadelphia: Fortress, 1982.

Cranfield, C. E. B. *A Critical and Exegetical Commentary on the Epistle to the Romans*. 2 vols. Edinburgh: T & T Clark, 1975–79.

Criswell, W. A. *Why I Preach that the Bible is Literally True*. Nashville: Broadman, 1969.

Curtis, Thomas F. *The Human Element in the Inspiration of the Sacred Scriptures*. New York: Appleton, 1867.

Dagg, J. L. *The Evidences of Christianity*. Macon, Ga.: Burke, 1869.

_____. *A Manual of Theology*. Charleston, S.C.: Southern Baptist Publications Society, 1858.

Daly, R. J. "The Hermeneutics of Origen: Existential Interpretation of the Third Century." *Word in the World*. Cambridge, Mass.: Weston, 1973.

Dana, H. E. *The Authenticity of the Holy Scriptures*. Nashville: Baptist Sunday School Board, 1923.

Dargan, E. C. *Doctrines of the Faith*. Nashville: Baptist Sunday School Board, 1905.

Davis, John Jefferson, ed. *The Necessity of Systematic Theology*. Grand Rapids: Baker, 1980.

_____. *Theology Primer*. Grand Rapids: Baker, 1981.

DeJonge, Henk Jan. "The Character of Erasmus' Translation of the New Testament as Reflected in His Translation of Hebrews 9." *Journal of Medieval and Renaissance Studies* 14 (1984): 81–87.

Demarest, Bruce A. *General Revelation: Historical Views and Contemporary Issues.* Grand Rapids: Zondervan, 1982.

Demarest, Bruce A. and Gordon R. Lewis. *Integrative Theology.* 3 vols. Grand Rapids: Zondervan, 1987–93.

Derrida, Jacques. *Writing and Difference.* Chicago: University of Chicago Press, 1978.

DeWolf, L. H. *A Theology of the Living Church.* New York: Harper and Brothers, 1960.

Dilday, Russell. *The Doctrine of Biblical Authority.* Nashville: Convention, 1982.

Dockery, David S. *Biblical Interpretation Then and Now.* Grand Rapids: Baker, 1992.

_____. "The Christological Hermeneutics of Martin Luther." *Grace Theological Journal* 4 (1983): 189–203.

_____. *The Doctrine of the Bible.* Nashville: Convention, 1991.

_____. "The Inerrancy and Authority of Scripture." *Theological Educator* 37 (1988): 15–36.

_____., ed. *Southern Baptists and American Evangelicals.* Nashville: Broadman and Holman, 1993.

Dockery, David S., Kenneth A. Mathews, and Robert B. Sloan, eds. *Foundations for Biblical Interpretation.* Nashville: Broadman and Holman, 1994.

Donnely, J. P. "Calvinist Thomism." *Victor* 7 (1976): 41–51.

Draper, James T. *Trusting Thy Word.* Nashville: Broadman, 1989.

Duduit, Michael, ed. *A Handbook for Contemporary Preaching.* Nashville: Broadman, 1992.

Dugmore, C. W., ed. *The Interpretation of the Bible.* London: SPCK, 1944.

Duke, J. O. "Pietism versus Establishment: The Halle Phase." *Classical Quarterly* 73 (1979): 3–20.

Elliott, Ralph. *The "Genesis Controversy" and Continuity in Southern Baptist Chaos.* Macon, Ga.: Mercer, 1993.

_____. *Message of Genesis.* Nashville: Broadman, 1961.

Ellis, E. Earle. *Prophecy and Hermeneutic in Early Christianity.* Grand Rapids: Eerdmans, 1978.

Elwell, Walter A., ed. *Evangelical Theologians.* Grand Rapids: Baker, 1993.

Erickson, Millard J. *Christian Theology.* 3 vols. Grand Rapids: Baker, 1983–86.

Estep, William R. "Baptists and Authority: The Bible, Confessions, and Conscience in the Development of Baptist Identity." *Review and Expositor* 76 (1979): 35–42.

Eusebius. *The History of the Church from Christ to Constantine.* Trans. G. A. Williamson. Minneapolis: Augsburg, 1965.

Evans, Gillian R. *The Language and Logic of the Bible: The Earlier Middle Ages.* Cambridge: University Press, 1984.

Farmer, William R. and Dennis M. Farkasfalvy. *The Formation of the New Testament Canon.* New York: Paulist, 1983.

Fee, Gordon D. *New Testament Exegesis.* Philadelphia: Westminster, 1983.

Fee, Gordon D. and Douglas Stuart. *How to Read the Bible for All Its Worth.* Grand Rapids: Zondervan, 1982.

Flesseman-Van Leer, Ellen. "Prinzipien der Sammlung und Ausscheidung bei der Bildung des Kanons." *Zeitschrift for Thelogie und Kirche* 61 (1964): 415–16.

France, R. T. "The Formula-Quotations of Matthew 2 and the Problem of Communication." *New Testament Studies* 27 (1981): 223–51.

————. *Jesus and the Old Testament.* London: Tyndale, 1971.

Froehlich, Karlfried. *Biblical Exegesis in the Early Church.* Philadelphia: Fortress, 1984.

Frost, J. M., ed. *Baptists: Why and Why Not.* Nashville: Baptist Sunday School Board, 1900.

Gadamer, Hans-Georg. "The Problem of Language in Schleiermacher's Hermeneutic." *Journal for Theology and the Church* 7 (1970): 68–95.

————. *Truth and Method.* Ed. G. Borden and J. Cumming. New York: Sheed and Ward, 1975.

Gamble, H. Y. *The New Testament Canon.* Philadelphia: Fortress, 1985.

Gamble, R. C. "Brevitas et Facilitas: Toward an Understanding of Calvin's Hermeneutic." *Westminster Theological Journal* 47 (1985): 1–19.

Garrett, Duane A. and Richard R. Melick, Jr., eds. *Authority and Interpretation: A Baptist Perspective.* Grand Rapids: Baker, 1986.

Garrett, James Leo, Jr. "Biblical Authority According to Baptist Confessions of Faith." *Review and Expositor* 76 (1979): 43–54.

————. "Theology of Walter Thomas Conner." Th.D. Dissertation, Southwestern Baptist Theological Seminary, 1954.

————. "Sources of Authority in Baptist Thought." *Baptist History and Heritage* 13 (1978): 47–49.

————. *Systematic Theology: Biblical, Historical, and Evangelical.* 2 vols. Grand Rapids: Eerdmans, 1990–95.

Geisler, Norman, ed. *Inerrancy.* Grand Rapids: Zondervan, 1979.

Gelvin, Michael. *A Commentary on Heidegger's "Being and Time."* New York: Harper and Row, 1970.

George, Timothy. *Theology of the Reformers.* Nashville: Broadman, 1988.

George, Timothy and David S. Dockery, eds. *Baptist Theologians.* Nashville: Broadman, 1990.

Gerhardson, Birger. *Memory and Manuscript: Oral Tradition and Written Transmission in Rabbinic Judaism and Early Christianity.* Trans. E. J. Sharpe. Lund, Sweden: Gleerup, 1961.

Gerrish, B. A. *The Old Protestantism and the New: Essays on the Reformation Heritage.* Chicago: University of Chicago Press, 1982.

Grant, Robert M. *Greek Apologists of the Second Century.* Philadelphia: Westminster, 1988.

_____. *The Apostolic Fathers.* 6 vols. New York: Thomas Nelson, 1964.

_____. *The Formation of the New Testament.* New York: Harper and Row, 1965.

_____. *The Letter and the Spirit.* New York: Macmillan, 1957.

Grant, Robert M. with David Tracy. *A Short History of the Interpretation of the Bible.* Philadelphia: Fortress, rev. 1984.

Grenz, Stanley J. *The Cry for the Kingdom.* Peabody, Mass.: Hendrickson, 1986.

_____. *Theology for the Community of God.* Nashville: Broadman, 1994.

Grier, James M. "The Self-Witness of the Bible." *Grace Theological Journal* 1 (1979): 71–76.

Guthrie, Donald. *New Testament Theology.* Downers Grove, Ill.: InterVarsity, 1981.

Hagner, Donald A. *The Use of the Old and New Testaments in Clement of Rome.* Leiden: Brill, 1973.

Hahn, H. F. and H. D. Hummel. *The Old Testament in Modern Research.* Philadelphia: Fortress, 1970.

Hanson, R. P. C. *Allegory and Event: A Study of the Sources and Significance of Origen's Interpretation of Scripture.* Richmond, Va.: John Knox, 1959.

_____. *The Bible as a Norm of Faith.* Durham, N.C.: University Press, 1963.

_____. *Tradition in the Early Church.* London: SCM, 1962.

Hanson, R. P. C. and A. T. Hanson. *The Bible Without Illusions.* Philadelphia: Trinity, 1989.

Hayes, Richard B. *Echos of Scripture in the Letters of Paul.* New Haven: Yale, 1989.

Hefner, P. "Theological Methodology in St. Irenaeus." *Journal of Religion* 44 (1964): 294–309.

Heidegger, Martin. *Being and Time*. Trans. J. Macquarrie. Oxford: Blackwell, 1962.

————. *On the Way to Language*. Trans. P. D. Hertz. New York: Harper and Row, 1971.

Helm, Paul. *Divine Revelation*. Westchester, N.Y.: Crossway, 1982.

Henry, Carl F. H. "The Authority and Inspiration of the Bible." *The Expositor's Bible Commentary*. Vol. 1. Ed. F. E. Gaebelein. Grand Rapids: Zondervan, 1979.

————. *God, Revelation, and Authority*. 6 vols. Waco: Word, 1976–83.

————. *The Identity of Jesus of Nazareth*. Nashville: Broadman, 1992.

Herring, Ralph, Frank Stagg, et al. *How to Understand the Bible*. Nashville: Broadman, 1974.

Hesselgrave, David. *Communicating Christ Cross-Culturally*. Grand Rapids: Zondervan, 1978.

Hirsch, E. D., Jr. *The Aims of Interpretation*. Chicago: University of Chicago, 1976.

————. *Validity in Interpretation*. New Haven: Yale, 1967.

Hobbs, Herschel. "Southern Baptists and Confessionalism: A Comparison of the Origins and Contents of the 1925 and 1963 Confessions." *Review and Expositor* 76 (1979).

Hoekema, Anthony A. *Created in God's Image*. Grand Rapids: Eerdmans, 1986.

Holmes, Michael W., ed. *The Apostolic Fathers*. Grand Rapids: Baker, 1989.

Honeycutt, Roy L. "Biblical Authority: A Treasured Baptist Heritage." *Review and Expositor* 83 (1986), 605–22.

Hooker, Morna D. *Studying the New Testament*. Minneapolis: Augsburg, 1979.

House, Paul, ed. *Old Testament Form Criticism*. Winona Lake, Ind.: Eisenbrauns, 1992.

Hughes, P. E. *Scripture and Myth: An Examination of Rudolf Bultmann's Plea for Demythologization*. London: Tyndale, 1956.

Hull, William. "Shall We Call the Bible Infallible?" *The Baptist Program* (1970).

Jackson, Belford D. "Semantics and Hermeneutics in Saint Augustine's De doctrina Christiana." Ph.D. Dissertation. Yale University, 1967.

James, Robison B., ed. *The Unfettered Word*. Waco: Word, 1987.

James, Robison B. and David S. Dockery, eds. *Beyond the Impasse?: Scripture, Tradition, and Interpretation in Baptist Life*. Nashville: Broadman, 1992.

Johnson, E. E. *Expository Hermeneutics: An Introduction*. Grand Rapids: Zondervan, 1990.

Johnston, Robert K., ed. *The Use of The Bible in Theology: Evangelical Options*. Atlanta: John Knox, 1985.

Juel, Donald. *Messianic Exegesis: Christological Interpretation of the Old Testament in Early Christianity*. Philadelphia: Fortress, 1988.

Kaiser, Walter C., Jr. *Toward an Exegetical Theology*. Grand Rapids: Baker, 1981.

Kantzer, Kenneth S., ed. *Applying the Scriptures*. Grand Rapids: Zondervan, 1987.

Kantzer, Kenneth S. and Stanley N. Gundry, eds. *Perspectives in Evangelical Theology*. Grand Rapids: Baker, 1979.

Käsemann, Ernst, ed. *Das Neue Testament als Kanon*. Gottingen: Vandenhoeck & Ruprecht, 1970.

Kaufman, Gordon D. "What Shall We Do With the Bible?" *Interpretation* 25 (1971): 90–96.

Kelly, J. N. D. *A Commentary on the Pastoral Epistles*. New York: Harper and Row, 1963.

————. *Early Christian Doctrine*. New York: Harper and Row, 1960.

Kelly, Joseph F., ed. *Scripture and Tradition*. Notre Dame, Ind.: Fides, 1976.

Kent, Homer A., Jr. *The Pastoral Epistles*. Chicago: Moody, 1982.

Klassen, W. and G. F. Snyder, eds. *Current Issues in New Testament Interpretation*. New York: Harper, 1962.

Klein, George L., ed. *Reclaiming the Prophetic Mantle*. Nashville: Broadman, 1992.

Klein, William W., Craig L. Blomberg, and Robert L. Hubbard, Jr. *Introduction to Biblical Interpretation*. Dallas: Word, 1993.

Kraus, Hans-Joachim. "Calvin's Exegetical Principles." *Interpretation* 31 (1977): 8–18.

Krentz, Edgar. *The Historical-Critical Method*. Philadelphia: Fortress, 1976.

Kubo, S. and W. Specht. *So Many Versions*. Grand Rapids: Zondervan, 1983.

Kugel, James L. and Rowan A. Greer. *Early Biblical Interpretation*. Philadelphia: Westminster, 1986.

Kuhatshek, Jack. *Taking the Guesswork Out of Applying the Bible.* Downers Grove, Ill.: InterVarsity, 1990.

Kümmel, W. G. *The New Testament: The History of the Investigation of its Problems.* Trans. S. M. Gilmour and H. C. Kee. Nashville: Abingdon, 1972.

Lampe, G. W. H., ed. *The Cambridge History of the Bible.* Vol. 2. Cambridge: University Press, 1969.

Lampe, G. W. H. and K. J. Woolcombe. *The Reasonableness of Typology.* London: SCM, 1957.

Latourette, Kenneth Scott. *A History of Christianity.* New York: Harper, 1953.

Lawrence, J. B. "The Bible, Our Creed." *Southern Baptist Home Missions.* Nashville: Convention, 1957.

_____. "The Word and Words of God." *Southern Baptist Home Missions.* Nashville: Convention, 1952.

Lee, R. G. *The Word of God: Not Broken and Not Bound.* Orlando: Christ for the World, 1930.

Leonard, Bill J. *God's Last and Only Hope.* Grand Rapids: Eerdmans, 1990.

Lewis, C. S. *Mere Christianity.* New York: Macmillan, 1952.

Lewis, Jack P. *The English Bible from KJV to NIV.* Grand Rapids: Baker, 1991.

Lietzmann, Hans. *Kleine Schriften II: Studien zum Neuen Testament.* Berlin: Akademic-Verlag, 1958.

Lindsell, Harold. *Battle for the Bible.* Grand Rapids: Zondervan, 1976.

Longenecker, Richard N. *Biblical Exegesis in the Apostolic Period.* Grand Rapids: Eerdmans, 1975.

Lumpkin, William L., ed. *Baptist Confessions of Faith.* Valley Forge, Penn.: Judson, 1959.

Lundin, Roger, Anthony Thiselton, and Clarence Walhout. *The Responsibility of Hermeneutics.* Grand Rapids: Eerdmans, 1985.

Luther, Martin, *Bondage of the Will.* Edinburgh: T & T Clark, reprint 1957.

_____. *Luther's Works.* Ed. J. Pelikan. St. Louis: Concordia, 1955.

Manly, Basil, Jr. *The Bible Doctrine of Inspiration.* New York: A. C. Armstrong and Sons, 1888.

Markus, R. A. *Saeculum: History and Society in the Theology of St. Augustine.* Cambridge: University Press, 1970.

Marshall, I. Howard. *Biblical Inspiration.* Grand Rapids: Eerdmans, 1982.

_____., ed. *New Testament Interpretation*. Grand Rapids: Eerdmans, 1975.

Martin, Ralph P. "Muratorian Canon." *New International Dictionary of the Christian Church*. Ed. J. D. Douglas. Grand Rapids: Zondervan, 1978.

_____. *Worship in the Early Church*. Grand Rapids: Eerdmans, 1964.

McCarter, Kyle P. *Textual Criticism: Recovering the Text of the Hebrew Bible*. Philadelphia: Fortress, 1988.

McCartney, Dan and Charles Clayton. *Let the Reader Understand*. Wheaton, Ill.: Victor/BridgePoint, 1994.

McDonald, H. D. *Jesus—Human and Divine: An Introduction to Christology*. Grand Rapids: Zondervan, 1968.

McDonald, Lee. *The Formation of the Christian Biblical Canon*. Nashville: Abingdon, 1988.

McKim, Donald K. *What Christians Believe About the Bible*. Nashville: Abingdon, 1985.

McNally, Robert E. *The Bible in the Early Middle Ages*. Westminster, Md.: Newman, 1959.

Mead, D. G. *Pseudonymity and Canon*. Grand Rapids: Eerdmans, 1988.

Metzger, Bruce M. *The Canon of the New Testament*. Oxford: Clarendon, 1987.

_____. *The Text of the New Testament*. Oxford: University Press, 1968.

Metzger, Bruce M., R. C. Denton, and W. Harrelson. *The Making of the New Revised Standard Version*. Grand Rapids: Zondervan, 1991.

Montgomery, John Warwick, ed. *God's Inerrant Word*. Minneapolis: Bethany, 1974.

Moo, Douglas J. *Romans 1–8*. Chicago: Moody, 1991.

_____. *The Old Testament in the Gospel Passion Narrative*. Sheffield: Almond, 1983.

Moody, Dale. *The Word of Truth*. Grand Rapids: Eerdmans, 1981.

Moody, Dwight. "Doctrines of Inspiration in the Southern Baptist Theological Tradition." Ph.D. Dissertation. The Southern Baptist Theological Seminary, 1982.

Morris, Leon. *I Believe in Revelation*. Grand Rapids: Eerdmans, 1976.

Mullins, E. Y. *Christianity at the Crossroads*. Nashville: Baptist Sunday School Board, 1924.

_____. *The Christian Religion in Its Doctrinal Expression.* Philadelphia: Judson, 1917.

Nash, Ronald. *The Word of God and the Mind of Man.* Grand Rapids: Zondervan, 1983.

Neill, Stephen and N. T. Wright. *The Interpretation of the New Testament 1861–1986.* New York: Oxford, 1988.

Nicole, Roger and J. Ramsey Michaels, eds. *Inerrancy and Common Sense.* Grand Rapids: Baker, 1980.

Nida, Eugene. *Message and Mission.* New York: Harper, 1960.

_____. *Toward a Science of Translating.* Leiden: Brill, 1964.

Nineham, D. E., ed. *The Church's Use of the Bible Past and Present.* London: Macmillan, 1963.

_____. *The Use and Abuse of the Bible.* London: SCM, 1976.

Noll, Mark A. *Between Faith and Criticism.* San Francisco: Harper and Row, 1986.

_____. "Evangelicals and the Study of the Bible." *Evangelicalism and Modern America,* ed. George Marsden. Grand Rapids: Eerdmans, 1984.

_____. *The Scandal of the Evangelical Mind.* Grand Rapids: Eerdmans, 1994.

Nowlyn, W. B. *Fundamentals of the Faith.* Nashville: Baptist Sunday School Board, 1922.

Origen. *On First Principles, and Contra Celsum.* Trans. Frederick Crombie. Vol. 4 of Ante-Nicene Fathers. Grand Rapids: Eerdmans, reprint 1976.

Osborne, Grant. *The Hermeneutical Spiral.* Downers Grove, Ill.: InterVarsity, 1992.

Packer, J. I. *"Fundamentalism" and the Word of God.* Grand Rapids: Eerdmans, 1958.

Palmer, R. E. *Hermeneutics.* Evanston, Ill.: Northwestern, 1969.

Pannenberg, Wolfart. *Basic Questions in Theology, I.* Philadelphia: Westminster, 1970.

_____. "Hermeneutics and Universal History." *History and Hermeneutics.* Ed. R. W. Funk. Tübingen: Mohr, 1967.

Patterson, Robert E., ed. *Science, Faith, and Revelation.* Nashville: Broadman, 1979.

Payne, J. B. *Erasmus: His Theology of the Sacraments.* New York: Bratcher, 1970.

Pelikan, Jaroslav. *Luther the Expositor.* St. Louis: Concordia, 1959.

_____. *The Preaching of Chrysostom.* Philadelphia: Fortress, 1967.

Pinnock, Clark. *Biblical Revelation.* Chicago: Moody, 1971.

_____. *A New Reformation.* Tigerville, S.C.: Jewel, 1968.

_____. *The Scripture Principle*. San Francisco: Harper and Row, 1984.

_____. "Three Views of the Bible in Contemporary Theology." *Biblical Authority*. Ed. Jack B. Rogers. Waco: Word, 1977.

Polhill, John B. *Acts*. In *New American Commentary*. Nashville: Broadman, 1992.

Poythress, Vern. "Divine Meaning of Scripture." *Westminster Theological Journal* 48 (1986): 241–79.

_____. "God's Lordship in Interpretation." *Westminster Theological Journal* 50 (1988): 27–64.

_____. *Science and Hermeneutics*. Grand Rapids: Zondervan, 1988.

Preus, James Samuel. *From Shadow to Promise: Old Testament Interpretation from Augustine to the Young Luther*. Cambridge: Harvard University Press, 1969.

Rabil, A. *Erasmus and the New Testament: The Mind of a Christian Humanist*. San Antonio: Trinity, 1972.

Radmacher, Earl D. and Robert D. Preus, eds. *Hermeneutics, Inerrancy, and the Bible*. Grand Rapids: Zondervan, 1986.

Ramm, Bernard. *Pattern of Authority*. Grand Rapids: Eerdmans, 1957.

_____. *Protestant Biblical Interpretation*. Grand Rapids: Baker, rev. 1970.

_____. *Special Revelation and the Word of God*. Grand Rapids: Eerdmans, 1961.

Reid, J. K. S. *The Authority of Scripture: A Study of Reformation and post-Reformation Understandings of the Bible*. London: Methuen, 1962.

Rice, John R. *Our God-Breathed Book*. Murfreesboro, Tenn.: Sword of the Lord, 1969.

Richard, R. P. "Application Theory in Relation to the New Testament." *Bibliotheca Sacra* 143 (1986): 210–16.

Richardson, Cyril C., ed. *Alexandrian Christianity*. Philadelphia: Westminster, 1953.

_____., ed. *Early Christian Fathers*. Vol. 1 of the Library of Christian Classics. Philadelphia: Westminster, 1953.

Ricoeur, Paul. *Essays on Biblical Interpretation*. Ed. L. S. Mudge. Philadelphia: Fortress, 1980.

_____. *Hermeneutics and the Human Sciences*. Ed. J. B. Thompson. Cambridge: University Press, 1986.

Roberts, R. C. *Rudolf Bultmann's Theology: A Critical Appraisal*. Grand Rapids: Eerdmans, 1976.

Robertson, A. T. *An Introduction to the Textual Criticism of the New Testament.* New York: Doubleday, 1925.

————. *Word Pictures in the New Testament.* 6 vols. Nashville: Broadman, 1934.

Rogers, Jack B. and Donald K. McKim. *The Authority and Interpretation of the Bible: An Historical Approach.* New York: Harper and Row, 1979.

Rogerson, John, Christopher Rowland, and Barnabas Lindars. *The Study and Use of the Bible.* Vol. 2 of *The History of Christian Theology.* Ed. Paul Avis. 3 vols. Grand Rapids: Eerdmans, 1988.

Rosas, Joseph. *Scripture in the Thought of Soren Kierkegaard.* Nashville: Broadman and Holman, 1993.

Runia, Klaas. *Karl Barth's Doctrine of Holy Scripture.* Grand Rapids: Eerdmans, 1962.

Ryle, H. E. *The Canon of the Old Testament.* New York: Macmillan, 1892.

Scalise, Charles J. "Allegorical Flights of Fancy: The Problem of Origen's Exegesis." *Greek Orthodox Theological Review* 32 (1987): 69–88.

Schaeffer, Francis. *The God Who Is There.* Downers Grove, Ill.: InterVarsity, 1968.

Schleiermacher, F. D. E. *Hermeneutics: The Handwritten Manuscripts.* Ed. H. Kimmerle. Trans. J. Duke and H. J. Forstman. Missoula, Mont.: Scholars, 1977.

Schneemelcher, Wilhelm. "Bibel I/III: Die entstehung des Kanons des Neuen Testaments und der Christlichen Bibel." *Theologische Real enzyklopadie* I. Ed. Gerhard Krause and Gerhard Muller. Berlin: de Gruyter, 1980.

————. "General Introduction" to *New Testament Apocrypha.* By Edgar Hennecke. Trans. and ed. R. M. Wilson. Philadelphia: Westminster, 1963.

Shelton, Raymond Berry. "Martin Luther's Concept of Biblical Interpretation in Historical Perspective." Ph.D. Dissertation. Fuller Theological Seminary, 1974.

Shotwell, Willis A. *The Biblical Exegesis of Justin Martyr.* London: SPCK, 1965.

Shurden, Walter B. *The Struggle for the Soul of the SBC.* Macon, Ga.: Mercer, 1992.

Silvia, Moises. *God, Language, and Authority.* Grand Rapids: Zondervan, 1990.

————. *Has the Church Misread the Bible?* Grand Rapids: Zondervan, 1987.

Skarsaune, Oskar. *Proof from Prophecy: A Study in Justin Martyr's Proof-Text Tradition.* Leiden: Brill, 1987.

Smalley, Beryl. *The Study of the Bible in the Middle Ages.* Oxford: Blackwell, 1952.

Sproul, R. C. "Controversy at Culture Gap." *Eternity* 27 (May 1975): 12–13.

Sproul, R. C., John Gerstner, and Arthur Lindsley. *Classical Apologetics.* Grand Rapids: Zondervan, 1984.

Stagg, Frank. *New Testament Theology.* Nashville: Broadman, 1962.

Stein, Robert H. *Playing by the Rules: A Basic Guide to Interpreting the Bible.* Grand Rapids: Baker, 1994.

Stein, Stephen J. "The Quest for the Spiritual Sense: The Biblical Hermeneutics of Jonathan Edwards." *Harvard Theological Review* 70 (1977): 99–113.

Steinmetz, David C. "The Superiority of Precritical Exegesis." *Theology Today* 27 (1980): 27–38.

Story, I. K. Cullen. *Nature of Truth in "The Gospel" and in the Writings of Justin Martyr: A Study of Orthodoxy in the Middle of the Second Century.* Leiden: Brill, 1970.

Stott, John R. W. *Between Two Worlds: The Art of Preaching in the Twentieth Century.* Grand Rapids: Eerdmans, 1982.

_____. *Decisive Issues Facing Christians Today.* Old Tappan, N.J.: Revell, 1990.

Strong, A. H. *Systematic Theology.* Old Tappan, N.J.: Revell, 1907.

Stuhlmacher, Peter. *Historical Criticism and Theological Interpretation: Toward a Hermeneutics of Consent.* Trans. R. A. Harrisville. Philadelphia: Fortress, 1977.

Sundberg, Albert C. "The Bible Canon and the Christian Doctrine of Inspiration." *Interpretation* 29 (1975): 352–71.

_____. "Canon Muratori: A Fourth-Century List." *Harvard Theological Review* 66 (1973): 1–41.

_____. *The Old Testament of the Early Church.* Cambridge: Harvard University Press, 1964.

_____. "Toward a Revised History of the New Testament Canon." *Studia Evangelica* 4 (1968): 452–61.

Temple, William. *Revelation.* Ed. John Baille and Hugh Martin. New York: MacMillan, 1937.

Thielicke, Helmut. *The Evangelical Faith.* Vol. I. Trans. G. W. Bromiley. Grand Rapids: Eerdmans, 1974.

Thiselton, Anthony C. *New Horizons.* Grand Rapids: Zondervan, 1992.

_____. "Truth." *New International Dictionary of New Testament Theology*. Ed. Colin Brown. Grand Rapids: Zondervan, 1979.

_____. *Two Horizons: New Testament Hermeneutics and Philosophical Description*. Grand Rapids: Eerdmans, 1980.

_____. "Understanding God's Word Today." *Christ the Lord*. Ed. John R. W. Stott. London: Collins Fontana, 1977.

Torrey, R. A. and A. C. Dixon, eds. *The Fundamentals*. 1917. Grand Rapids: Baker, reprint 1980.

Trigg, Joseph Wilson. *Origen: The Bible and Philosophy in the Third-Century Church*. Atlanta: John Knox, 1983.

Tucker, G. M. and Douglas A. Knight. *Humanizing America's Iconic Book*. Chico, Calif.: Scholars, 1982.

Turner, H. E. W. *The Pattern of Christian Truth*. London: Maybrays, 1954.

Turner, Helen Lee. "Fundamentalism in the Southern Baptist Convention." Ph.D. Dissertation. University of Virginia, 1990.

Turner, J. Clyde. *Things We Believe*. Nashville: Convention, 1956.

Van Ness, J. *The Baptist Spirit*. Nashville: Baptist Sunday School Board, 1914.

Verhoef, P. A. "Luther and Calvin's Exegetical Library." *Concordia Theological Journal* 3 (1968): 5–20.

Wainwright, Geoffrey. "New Testament as Canon." *Scottish Journal of Theology* 28 (1975): 551–71.

Wald, Oletta. *The Joy of Discovery*. Minneapolis: Bible Banner, 1956.

Walenbach, John R. "John Calvin as Biblical Commentator: An Investigation into Calvin's Use of John Chrysostom as an Exegetical Source." Ph.D. Dissertation. University of Pittsburgh, 1974.

Wallace, O. C. S. *What Baptists Believe*. Nashville: Baptist Sunday School Board, 1934.

Warfield, B. B. *The Inspiration and Authority of the Bible*. Philadelphia: Presbyterian and Reformed, reprint 1948.

Weatherspoon, J. B. *The Book We Teach*. Nashville: Baptist Sunday School Board, 1934.

Wellhausen, Julius. *Prolegomena to the History of Israel*. Edinburgh: T & T Clark, 1885.

Wells, David F. *No Place for Truth*. Grand Rapids: Eerdmans, 1993.

_____. *The Person of Christ*. Westchester, Ill.: Crossway, 1984.

Wenham, John W. *Christ and the Bible*. Downers Grove, Ill.: InterVarsity, 1972.

Westcott, B. F. *A General Survey of the History of the Canon of the New Testament*. London: Macmillan, 1870.

White, James E. *What Is Truth?* Nashville: Broadman and Holman, 1994.

White, W. R. *Baptist Distinctives*. Nashville: Convention, 1950.

Wood, A. Skevington. *Captive to the Word: Martin Luther's Doctrine of Sacred Scripture*. Grand Rapids: Eerdmans, 1969.

_____. *Luther's Principles of Biblical Interpretation*. London: Tyndale, 1960.

_____. *The Principles of Biblical Interpretation as Enunciated by Irenaeus, Origen, Augustine, Luther, and Calvin*. Grand Rapids: Zondervan, 1967.

Wood, Charles M. *The Formation of Christian Understanding: An Essay in Theological Hermeneutics*. Philadelphia: Westminster, 1981.

Woodbridge, John D. *Biblical Authority*. Grand Rapids: Zondervan, 1983.

Woodward, Kenneth L., et al. "The Evangelicals." *Newsweek* 25 (1976): 75–76.

Wright, G. Ernest. *God Who Acts: Biblical Theology as Recital*. London: SCM, 1952.

Zuck, Roy B. "The Role of the Holy Spirit in Hermeneutics." *Bibliotheca Sacra* 141 (1984): 120–30.

GLOSSARY

Alexandrian school: Alexandria was a center of great learning. Here Philo developed his allegorical hermeneutics. The school of thought represented in Alexandria had streams of Platonic, neo-Platonic, and Gnostic thought, and these streams of thought influenced the way Judaism and Christianity were articulated. At the beginning of the third century A.D. Alexandria became important as a seat of Christian theology. The school was characterized by its dependence upon neo-Platonic philosophy and its application of the allegorical method of biblical interpretation.

allegorical interpretation: That kind of interpretation which assumes that the text to be interpreted says or intends to say something other than its literal wording suggests. It seeks to draw out a deeper, mystical sense not derivable from the words themselves.

already/not yet tension: The belief that the eschatological life may be enjoyed here and now in the "already," but that the full consummation of this life is "not yet" complete and awaits a future fulfillment. There is an indeterminate interval between Christ's resurrection and second coming. During this interval the age to come overlaps the present age. Believers "already" live spiritually in the new age, though temporally they do "not yet" live in that age. This dialectic is called the "already/not yet" tension.

anagogical interpretation: A method of biblical interpretation that seeks to unfold the spiritual meaning of a Scripture passage as it relates to eternal or future realities.

Antiochene school: An approach to or school of biblical interpretation and theology popular from the third to the eighth centuries A.D. that developed in Antioch of Syria. The approach tended to be rational, historical, and literal, in contrast to that which had previously developed in Alexandria. Interpreters who followed this approach seemed to be critical in their methodology, with some dependence upon Aristotle and that philosophical tradition.

apocalyptic literature: A collective term to designate those ancient visionary writings or parts of writings that, like the Book of Revelation, claim to reveal the mystery of the end of the age and the glories of the age to come. It is a distinctly Jewish and Christian phenomenon that goes back to the sixth century B.C., but it flourished between 200 B.C. and A.D. 100.

Apostolic Fathers: A group of early Christian writers believed to have had direct contact with the apostles of the early church. The term is used to describe the earliest noncanonical writings of the late first and early second centuries.

Arius/Arianism: Arius (A.D. 250–336) was an elder in an urban parish in Alexandria (A.D. 318–325). He taught that God the Father alone is God. This God could not possibly have communicated His essence to any other: thus the Son is a being created by the will and power of the Father. Unlike the Father, Jesus was not without beginning. Arianism was declared heretical at both the Council of Nicea (A.D. 325) and the Council of Constantinople (A.D. 381).

authoritative hermeneutics: A way of interpreting Scripture to point out the false beliefs of heretics. This was accomplished by establishing the correct theological meaning of Scripture by the authority of the bishop or the *regula fidei* (rule of faith).

authority: The right or power to command belief and/or action.

canon/canonical: The term canon refers to the group of books acknowledged by the early church as the rule of faith and practice. Both Jews and Christians have canons of Scripture. The Jewish canon consists of thirty-nine books called the Old Testament or Hebrew Scriptures. The Christian canon consists of sixty-six books (thirty-nine Old Testament and twenty-seven New Testament) for Protestants and eighty books for Catholics, whose canon includes the Apocrypha.

Chalcedonian christology: The belief about Jesus Christ adopted at the Council of Chalcedon (A.D. 451) and considered by most today as the foundation of classical orthodox christology. The confession affirms Jesus as the one and the same Christ, Son, Lord, Only Begotten—to be acknowledged in two natures, without confusion, without change, without division, without separation; the distinction of the natures being in no way abolished because of the union, but rather the characteristic property of each one being preserved, and concurring into one person and one being.

christocentric interpretation: A term often used synonymously with "christological," but more specific or focused, seeing Jesus Christ as central to all interpretation of the Old Testament.

christological interpretation: The Greek word *Christos* means "anointed one" and is the equivalent of the Hebrew *Mashiah* (Messiah). Christological interpretation reads the Old Testament in light of the belief that Jesus of Nazareth is the Messiah/Christ and the fulfillment of the Old Testament promises and prophecies.

christology: The word refers to the teaching of Christ, His person and natures. In earlier times, christology also included the work of Christ, now usually treated under the doctrine of salvation.

christology from above: Used in this volume to suggest that the study of Jesus Christ should begin with His divine nature and heavenly preexistence.

christology from below: Used in this volume to emphasize that the study of Jesus Christ should begin with His human nature and earthly life.

coherence view of truth: A theory holding that truth consists in coherence with other statements known to be true. The theological, ethical, and historical message of Scripture is known to be true because of the general, overall consistency of the biblical writings, even though this consistency is expressed in great variety.

concursive inspiration: A term communicating that inspired Scriptures are at the same time divine and human words. Since Scripture has a dual authorship, it is a product of God as well as of human authors.

contextual: A term denoting that some portions of Scripture have adapted certain life situations or cultural or temporal contexts to communicate their message.

correspondence view of truth: A theory maintaining that truth consists in some form of correspondence between one's belief and actual conditions in the world. Although Christian faith is deeply rooted in history, the correspondence of the Christian position as a whole to ultimate reality will be verified only by the return of Christ at the end of history.

Dead Sea Scrolls: The name given mainly to parchment and papyrus scrolls written in Hebrew, Aramaic, or Greek and discovered in eleven caves along the northwestern coast of the Dead Sea between 1947 and 1956. The scrolls date from 250 B.C. to A.D. 68 and are assigned to an Essene community located at the site or area known as Qumran.

docetic view of Scripture: A view suggesting that the human authorship of Scripture is only apparent or imaginative.

docetists: A group in the early church who regarded the human nature of Christ and His sufferings as imaginary rather than part of a real incarnation.

early church: A rather broad and somewhat ambiguous term used to describe the Christian church from its inception through its development in the first five centuries. Sometimes the terms earliest church, earliest Christianity, primitive church, or primitive Christianity are more focused upon the first-century church.

Ebionites: An early Christian sect that accepted Jesus as the prophetic successor to Moses but denied His deity and preexistence.

Enlightenment philosophy: A philosophical movement during the seventeenth and eighteenth centuries, sometimes identified as the Age of Reason. Characterized by rationalism and self-sufficiency, it rejected external authorities such as the Bible, the church, and the state.

epistemological: That which is concerned with the possibility, nature, and conditions of human knowledge. Knowledge of God becomes a possibility for humans at God's initiative by grace through faith.

exegesis: Exegesis means "to explain the meaning of a text in its original context." In Christian theology, exegesis is based on the presupposition that the Bible is in some sense the Word of God and that humanity is the recipient of its message. Exegesis and hermeneutics are sometimes used synonymously, but we can distinguish that exegesis asks "What did a text mean to the original sender or receiver?" while hermeneutics asks "What does a text mean for the present reader?"

functional hermeneutic: A way of describing how readers apply biblical text to their own context and situation without attention to its original context or situation. Meaning is thus bound up with Scripture's functional application.

Gemara: A commentary work of the rabbis known as *Amoraim* (expounders). It developed primarily in two centers, Babylon and Palestine (Tiberias) from the third to the fifth centuries.

general revelation: God's self-disclosure in a general way to all people at all times in all places. God reveals Himself through nature, history, our experience, and our conscience.

harmonization: An attempt to rearrange historical materials as they are presented in such books as Samuel, Kings, Chronicles, the Gospels, and Acts so that similar accounts present a unified meaning.

hermeneutic: The name ascribed by scholars to a school of thought beginning principally with the later Heidegger but whose roots go back to Dilthey and Schleiermacher, sometimes called ontological hermeneutics. It differs from traditional hermeneutics in that it is no longer equated with a theory of exegetical method, but is a description of what constitutes the phenomenon of understanding as such. It rejects the idea that a text has meaning autonomous of the interpreter.

hermeneutics: From the Greek *hermeneuein:* to express, to explain, to translate, to interpret. It is variously defined, but refers to a theory of interpretation. Traditionally, hermeneutics sought to establish the principles, methods, and rules needed in the interpretation of written texts, particularly sacred texts.

historical-critical models: A term used broadly to describe all methodologies related to the study of biblical texts. It emphasizes historical, philological, and archaeological analysis of biblical texts to discover the historical setting of a document, such as the time, place, and sources behind the text.

indicative/imperative: The shape of New Testament theology and ethics. It recognizes that often the New Testament writers explain the individual believer's or the church's position before God (in the indicative mood). This is followed by an exhortation to live out this teaching in practical terms (in the imperative mood). For example, in Romans 6, Paul says, "Anyone who has died has been freed from sin. . . . Therefore do not let sin reign in your mortal body" (6:7,12).

inerrancy: The idea that when all the facts are known, the Bible (in its autographs, that is, the original writings), properly interpreted in light of the culture and the means of communication that had developed by the time of its composition, is completely true in all that it affirms, to the degree of precision intended by the author's purpose, in all matters relating to God and His creation.

infallibility: The view that the Bible is incapable of error and cannot deceive or mislead. Some contemporary scholars want to apply the term infallible only to the message of the Bible to avoid the affirmation that the Bible is also truthful in matters relating to history, geography, and related matters. The meaning given to infallible in this volume is consistent with the classical meaning of the term, not with the revised meaning of some contemporary scholars.

inspiration: The superintending influence the Holy Spirit exerted on the biblical writers, so that the accent and interpretation of God's revelation have been recorded as God intended so that the Bible is actually the word of God.

kerygma: A Greek term for the apostolic preaching of the gospel found in the New Testament. The six basic aspects of this preaching include:

1. Jesus is the fulfillment of the Old Testament messianic promises.

2. This fulfillment has taken place through the ministry, death, burial, and resurrection of Jesus Christ.

3. By virtue of the resurrection Jesus has been exalted to the right hand of God.

4. The presence of the Holy Spirit in the church is a sign of Christ's present power and glory.

5. This messianic age will reach its consummation at the return of Christ.

6. A call to repentance issues in the forgiveness of sins and the gifts of the Holy Spirit.

late Judaism: Judaism from the closing of the Old Testament to the third century A.D., specifically its different groups (Pharisees, Sadducees, Essenes, and Zealots) during the intertestamental period and the first century A.D.

literal interpretation: An attempt to understand Scripture in its plain and ordinary sense without seeing a deeper or spiritual meaning.

Marcionism: A movement in the early church based on the teachings of Marcion, a second-century heretic. Marcion rejected the Old Testament and issued his own New Testament consisting of an abbreviated Gospel of Luke and ten Letters of Paul (excluding the Pastorals). Marcion set forth stark contrasts between the God of the Old Testament and the Christ of the New Testament.

Masoretic text: The text of the Hebrew Bible that added vowel points to the Hebrew consonantal prepared by a group of Jewish scholars around A.D. 700 to preserve the oral pronunciation of the Hebrew words.

Meaning: Meaning is a highly ambiguous term, and the only safe way of handling it is to identify the various senses in which it is used. One way of discussing meaning is by use of the terms sense and referent. The sense is what is being said and the referent is what is being talked about. Meaning can also be discussed in terms of value and entailment. Meaning as a value does not imply a greater understanding of a subject, but instead a greater appreciation. For instance, we can say that Paul means more to one person than does John. This person may not understand Paul better, but she or he does prefer Paul to John. By entailment, we are not indicating that meaning expresses synonymous relationships between two ideas, but that one idea leads inexorably to the other. When we discuss meaning in terms of the author's intentions or results, it is more than understanding why writers say what they say. To understand why writers say what they do is not the same thing as understanding what they are saying. The author's results can be discussed in terms of historical meaning, objective meaning, and normative meaning. Historical meaning is grounded in the historical sense of the text. When the genre so indicates, the historical meaning also refers to the historicity of the event behind the text. An objective meaning is a meaning determined primarily by the author or text, rather than the reader. An objective meaning refers to the interpreter's attempt to ground meaning in either the author's intention or the author's result (the text itself). Often the historical meaning and the objective meaning are identified as synonymous concepts, but this is not mandatory. A normative meaning suggests that the interpreter's findings have authority for the interpreter and may even be binding upon the interpreter.

midrash: Jewish interpretation of Scripture; more precisely, a commentary that contemporizes Scripture for current and practical situations.

Mishna: From the Hebrew *shanah*: to learn, to repeat. The Mishna was an authoritative collection of rabbinic *halakic*—legal or procedural material developed within the oral traditions of pharisaic and rabbinic Judaism, arranged and revised by Judah ha-Nasi in the first decades of the third century. The Mishna provides the foundation for the structure of the Talmud and is of great significance for understanding the Judaism of the intertestamental and early church period.

Montanism: A prophetic movement or sect that developed in Phrygia in Asia Minor around A.D. 172. It emphasized an ecstatic manner of utterance that ran counter to the tradition of Israelite and Christian prophecy.

241

Muratorian fragment: A fragmentary list of New Testament books known in Rome around A.D. 200. The list attests that the canonical books that were received in the church in the west were authorized to be read in public worship services. The list is named after L. A. Muratori, who discovered and published the document in the middle of the eighteenth century.

Nestorian christology: The teaching about Jesus associated with Nestorius of Antioch. Nestorianism maintained that Christ was a conjunction (*synapheia*) of two distinct natures. It was believed that before the union, there had been the Son of God, with His divine nature, and a human embryo, with His human nature. The Son of God entered the human fetus at the moment of conception, but did not mix with it in any way. God and man were linked in symmetrical union in which the whole was greater than its parts. The whole was the person of Christ, the appearance of a union which could theoretically be dissolved without destroying either the Son of God or the man Jesus. Nestorius and his teaching were condemned at the Third Ecumenical Council (Ephesus, A.D. 431) and again at Chalcedon (A.D. 451).

Nicene christology: The teaching of the fourth-century church derived from the Council of Nicea (A.D. 325) and confirmed at Constantinople (A.D. 381). This teaching was articulated by Athanasius (ca. A.D. 297–373). The Council of Nicea condemned Arius by insisting that the Son was not simply the "firstborn of all creation," but was indeed "of one essence with the Father." Against Arius, Athanasius sought to uphold the unity of essence of the Father and Son by basing his argument not on a philosophical doctrine of the nature of the Logos, but on the nature of the redemption accomplished by the Word in the flesh. Only God Himself, taking on human flesh and dying and rising in human flesh, can effect a redemption that consists in being saved from sin and corruption and death, and in being raised to share the nature of God Himself. After Nicea, it became apparent that there were two main schools of thought in the church, centered in Alexandria and Antioch respectively. In doctrinal terms, Alexandria claims priority, and Antioch is best regarded as a reaction against what were believed to be Alexandria's excesses.

normative meaning: An expression suggesting that the interpreters' findings have authority for the contemporary interpreters of Scripture and may even be binding on the interpreters.

normative Scripture: A term indicating that Scripture's power is not limited by temporal or contextual matters. It indicates that the message of Scripture has binding authority for the contemporary church.

Papyri fragments: Writings on sheets that were formed by cutting the stems off an Egyptian plant into long, thin strips placed in two crosswise layers and glued together by hammer blows.

patristics: The study of the fathers of the church. The leaders, particularly the bishops, were known as the Fathers. More specifically, the term has come to be applied to the first Christian writers of acknowledged eminence. The outstanding thinkers and theologians of the first six centuries of the church have come to be regarded as the Fathers and the study of these leaders is known as patristics.

pericope: A term adopted from Hellenistic rhetoric and used to refer to a short section or passage of Scripture. It was first used in Christian circles by Jerome to designate a portion of Scripture. This usage preceded the division of Scripture into chapters. In contemporary biblical criticism, the term is used to refer to any self-contained unit of Scripture.

personal revelation: Revelation viewed primarily as a personal experience or encounter with God in Christ. It focuses attention on the dynamic and personal characteristics of God's manifestation of Himself to men and women.

pesher: An approach to commenting on the Scripture, particularly the Old Testament prophets, by the Qumran sectarians who believed themselves to be living in the last days. Pesher is a divinely illuminated interpretation of the divine mysteries of Scripture, relating such texts to the last days.

Pharisees: An important Jewish group that flourished in Palestine from the late second century B.C. to the late first century A.D. The Pharisees were strongly committed to the daily application and observance of the law. They accepted the traditional elaborations of law, making specific and daily application possible. They believed in the existence of spirits and angels, the resurrection, and the coming of a Messiah.

plenary: A Latin term meaning full. When applied to the concept of inspiration, it means that the Bible is inspired in all parts.

progressive revelation: A term indicating that God's self-disclosure unfolds and develops over time. This revelation interprets and amplifies the previous revelation but does not contradict it in any way.

prophecy: The speaking, proclaiming, or announcing by prophets under the influence of divine inspiration. The primary ways the prophets received revelation included direct encounter with God, dreams, and visions. The sayings of prophets at times had direct application for their own settings, whereas at other times they are best understood as foretelling future events.

propositional revelation: God's self-manifestation understood as information about God, including the divine interpretation of revelatory events. A proper view of Christian truth distinguishes between the personal and propositional aspects but does not separate them.

Qumran: The name given to the ruins of an Essene community of fanatic Jewish monastics on the northwestern coast of the Dead Sea. It was first occupied in approximately 150 B.C. and destroyed in A.D. 68 by Rome during the first Jewish revolt.

rabbinic literature: Commentary and prescriptive writings based on Scripture for the various Jewish communities. "Rabbi" is a title used to honor Jewish religious teachers. As the title given to teachers of the law in the Jewish community, it passes on from teacher to pupil by ordination, qualifying one who has the proper training to function as preacher, teacher, and pastor in the Jewish synagogue. The writings of the rabbis are broadly grouped under the title rabbinic literature.

redaction criticism: From the German *Redaktionsgeschichte*, the term refers to a method of biblical criticism that seeks to determine the theological perspectives of a biblical writer by analyzing the editorial and compositional techniques and interpretations employed in shaping and framing the written and oral traditions about Jesus (see Luke 1:1–4).

revelation: An uncovering, a removal of the veil, a disclosure of what was previously unknown, God's manifestation of Himself to humankind in such a way that men and women can know and have fellowship with Him.

sensus plenior: A Latin term indicating that God intended a fuller meaning of a passage of Scripture, although it was not clearly understood by the human author or by the original hearers/readers.

Septuagint: From the Latin term meaning seventy, a term referring to the Greek translation of the Old Testament made by the Jews of Alexandria, Egypt, around 250 B.C. Tradition maintains that the text was translated by seventy-two scholars.

slippery-slope arguments: A popular term suggesting that after one generation abandons an orthodox view of Scripture, succeeding generations will continue to abandon other important orthodox beliefs.

soteriology: The term referring to the church's teaching about salvation of humans from the power and effects of sin. From the Greek term *soteria*, it relates to the comprehensive doctrine of salvation—past, present, and future.

special revelation: God's self-manifestation in a particular way to particular people at particular times and places.

Talmud: From the Hebrew *lamad*: study or instruction. Talmud is the comprehensive term for the Mishna (proverbs, tales, custom, folklore, etc.) as well as strict exposition of the text. The structure of the Talmud is therefore that of the Mishna, having six orders divided into sixty-three tractates, the form it obtained by the third century.

Targum: In broad terms, the word *Targum* means "translation or interpretation"; more specifically it refers to Aramaic translations of the Old Testament. In rabbinic literature it often refers to Aramaic phrases that are found in the Old Testament books of Ezra, Nehemiah, and Daniel. The Targum developed from the synagogue practice of translating the Hebrew Scriptures into Aramaic, for the Aramaic-speaking Jews, usually with an accompanying commentary or expanded paraphrase.

textual criticism: A discipline that attempts to reconstruct the original text of the Scriptures as closely as can be determined.

theopneustos: A Greek term translated "divinely inspired" or "God-breathed" (2 Tim. 3:16), indicating that the Scriptures are the product of God's creative breath and thus divine.

typological interpretation: A type of biblical interpretation in which persons, events, or things in the Old Testament are interpreted as foreshadowings of persons, events, or things in the New Testament. Typological interpretation differs from an allegorical one in that the latter sees the hidden meaning of a text, whereas the former understands a revelatory connection between two historically distinct but spiritually significant persons or events.

Vulgate: A Latin translation of the Bible by Jerome near the close of the fourth century A.D. It became the common version of the Catholic Church during the Middle Ages.

NAMES INDEX

A

Abraham, William 12, 54, 60
Achtemeier, Paul 54, 60
Ackroyd, P. R. 94
Aldridge, J. W. 145
Alexander, J. A. 144
Allen, Clifton J. 213
Ammerman, Nancy T. 12, 209
Aquinas, Thomas 33, 118, 123
Arminius, J. 145
Ashcraft, Morris 206, 214
Athanasius 89, 111
Augustine 111, 116, 118–119, 127, 131, 151
Avis, Paul 124

B

Bahnsen, Greg L. 74
Baillie, John 33
Baker, D. L. 56, 125

Bangs, C. 145
Barker, Kenneth L. 95
Barr, James 4–5, 12, 13
Barrett, C. K. 34, 35
Barrow, R. H. 127
Barth, G. 139
Barth, Karl 33–34, 53, 60, 143, 148, 184
Basden, Paul A. 209, 213
Baur, F. C. 137
Beare, F. W. 92, 96
Beckwith, R. T. 86, 95
Beekman, John 94
Bell, William E. 206
Belleville, Linda 95
Bengel, Johann Albert 135, 146
Bentley, J. H. 145
Berkouwer, G. C. 12, 32, 54, 60, 185
Bernard of Clairvaux 123
Black, David Alan 59, 94, 125, 147, 213
Black, Matthew 35, 125

247

Scripture Index